Keep being
Awesome!

E

THE **PRINCIPLES** OF
DAVID & GOLIATH

MINDSET & BELIEF SYSTEMS

FEATURING

Erik Swanson ~ Brian Tracy
Alec Stern ~ Cynthia Kersey ~ Rob Angel

Orders by U.S. trade bookstores and wholesalers.
Email info@BeyondPublishing.net

Manufactured and printed in the United States of America and distributed globally by Beyond Publishing and Integrity Publishing.

Library of Congress Control Number: 2022907797

Hardback ISBN: 978-1-63792-301-6

Paperback ISBN: 978-1-63792-300-9

Acknowledgement to our Artist!

We would like to thank The Artiste, Patrick Carney, for his amazing art work and contribution to our book series, The Principles of David & Goliath. We are honored to include his artwork on the covers of each of the book in the series. (Photo credit: Ann Landstom)

"The Artiste"

Patrick Carney, The Artiste, is an indomitable spirit who has shared his creative talent with the world in ways that are sometimes beyond measure. No one captures the 'Essence of Women,' the aura of their souls, the contours of their brilliance in the way this artist can. Carney captures the legacy that these women leave as footsteps on this earth.

While attending the School of Visual Arts in New York City, Patrick Carney had the privilege to study with Chuck Close, Marge Anderson, Robert Israel, Burne Hogarth and Milton Glaser; each of these teachers having a profound impact on his life.

As a youth he read voraciously–searching for answers which led to more questions. While pursuing studies at Buffalo State, he worked as a specialist in media at the Communications Center. Later he was named the Art Director of the Lafayette Community Center where he taught art to inner city children. For a time he traveled throughout the NY State as an Artist in Residence at underprivileged high schools as a representative of the Arts Council, and volunteered as a art teacher in the state prison system, believing that it was his obligation to give back and "Pass On" his given talents.

Starting in 1964 in NY's West Village, Mr. Carney dedicated his time to drawing and painting the world of rock n' roll music, it's passion and creativity caught in real time forever. He traveled throughout the US attending rock concerts and painted whatever star excited him – and thus his work is a varied series of welcome surprises.

Hanging out at what he calls "the corner of Art and Soul," the Artiste Patrick Carney creates the images of your youth, capturing on canvas the music you grew up with.

Not only are Patrick Carney's Acrylics and Pen & Inks purchased by collectors all over the world, his paintings are displayed in the personal collections of such luminaries as Dick Clark, John Lennon, Bob Dylan, Stevie Nicks, Bruce Springsteen, JD Souther, Tom Russell, Judy Collins, Al Kooper, Pete Seeger, Sharon Lechter, Erik Swanson and Kevin Harrington.

PEOPLE LOVE
THE PRINCIPLES OF DAVID & GOLIATH

"Read this book series and change your life! Create your blueprint to success by learning the secrets revealed in *The Principles of David & Goliath*. This book series will take you through the journey with us as you experience stories of triumph and conquer the Goliaths of your life."

~ **Brian Tracy** ~ World Renowned Leader and Speaker in Personal Development

"*The Principles of David & Goliath*, the story of a contest where a smaller, weaker David faces a much bigger, stronger adversary Goliath and succeeds is more important today than ever. This book series takes a modern day look at this age old principle as the contributors share their own stories of victory and success even in the face of extreme odds and seemingly unsurmountable obstacles. Erik Swanson has curated this series so that you may more quickly conquer the Goliaths in your life. If you are looking for inspiration and heavy doses of courage, read *The Principles of David & Goliath*."

~ **Sharon Lechter** ~ Global Financial Literacy Expert and New York Times Bestselling Author

"The underdog truly has the advantage! Allow yourself to open your eyes, your hearts and your energy to the stories of some fantastic leaders who share their journeys in how they, too, beat the 'Goliaths' of their lives by implementing these timeless principles of success."

~ **Dr. Joe Vitale** ~ New York Times Bestselling Author, Featured in *The Secret*

"Do you want to enhance your life? If the answer is yes, then grab a copy of The Principles of David & Goliath and harness the time tested truths in this book. I highly recommend it and am honored to be one of the contributing celebrity authors in the series."

~ **Cynthia Kersey** ~ Bestselling Author of *Unstoppable*,
Founder & CEO of Unstoppable Foundation

"In this inspiring book series, you will find others with experience sharing their stories and offering insight, suggestions and object lessons to help you create your own framework so that you can overcome the Goliaths that we face in everyday life."

~ **Alec Stern** ~ America's Startup Success Expert,
Co-Founder of Constant Contact

"We all have events in our lives that in the moment we feel are insurmountable, yet we have dig deep to overcome those challenges. *The Principles of David & Goliath* gives you stories and habits to help you navigate through and create the success in your life that you desire."

~ **Rob Angel** ~ Bestselling Author of *Game Changer*,
Creator of *Pictionary*

"In every one of us there is a David who can conquer our own Goliath. We have a choice in life to be a victim of our circumstances or be the David and believe in ourselves. For me it has been a journey of overcoming being raped and thrown off of a 75 foot cliff and left for dead. This left me paralyzed from the neck down in the beginning. But, I chose to slay my Goliath to now walking for exercise and still gaining function in my body. It took having the courage to turn the Impossible to I'M POSSIBLE through grit, hard work and the right mindset. What's your Goliath? Read this book and learn how to slay your Goliaths just like I did!"

~ **Dana Liesegang** ~ Motivational Speaker & Conquering Survivor

"People all around the world owe it to themselves to learn the secrets and steps to effectively work with the obstacles they encounter throughout their lives. That is exactly what you will learn in this marvelous book series called *The Principles of David & Goliath*."

~ **Blaine Bartlett** ~ Bestselling Author and Bloomberg TV Co-Host

"The book series, *The Principles of David & Goliath*, is filled with brilliant nuggets from brilliant authors who share their stories about triumphing in the face of challenges that are inspiring, motivating, and educational reminders that we can utilize to help us with our own challenges and triumphs every day!"

~ **Natalie Susi** ~ #1 Bestselling Author, Speaker,
Professor of Conscious Conversations

"Uh oh, here comes another Goliath! No worries, this book will show you how to slay the Goliaths, those obstacles and forces that try to stop you or slow you down from living your BIG life. Read these ideas and win!"

~ **David M. Corbin** ~ Two Time *Wall Street Journal*
Bestselling Author, Mentor to Mentors

"A must-read for anyone looking to unleash their amazing confidence and their full potential."

~ **Greg S. Reid** ~ Award Winning Bestselling Author, Filmmaker, Speaker

"There is a David in all of us willing to face and ultimately overcome seemingly insurmountable odds. Like the rock from the sling, one simple choice can change the course of your life. Choose to read this powerful book."

~ **Doug Grady** ~ Speaker, Bestselling Author on Human Performance

"The principles of David and Goliath are as powerful today as they were when they were exemplified all those years ago. Today, this book series will help us all to rise above the obstacles and conquer the giants in our lives once and for all."

~ **Bob Donnell** ~ Founder of Everything Next Level
& Next Level By Association

"You and I are often 'David' in various parts of life. It is easy to feel overwhelmed or outgunned. Let this book erase your fears and show you the slingshots available right now!"

~ **Jim Cathcart** ~ Certified Speaking Professional (CSP) and Former President of the National Speakers Association (NSA), Going Pro Mentor

"This is a great book series! It all starts in our mind and we can choose to be a 'David' by planning and developing a strategy and then acting upon it by using persistence to become our true selves. We need to take responsibility and look in the mirror and repeat, 'If it is to be, it is up to me.' What are you waiting on?"

~ **Don Green** ~ Bestselling Author & President of The Napoleon Hill Foundation

"This book shows you how to be a David to the Goliaths in your life. The best way to predict the future is to create it. Every 'David' I've ever met steps into their power and are always guiding and enlightening people they meet. If you're passionate about what it is you do, then you're going to be looking for everything you can to get better at it and be a David, too."

~ **Patrick Carney** ~ The Artiste and Founder of YES Mastermind

"When we think we're down and out we can definitely position ourselves there. When we believe we can triumph and overcome, it does not matter how big the obstacle, what matters is that we're willing to work through the obstacle."

~ **Steven Wener** ~ Speaker, Coach, Founder of The Primer Morning Master-Calls

"Erik Swanson is a wonderful guide to empower you with the mindset and strategies to turn obstacles into opportunities!"

~ **Niurka** ~ Speaker, Coach, Energy & Thought Leader

"There are times when we question our calling even though it speaks to us. This book series reminds us that listening to the voice within us is just the first step. *The Principles of David and Goliath* help inspire you to create a strategy and an action plan to help fulfill that calling.

~ **Brian Galke** ~ Founder of Subtle Skills

"As a Habits & Behavioral Coach, Erik "Mr. Awesome" Swanson has harnessed a very difficult life matter in his AWESOME book series where the David in our lives learn how to conquer the Goliaths that we all face… truly, a MUST-READ!"

~ **Jesse & Lisa Ferrell** ~ International Speakers & Success Coaches

"What's the difference between someone who takes a beating and learns to not stand out again vs someone who looks at insurmountable odds and follows the gospel of Nike: Just Do It? This book contains a collection of invaluable advice that will make sure you land in the latter group, aka David's winner camp."

~ **Dr. Marissa Pei** ~ #1 Bestselling Author, #1 Host & Producer of Award-Winning NBC News Radio KCAA AM FM show Take My Advice, I'm not using it: Get Balanced with Dr. Marissa

"David & Goliath is one of the greatest principles taught in history. As its story perpetuates inspiring examples of triumph to anyone in modern times, I'm honored to be a contributing author and to sit side-by-side with these amazing co-authors and celebrities who want to help readers all over the world overcome their greatest challenges."

~ **Jon Kovach Jr.** ~ #1 Bestselling Author, Speaker, Global Mastermind Team Leader

"Adversity introduces us to ourselves! We need 'Goliaths' in our lives to bring out the David in us! The bigger the challenge, the greater character development we experience. No one ever knows how strong we are until being strong is our only choice!"

~ **Dan Clark** ~ Speaker Hall of Fame & N.Y. Times Bestselling Author

"There is an old Italian saying that goes like this: Finché C'È Vita C'È Speranza. It means 'While There's Life, There's Hope!' in *The Principles of David & Goliath*, there are so many stories and lessons of hope which ultimately gives you life! Read this book, grow and blossom with your new found success."

> ~ **Sir Bruno Serato** ~ 2012 CNN Man of the Year,
> Owner of Anaheim White House

"An awesome account of how to overcome obstacles and what I call 'situations.' Wise words to live by. I strongly recommend these books in this series. A truly enlightening read."

> ~ **Ron Klein** ~ The Grandfather of Possibilities,
> Inventor of the credit card magnetic strip

"There are a lot of people in the world doing awesome things every day, but it takes a truly special person to make people feel **awesome** every day! Erik Swanson is one of these special people and the world is more awesome because he is in it. Pick up his latest #1 bestselling book and learn the secrets to success and happiness."

> ~ **Tim Conners** ~ America's Ambassador of Hope, Adventurer,
> Motivational Speaker, Cancer Survivor, Sightless Visionary

"Are you ready to up-level and stop playing small? Then, grab your copy of *The Principles of David & Goliath*! I highly recommend it as the stories from these incredible authors will inspire you to take action through subtle shifts by thinking outside the box to enhance your life! A must-read!"

> ~ **Fatima Hurd** ~ 6 Time #1 Bestselling Author in
> *The 13 Steps to Riches*, Branding Photographer

"If you were looking to up-level your life, then look no further! *The Principles of David & Goliath* book series will do just that. I highly recommend reading the whole series!"

> ~ **Jeff Fagin** ~ Founder & CEO of 2PercentClub

"When you get punched in the face by life, you swallow the damn blood and punch back! This book is about the massive fight it takes inside you and out to overcome your fears, doubt's and insecurities while ultimately achieving what only you can define as success"

~ **Eric Louis Power** ~ Speaker and Bestselling Author of
Don't Shoot Your Future Self

"It took courage, strategy and strength for David to step up and conquer the giant, Goliath. In *The Principles of David & Goliath*, you will learn how to harness each of the 3 critical fundamental areas for your success."

~ **Adam Markel** ~ #1 Bestselling Author of *Change Proof: Leveraging the Power of Uncertainty to Build Long-Term Resilience*

FREE GIFT!
GRAB YOUR SPECIAL
& AWESOME FREE GIFT!

We have a very special gift for those who want to surround themselves with a tribe of people creating magic in supporting each other and their growth in their personal and professional lives! It's time for you to be up-leveled in such a fantastic way! You deserve to reward yourself and join us. "NDSO!" No Drama - Serve Others!

Visit the QR code link above to get your FREE GIFT!
www.RideAlongGuestPass.com

Global Speakers Mastermind & Habitude Warrior Masterminds

Join us and become a member of our tribe! Our Global Speakers Mastermind is a virtual group of amazing thinkers and leaders who meet twice a month. Sessions are designed to be 'to the point' and focused, while sharing fantastic techniques to grown your mindset as well as your pocketbooks. We also include famous guest speaker spots for our private Masterclasses. We also designate certain sessions for our members to mastermind with each other & counsel on the topics discussed in our previous Masterclasses. It's time for you to join a tribe who truly cares about **YOU** and your future and start surrounding yourself with the famous leaders and mentors of our time. It is time for you to up-level your life, businesses, and relationships.

For more information to check out our Masterminds:
Team@HabitudeWarrior.com
www.DecideTobeAwesome.com

CONTENTS

Acknowledgement	To Patrick Carney	5
Testimonials	People Love The Principles of David And Goliath	7
Introduction	The Principles Of David And Goliath	19
Foreword	By Alec Stern	23
Erik Swanson	Creating Your Bank Of Positivity	25
Brian Tracy	The Way To A Wealthy Mindset	35
Alec Stern	The Mindset Of Life, Health, & Business	49
Cynthia Kersey	The Gift Of Giving	57
Rob Angel	Picture This!	67
Adrienne Micali	Trust What Comes Into Your Life	73
Angela Harden-Mack	Slay The Giant	80
Angelika Ullsperger	Mind Power	85
Anthony Manzon	Success Starts With Mindset	91
Bonnie Lierse	No Time For Fear	97
Bryce Mckinley	Uncertainty Creates Opportunity	103
Charlson Gaines	Freedom To Choose	107
Crystal Lindsey	Rejected	112
Darrell David Stern	You Are A Gift To The World	118
Dawnese Openshaw	Fastballs And Facing Fears	125
Derika & Christopher Faamausili	Powers Inside You Beyond Your Belief	131
Diana Smith	Life At The Back Of The Room	138
Eileen Galbraith	Live Your Dreams	144
Erin Ley	Conquering Self-Doubt With Self-Confidence	150
Fabiola Gonzalez	Achieve All That You Visualize	155
Fred Moskowitz	Secrets To Developing An Unshakeable Mindset	161
Gigi Sabbat	Resilience Defeats The Giants	167
Gwen Mitchell	How Can You Master Your Internal Goliath?	171

Jen Du Plessis	The Empty Space	176
Jessa Carter	Our Greatest Asset	183
Jessica Bojorquez	The Wounded Woman	189
Jon Kovach Jr.	Stones To A Sword Fight	195
Kearn Cherry	Sometimes A Giant Must Fall	201
Maris Segal & Ken Ashby	Goliaths Happen, David Chooses	205
Mary Beth Kellee	Just A Small-Town Girl	212
Maureen Vincenty	Dream And Be Obsessed	217
Michelle Crites	The Gift Of Trust	223
Michael Wolf	4 Minutes Each Day Can Change Your Life	228
Monica Pandele	Does Nature Love You?	235
Neetu Sing	From Frozen In Fear To Finally Flying Free	241
Nicki Hu	Testing My Relationship With Self-Worth	247
Dr. Onika Shirley	Resiliently Facing One Of Many Giants	253
Peter Mendiola	A Winner's Mindset	259
Phillip McClure	The Wolf Goliath	264
Rachel Diamond	Lost At Sea: A Lighthouse Of Love	270
Rachel Ivanovich	Mind The Gap	276
Roxanne Felton	The Truth Will Set You Free	282
Samantha Roberts	Your Challenges, Your Great Contributions	288
Shane Laufman	A Sixth-Grader Can Do It	294
Steven Wener	Transformations	300
Susan Carpio	Believe In Yourself—And Be Open	305
Thomas Malagisi	Development Of A Mindset And Belief System	311
Valeria Mironov	Find Your "Enough" Point	316
Vera Thomas	The Mind of David	322

THE PRINCIPLES OF
DAVID AND GOLIATH

In the famous story of David and Goliath, David goes to fight in one of the greatest battles in history. David's countrymen were troubled by the stature and size of their foe, Goliath. David's kingdom could not find anyone to match the size and strength to go battle against the giant. David believed he would be protected if he went up against Goliath in battle. David was surprised that the rest of his army was afraid and petrified of Goliath. David was angered by Goliath's mocking of his army and took Goliath's challenge to come to him and battle him. The challenge proposed by Goliath was that if an Israelite defeated Goliath, then all of the Philistines would become servants to David's kingdom. If Goliath beat the Israeli soldier, then all of Israel would be servants to the Philistines. This put pressure on King Saul and his army, who felt they had nobody in the entire kingdom who could match the giant's strength. David, who was only sent to feed his brothers, remained baffled that nobody else would call upon their powers and beliefs to face the giant to defend their country.

David was firm in his beliefs in himself and knew that he would be protected. He willingly went to battle against Goliath. For David, it wasn't a moment of valor or heroism, whereas all he wanted to do was take down the beast that was mocking his people. King Saul attempted to put his best armor and weapons on David to protect him in battle. But David knew all he needed was his sling and his staff. David faced the giant without hesitation and without any of the armor and weapons from his king. Even when the odds were stacked against David, he knew that he had the ability and the power to take down the giant with just one sling of a rock. David hit the giant right in the forehead, killing him outright.

In *The Principles of David and Goliath*, we honor those who never waver in their mindset and beliefs, and for those who choose to take on the giants, even when it is not in their favor. Whether you are an underdog, faced with challenges, and unprepared, every battle and challenge can appear to be as big as a giant.

In this three volume book series, you will come to read and learn the words and principles of inspired leaders from around the world who have overcome their most significant challenges and obstacles. They share their stories and journeys of triumphs to teach others how to accomplish their own successes. Created by Erik "Mr. Awesome" Swanson, 13 time #1 Bestselling Author and Founder of Habitude Warrior International and Habitude Warrior Masterminds, his hope and desire is to inspire you, the reader, to realize your full potential and put faith in your abilities to conquer and overcome your own Goliaths in your life. Erik has invited 33+ Bestselling Authors and 13 Celebrity Authors to share their wisdom and share their stories with you. You will find yourself embracing many different emotions while reading each chapter. Our goal is to have you realize if we can do it, you can as well! We look forward to your successes and also look forward to you sharing these books with your friends and family. One of the best gifts to give someone is the gift of success and courage. You will find these chapters are filled with exactly that.

Volume 1 - *The Principles of David and Goliath* - *Mindset & Belief Systems*

In the first book in the series, our authors dive deep in to what it takes to have a clear and concise mindset. They teach the value of believing in yourself, as we can move mountains. Too many of us allow other people to determine our mindset for us. We are here to share the principles of developing a great mindset that encourages you to go that extra mile. We share steps for you to create your own all-powerful belief system.

Volume 2 - The Principles of David and Goliath
- Strategy & Goal Methods

In the second book in the series, we share the realization that attitude is not everything. Having a great mindset is the first step, but, it needs to be followed up by a strategic method for your success. Our authors teach the strategies and goal methods that they have implemented over their lives to reach the summits of success. Success leaves clues. We are here to share with you our stories which not only will inspire you to take action, but will give you a blueprint to follow that will directly lead you to your ultimate goal.

Volume 3 - The Principles of David and Goliath
- Action & Implementation

In the third book in the series, our authors share the principles and methods to take massive and laser focused action. Through our stories, we teach you how to develop a new habit or muscle to take action on your thoughts and strategies. It is not enough to simply have a great mindset and know what to do. The next step is 'to do it!' And implement your strategies. Too many people around the world suffer from 'analysis of paralysis.' It's YOUR time! Time for you to take action on your new habits of success. Welcome to your new and amazing life!

www.ThePrinciplesofDavidandGoliath.com

ALEC STERN
"AMERICA'S STARTUP SUCCESS EXPERT"

Foreword

In everyday life and in business, most of us have, or will, find ourselves in situations where we feel we're the underdog, like David, facing a much stronger adversary, like Goliath. In these moments, especially if you're having this kind of experience for the first time, it is easy (and understandable) to feel small, weak, or otherwise unequipped to overcome the challenges or obstacles facing you. It can seem, at the moment, that the odds are against you, even insurmountable. Honor these feelings as they are all valid.

You may be facing a Goliath for the first time, or you may have been either successful or defeated in the past. What do you do? When facing such a challenge, it's important to look inward and take stock of yourself, your business, your capabilities, etc. Because in the secularized story of David and Goliath, it wasn't size or strength that was the deciding factor; rather, it was David's mindset, perseverance, expertise, and choice of weapon that secured his victory against the odds.

Your own challenges in life can be around getting or staying in good health, maintaining perspective, a positive mindset, minimizing stress and pressure, succeeding in business or in love, etc. While a Goliath may be in the mix, don't let your Goliath be of your own making. Seek and learn from your own and others' experiences, but while doing so, be sure to maintain perspective. If friends, family, business associates, or mentors are not especially supportive, sometimes it is because of their own perceived failures.

In business, we face growth and scale concerns, hiring needs, economic conditions, world events, etc. In most instances, you will be working in a space where there is competition, others who are entrenched with more time in the market or an industry with a set way in which things have been done in the past.

It's important to remember you are not alone; you are not the first or the last to face a Goliath. And, past failures do not have to be the preface for today's or tomorrow's outcomes. Moreover, this is unlikely to be the last time you will face such a challenge.

In this inspiring book, you will find others with experience sharing their stories and offering insight, suggestions, and object lessons on how to set yourself on a path to victory.

What did others do that led to success or failure in removing the obstacle or challenge? What worked and why? You will hear many amazing stories of how others have faced their Goliaths and conquered them.

As we face obstacles and challenges in life and business, it is beneficial to have a framework to tackle them.

In *The Principals of David and Goliath,* you will learn how to create your own framework in three key stages: Mindset & Belief Systems, Strategy & Goal Methods, Action & Implementation. This is the framework that can help you overcome the Goliaths that we face in everyday life.

Erik Swanson

CREATING YOUR BANK OF POSITIVITY

As far as I can remember, I always felt that I had the power to control what I was thinking at any given time. Even as a young kid growing up, I felt that I had the ability to change my mindset and direct it towards what I wanted to think about. This was so powerful and useful and still serves me today in so many areas of my life.

As human beings, we tend to allow others to shape our minds. We allow other people and their thoughts to direct what we perceive as reality. I read somewhere that research had determined we have over 6,000 thoughts going through our minds per day. That is a ton of thoughts! Wow, how do we control them?

There within lies the issue. Controlling our thoughts is imperative to a successful outcome in life. Most of us allow others to creep into our thoughts every single day. We allow them to bring in all types of unwanted negativity. We allow them to rent space in our minds, yet we don't even charge them rent for it.

Reframing Our Thoughts

One major secret to success is to reframe our minds to consistently have positive thoughts that are leading towards the direction of our desired outcomes. It may be easier said than done. But, with practice, I'm confident you can succeed.

Three Keys to Reframing Our Thoughts

First, you must make a conscious decision always to think positive thoughts. This doesn't mean you can't have negative thoughts come into your mind. Trust me, they will try to break in. But you must vow to yourself that if a negative thought does seep into your mind, you will acknowledge it and decide not to allow it to stay.

Second, you will replace this negative thought with a positive thought immediately. Literally tell yourself, out loud if you must, that you are changing this negative thought into a positive one!

Third, you must remind yourself that you only allow positive thoughts into your mind each and every day. You are a bank of positivity. Remind yourself that in order to accomplish your ultimate awesome goals, you must keep your mind clear and positive.

Some of the greatest grandfathers of leadership, such as Napoleon Hill, Earl Nightingale, and Jim Rohn, used to remind us that weeds will always try to grow in your gardens. We must vow to always keep the weeds of negativity out of our mental gardens.

Creating Your Bank of Positivity

There is one specific Habitude Warrior technique I have used for years to create your Bank of Positivity. First off, you may ask, "what is a Bank of Positivity?" It is simply a list of great, positive thoughts you have ready to feed into your mind. These are thoughts you have developed over time that you 'deposit' into your Bank of Positivity. You must, just like any other bank, make consistent deposits before you expect to take any withdrawals out.

Step One: Grab a notebook that you determine will hold all of your positive thoughts. Keep it all in one place and readily available. You can even give your notebook a name!

Step Two: Start journaling by writing down each and every positive thought you have each day for seven days straight.

Step Three: After the seven days, review your notebook and start circling the most common positive thoughts you have had over the past week. Create a new list with those dominant positive thoughts.

Step Four: Read your dominant positive thoughts out loud every morning when you wake up and every night before you go to sleep. These will start to turn into your Bank of Positive Affirmations.

Step Five: Whenever you have a negative thought arise in your mindset, refer back to your Bank of Positivity and read them aloud to yourself.

Your Mindset and Belief Systems need to be in Congruence

In order to have your positive mindset actually work in your favor and create long-lasting change, you must create the congruency and sync your beliefs systems with your mind. It is not enough to simply have a positive mindset if you don't put a true conviction or belief system behind it.

In other words, you must believe in yourself! Too many people walk this earth not believing in themselves. They act as if others should believe in them, yet they lack a true sense of belief in their own abilities.

My rule of thumb is to fill up your cup to the top for yourself and your own belief systems and have it overflow for others.

Four Strategic Habitude Warrior Ways to Believe in Yourself

1. Leaders Game - Leaders and successful people leave clues. Start looking at those successful leaders you look up to and start reminding yourself that you are just like them.

2. Affirmations - Keep affirming to yourself that you truly are the best. You are the type of individual who can handle any and every situation that comes your way. You are powerful!

3. Remind - Remind yourself that you are the type of person who wins. Remind yourself of some of your past wins and successful moments and relive them in your mindset. Your subconscious mind doesn't know the difference between something you are visualizing or something that is real. Therefore, your visualization turns into reality in your mind.

4. Concentration – Concentrate on the positive outcome and view it in your mind. Concentrate and use all of your senses. If you can include all five of your senses to concentrate on the positive outcome, your belief systems will start working in your favor and start becoming in alignment with your conscious mind.

Once you truly believe in yourself, you can start moving mountains! A confidence will come over you and will shine through you to the world. It is one of the most beautiful things to watch. Have you ever noticed that some people can walk into a room without saying a word and have the whole room turn to see who this person is? Just the mere fact that they walked into the room with an all-knowing confident attitude will literally capture everyone's attention.

I love it when I go to coffee shops. I don't even drink coffee, but I still love to go to them. I will walk in and not even say a word to anyone, yet I have a huge smile on my face. Why? It's because I know that I am probably the most confident and positive person in the room at the moment. I smile because I know that I have something to smile about. People think I am smiling at them to be nice. In reality, I'm smiling at myself. My internal belief system is kicking in and reminding me to enjoy this moment.

You, too, can have moments like this. In fact, you can create each and every moment of your life to reflect how you would like it to be. I call this a "Positive Mental Environment!" This is when you decide to create your environment to reflect a positive and amazing feeling no matter where you are. Some people refer to the phrase "fake it until you make it." That's fine to start off with. But, once you go through the steps I've outlined above, you start to realize that you are not faking it anymore. You genuinely are creating your own environment of success. This is a space that I call Utopia. This space is where you believe in yourself so much that nothing can deter you.

Nothing can bring you down. Even if something negative arises, you now have the ability and the power to change that moment. This is a powerful space to be in. Cherish it and live it as it is yours to keep.

Moments of Triumphs

One of the most important things to realize is that in life is that we will all have those moments which we feel are way too difficult. You know those moments which feel insurmountable? Just like in the story of David & Goliath, we have to access our amazing mindset and belief systems to conquer our fears and obstacles.

The very first step in conquering the obstacles in our lives is not a physical action at all. It is a mental action! Just like David, we need to access our minds and beliefs in ourselves before we can ever pick up a physical object. Our friend, who recently passed, Bob Proctor, wrote a book with another friend of mine,

Greg Reid, titled *Thoughts Are Things*. This is so true. Thoughts truly are things. It has been scientifically proven over recent years. In fact, 'things' are merely energy vibrating at a very high speed. The only difference between a Porsche car and a possum is the speed or rate of vibration.

You know the saying, "Sticks and stones may break my bones, but names will never hurt me." This is true and false all at the same time. If you think about it, sticks and stones may break my bones; true. But, depending on your level of belief in yourself, names may actually hurt you. That's the key component—YOU! If you allow yourself to be hurt by names from others, then you will allow them to hurt you. But, if you decide to honor yourself and believe in yourself so much that even if others call you names or say negative things, you have the ultimate last word to your own mindset to accept it negatively or not to accept it at all.

To triumph over the obstacles in life, you must commit to believing in yourself more than anyone on this green earth will. My main mentor, Brian Tracy, used to remind me all the time that your success and mindset are very similar to a bicycle tire. You must pump up your own tires before you can expect to ride a bike smoothly. This principle is so applicable. Think about it. In order to have a smooth day, you must pump up your mental bicycle tire. Give yourself the amazing feeling of being proud of yourself. Believing in yourself will allow you to walk taller, faster, swifter, and more in a laser focus. People will soon look to you for answers that they have struggled with for years. You will soon be the talk of the town as someone who has a clear head on your shoulders. This is a great feeling and one that you want! Trust me! It's an amazing feeling.

First Things First

Keep in mind that the first step, as I've described earlier in this chapter, is to create, develop, and maintain a great, successful attitude and mindset; It is NOT to pick up the slingshot and stone first… It is NOT to pick up the bow and arrow first.

The way to a healthy relationship with success is to create and accept it in your mindset and belief systems. Most people get the order wrong in this respect. Most people simply try to pick up anything they can throw at the obstacle or the Goliath. This is a primitive way of thinking and not one you want to adopt. We have all been there before. We have all tried to fit the triangle into the square, only to get frustrated and give up.

Vow to yourself you will adopt a new, successful way of thinking that yields far more successful results. Decide to be a person who brings a positive outlook to each and every circumstance that is presented to you. Vow to create a loving and nurturing relationship with yourself as this is the way of true love. It is true that you can't love anyone more than you love yourself. Fill your cup of belief in yourself first and allow the overflow to change the world!

ERIK SWANSON

Habits & Attitude Coach

As an Award-Winning International Keynote Speaker and 13 Time #1 Best-Selling Author, Erik "Mr. Awesome" Swanson is in great demand around the world! He speaks to an average of more than one million people per year. Mr. Swanson has the honor to have been invited to speak to many schools around the world including the prestigious Harvard University. He is also a recurring Faculty Member of CEO Space International as well as an Alumni Keynoter at Vistage Executive Coaching. Erik's speeches can be found on Amazon Prime TV as well as joining the Ted Talk Family with his latest speech called "A Dose of Awesome."

Erik got his start in the self-development world by mentoring directly under Brian Tracy. Quickly climbing to become the top trainer around the world from a group of over 250 handpicked coaches, Erik started to surround himself with the best of the best and very quickly started to be invited to speak on stages alongside such greats as Jim Rohn, Bob Proctor, Les Brown, Sharon Lechter, Jack Canfield, Lisa Nichols, and Joe Dispenza... just to name a few. Erik has created and developed the super-popular Habitude Warrior Conference, which has a two-year waiting list and includes 33 top-named speakers from around the world. It is a 'Ted Talk' style event which has quickly climbed to one of the top ten events not to miss in the United States! He is the creator, founder, and CEO of the Habitude Warrior Mastermind and Global Speakers Mastermind. He is also the creator and publisher of *The 13 Steps To Riches* book series as well as The Principles of David & Goliath book series. His motto is clear... "NDSO!": No Drama – Serve Others!

www.SpeakerErikSwanson.com
www.ThePrinciplesofDavidandGoliath.com

Message from the Creator of
The Principles of David & Goliath

When I was in my twenties, I had the pleasure of meeting an individual who would turn out to be one of the biggest influencers in my life and quickly became my main mentor. That individual is none other than Brian Tracy! I started working for him close to 25 years ago. He had taught me many lessons in how to cultivate my mindset throughout the years. I learned that mindset plays an absolute huge part in all areas of our lives.

Brian has been a master at teaching leadership, connection and sales skills to business professionals all around the world. He has helped millions upon millions of people grow professionally as well as personally for over 50 years.

I thought it only fitting to ask Brian Tracy to grace our book series as one of our celebrity authors and share amazing techniques with us to build our businesses while we learn the value of becoming the 'David' to our 'Goliaths' in our lives. Please enjoy the principles Brian shares in this chapter in how a wealthy mindset turns into a way of wealth.

I would like to thank you, Brian, for allowing us to all learn from your years of knowledge and expertise. We are all honored to be part of this journey with you.

Speaker Erik Swanson ~ 13 Time #1 Bestselling Author

Brian Tracy

THE WAY TO A WEALTHY MINDSET

There are more than eight million millionaires in the United States today. Most of them are self-made. They started with nothing and earned all their money within one generation. The ten wealthiest multi-billionaires in the US all started with nothing and earned their money in a single lifetime.

Fully 80% of self-made millionaires are entrepreneurs or salespeople. Starting and building your own business is and always has been the high road to wealth in the United States.

The good news is that the United States is today the most entrepreneurial country in the world. Fully 70% of Americans dream about starting their own business someday. Fully 1/12th of Americans working today are working in a business start-up.

Entrepreneurship is natural and normal for most people. You have within you, right now, the talents and abilities that you need to start and build a successful business, to take complete control over your life, and achieve financial freedom. You just need to learn how.

If you can drive a car, you can learn to be a successful entrepreneur. As Richard Branson, founder of Virgin Records and Virgin Airlines said, "Once you learn how to start and build a business, you can do it over and over again. The principles are the same."

The good news is that all business skills are learnable. You can learn any business skill you need to achieve any business or financial goal you can set for yourself.

Once you learn a skill, you can use it over and over again. Each time you use it, you get better and better, and as you get better you achieve the same financial goal with less time, effort and energy.

To succeed in your own business, you need a range of skills. The absence of one key skill can hold you back, or even be fatal to your dreams of business success. Fully 80% of new businesses go broke within the first four years; 86% of current businesses are under-performing.

The Purpose of a Business

The purpose of a business is to create and keep a customer in a cost-effective way. Profits are not the purpose of a business. Profits are the result of skillful, successful customer acquisition and customer service.

Business is quite simple. It consists of three basic activities. First, you must find or create a product or service that people want, need and are willing to pay for. Second, you must market and sell the product or service in sufficient quantities to cover all your costs and make a profit. Third, you must manage and administer the people, money and business activities. Give yourself a grade on a scale of 1-10 in each of these three areas. Wherever you are weak, that will be the source of all your problems.

Three Qualities of Successful Entrepreneurs

There are three qualities of successful entrepreneurs, based on studies of many thousands of them. First, they have the courage to launch, to step out in faith, with no guarantees of success. They are willing to face the prospect of temporary failure in the pursuit of opportunity, freedom, control and financial independence.

Second, they have the quality of optimism. They have a positive mental attitude toward themselves and their business opportunities. They have the self-confidence to keep moving forward.

Third, entrepreneurs are persistent. They never give up. As far as they are concerned, "Failure is not an option!"

Three Keys to a Successful Business

If you are not now in business, how do you determine what business to go into? Jim Collins, in his book *Good to Great*, analyzes more than 1000 companies to determine what makes a business great. He finds that the ideal business is one that has three qualities. First, it is something that you have a passion for. It is a product or service that you really like and enjoy, and you want other people to experience it as well.

Second, a successful business is something in which you have the potential to be the best in your area. You may not be the best when you start or at the moment, but you have the potential to be the best if you keep improving.

The third quality of a successful business is that you are offering a product or service that is highly profitable. If you do become the best in your field, you will make a lot of money as a result.

The way you find a product or service is first, find something that you really believe in, care about and want other people to use and enjoy. You must be excited about your product or service if you want your customers to become excited about it. Second, go to a potential customer for your product or service idea and ask him or her if they would buy it, and how much they would pay for it. This is called "Fast, cheap, market research." The only true test is a customer test. When you ask a customer for their opinion, they will always tell you the truth. This can make or save you a fortune in the course of your business career.

The three questions you ask before you introduce a new product or service, or start a business, are these. First, is there a market for your product or service? Is it something that is better, faster, or cheaper, or all three, than anything else available? Never assume. Always test your assumptions before you invest.

Second, is the market large enough? Are there enough people to buy enough of what you sell to make it a prosperous business? Third, is the market concentrated enough? Is it possible for you to reach your market with conventional advertising or promotional methods?

The key question in marketing is always this: "What exactly is to be sold, and to whom is it to be sold, and how is it to be sold, and at what price, and how is it to be billed, produced, distributed and serviced?"

You can ask and answer this question over and over again throughout your business career.

Three Ways to Increase Sales

There are only three ways to increase sales: first, you can make more individual sales. Second, you can make larger sales per customer. Third, you can make more frequent sales to the same customer. You must be continually thinking of ways to do all three.

Customer Satisfaction

The primary job of the entrepreneur, which determines his success, is to innovate and market. Innovation means finding faster, better, cheaper, easier ways to serve customers. Marketing is to find better, faster, cheaper and more efficient ways to sell your product or service to your customers. Innovation and marketing goes on throughout your business life.

There is one primary job, goal and measure of business success. It is "Customer Satisfaction." The entire purpose of your business, and your success, will be determined by how well you satisfy your customers in comparison with other people who want to satisfy the same customers.

The key measure of customer satisfaction is "repeat business." This means that your customers come back and buy from you again and again.

The ultimate question for customer satisfaction is this: "Would you recommend us to others?" Your customer's answer to this question will tell you everything you need to know about the efficiency and effectiveness of your business operations and your products or services.

Your goals in building your business are three. They are, 1) To get the customer to buy from you for the first time. This is the major focus of your sales and marketing efforts. 2) They are to get the customer to buy again because he or she was so satisfied with the first purchase. In reality, the second purchase is the most important because it is proof that you delivered on the promises you made to get the first sale. The most important is number three, that your customers bring their friends and recommend their friends and refer their friends to buy from you as well.

The primary purpose of marketing and advertising is to make selling unnecessary. If you have chosen your market accurately and you have advertised effectively, people will automatically say, "That's for me!"

The rule is that "good advertising sells." If your advertisement is a good advertisement, it will trigger immediate sales. If it does not trigger immediate sales, you must stop that advertising immediately and start advertising in a different way or a different place.

Four Strategic Marketing Principles

There are four keys to successful sales and marketing.

1. Specialization – you must specialize in a particular customer, or market area. It must be clear to you and to everyone who deals with you that this is your area of specialization.

2. Differentiation – the title of the book *Differentiate or Die* is quite true. To be successful in business, you must have a competitive advantage, an area of superiority that makes you different and better than any of your competitors. Your competitive advantage must be something that your customer wants, needs, values and is willing to pay for.

   This is often called your "value offering." It is what makes you the "only supplier" for the customers you have chosen to serve. Sometimes it is called your "area of excellence."

   Finally, in differentiation, you need a "Unique Selling Proposition." This is something that you do or offer that no one else in the world can offer to your customers.

   As Jack Welch of General Electric said, "If you don't have competitive advantage, don't compete." Your ability to develop a competitive advantage, a unique selling proposition, is the key to your success in business.

3. Segmentation – this is the process of identifying your ideal customers, the customers who will most appreciate the product or service in which

you specialize, and the way in which your product or service is superior to anyone else's.

4. Concentration – this requires that you concentrate all of your sales, marketing and business efforts on contacting and selling exactly those customers who can most benefit and enjoy from what it is you do better than anyone else.

Seven Strategic Questions

There are seven strategic questions you need to ask in the process of specialization, differentiation, segmentation and concentration. Here they are:

1. Who is my customer? Who is my ideal customer? Who is my perfect customer? You must be absolutely clear about the age, income, education, tastes, history, background and desires of your ideal customer before you begin a business, and especially before you begin advertising.

2. Why does he or she buy? What need or desire does he or she have that causes him or her to buy in the first place?

3. What value, result or reward does he or she expect when he or she buys from me? What is my value offering to my customer?

4. What do you do better than anyone else? What is your competitive advantage? What makes you superior to any other choice the customer can make?

5. Who or what is your competition? Not only your direct competition, but any other use of the same amount of money, or any other way to satisfy the same need. You must be crystal clear about who you are competing against if you are going to compete successfully.

6. Why does your customer buy from your competitor? What value does he perceive that he receives from your competitor that he does not receive from you? How could you counteract this?

7. What does your customer need to be convinced of to buy from you, rather than from anyone else?

Once you have answered the above questions, ask yourself, "What are the 20% of your activities that could account for 80% of your results?" Remember, only a small number of your decisions and actions account for most of your financial results. What are they?

Seven Key Result Areas of Selling

There are seven steps to selling more of your product or service.

1. Prospecting – this is the process of lead generation. Where are your prospects? Who are they? How do you get to them?

2. Establishing rapport – your ability to build trust, credibility and confidence in your prospective customer is the key to making the sale.

3. Identifying needs accurately – this is the process of asking focused, targeted questions to make sure that you fully understand what your customer wants and needs and is willing to pay for.

4. Presenting – this is where you show, teach and explain the benefits of what you sell. You focus on what your product "does" rather than what your product "is."

5. Answering objections – this is where you answer the normal and natural concerns that prospects have about price and capability.

6. Closing the sale – you must learn how to ask for the order and tell the prospect exactly what he or she has to do to complete the sale.

7. Getting resales and referrals – this is the "acid test" of success. Do your customers buy from you again, and recommend you to their friends and associates? This is the key to the future.

The Law of Three says that there are three activities that account for 90% of your sales results. They are prospecting, presenting and closing. All sales activities are essential, but prospecting, presenting and closing are the keys. All your business problems will arise from a weakness in one of these three areas.

The good news is that these are all learnable skills. You can become excellent in prospecting, presenting and closing, and you must commit yourself to excellence in these areas if you want to build a successful, profitable business.

The Marketing Mix

There are seven parts of the marketing mix that you must continually think about and revise in the face of fast-changing market conditions.

1. Product/Service – what exactly do you sell? What exactly does it do to improve the life or work of your customers? Is this the right product for you, and for your market, at this time?

2. Price – how much do you charge, and how do you charge it? Could there be a better way to price and charge for your products?

3. Promotion – these are your methods of marketing, advertising and selling. What revisions do you need to make in your promotional activities to increase the sales of your products or services?

4. Place – where exactly do you sell and deliver your product? Could there be a better place?

5. Packaging – this refers to the external appearance of your product or service, your business, the way your people dress and groom, and every visual image that your customers see or experience. 95% of the first impression that you make on your customers will be visual, and the visual appearance can often determine whether you make the sale or not.

6. Positioning – how are you positioned in your customer's mind? How do they think about you when you are not there? What do they say about you

when they think of you? What words do you trigger in your customer's mind when your name is brought up?

7. People – who are the key people in your business who deal with customers? Who are your key salespeople? Who are your key service people? The fact is that people do not buy products or services; they buy the people who sell those products or services. Sometimes, one change in your key people can change your entire business.

One of the most important business skills you will ever learn is called "Zero-Based Thinking." In zero-based thinking, you continually ask this question, "If I were not now doing what I am doing, knowing what I now know, would I get into it again today?"

Is there any part of your business, your product, price, promotion, place, packaging, positioning or people that, knowing what you now know, you would not start up again today, if you had to do it over?

It takes tremendous courage to admit that you have made a mistake, or that you are doing the wrong thing based on the current market. But facts are facts. If you would not get into it again today, your only question is, "How do I get out of this, and how fast?"

The only measure of any business activity is this: Is it working? Are you getting results? Are you generating sales, revenues and positive cash flow? If you are not, be prepared to change or even abandon the product, service or activity.

In your business, there are only two types of activities – revenue and expense. You should only invest money in your business to increase revenues. To increase sales.

There are four ways to move faster down the road to wealth.

1. You can do more of certain things.

2. You can do less of other things.

3. You can start up something brand new, something that you have never done before.

4. You can stop certain activities altogether.

Always ask yourself, "What should I do more of, less of, start or stop?"

On the road to wealth, you have three key concerns. First, apply the 80/20 Rule to all of your activities, customers, prospects, methods of sales and advertising, services, cash flow and people. Remember, 20% of your activities will account for 80% of your results. That is where you must focus and concentrate.

Second, profitability – examine every activity of your business to determine the most profitable things you sell or do. What is number one? What is the second most profitable? What is the third most profitable?

You must know, with unerring accuracy, where your best profits are coming from so you can do more of those things.

Third, efficiency – keep asking yourself, "If I could only do one thing all day long, what one activity would it be? What one activity would have the greatest impact on sales, revenues and cash flow?" Whatever your answer to that question, focus on that single-mindedly every single day.

The Road to Wealth

The key to success on your road to wealth is very simple. It is to "add value." All success in life, and in every area, comes from adding value in some way. The more value you add, the more you will be able to capture some of that value for yourself, in the form of commissions, profits and ultimately business success.

You add value by finding a product or service that people want and need, and then by offering that product and service in a quality and quantity that people are willing to pay for. You sell it effectively, deliver it efficiently and service your customers in an excellent way.

The way to wealth is, and always has been, your ability to start and build a successful business through a clear and concise mindset. Much like David in the famous story of "David and Goliath," you must create and maintain the best possible mindset to laser focus on your desired outcome. You may feel that the weight of the challenges in front of you are so insurmountable, but it is your job to vow to yourself that you are strong enough mentally to conquer through any challenge placed in front of you. It is my wish and desire for you to have ultimate success. Be strong mentally and win the game of obtaining the way to a wealthy mindset.

BRIAN TRACY

Brian Tracy is Chairman and CEO of Brian Tracy International, a company specializing in the training and development of individuals and organizations. Brian's goal is to help you achieve your personal and business goals faster and easier than you ever imagined.

Brian Tracy has consulted for more than 1,000 companies and addressed more than 5,000,000 people in 5,000 talks and seminars throughout the US, Canada and 70 other countries worldwide. As a Keynote speaker and seminar leader, he addresses more than 250,000 people each year.

He has studied, researched, written and spoken for 30 years in the fields of economics, history, business, philosophy and psychology. He is the top selling author of over 70 books that have been translated into dozens of languages.

He has written and produced more than 300 audio and video learning programs, including the worldwide, best-selling *Psychology of Achievement*, which has been translated into more than 28 languages.

He speaks to corporate and public audiences on the subjects of Personal and Professional Development, including the executives and staff of many of America's largest corporations. His exciting talks and seminars on Leadership, Selling, Self-Esteem, Goals, Strategy, Creativity and Success Psychology bring about immediate changes and long-term results. Brian Tracy is the recipient of many awards including The Habitude Warrior Lifetime Achievement Award.

He has traveled and worked in over 107 countries on six continents, and speaks four languages. Brian is happily married and has four children. He is active in community and national affairs, and is the President of three companies headquartered in Solana Beach, California.

www.BrianTracy.com
www.ThePrinciplesofDavidandGoliath.com

Alec Stern

THE MINDSET OF LIFE, HEALTH, & BUSINESS

In *The Principles of David and Goliath*, the first stage is Mindset & Belief Systems. In life, health, and business, I have learned how to create a mindset or way of thinking that focuses on setting affirmations and intentions which lead to outcomes. I visualize the outcomes I am looking for and see my vision through to reality. I find that if I can see the outcome play through in my mind, it provides me with the path and steps I will take to get the outcome I desire. It also helps with identifying obstacles that may hinder you from achieving the desired outcome. For example, if I were running a road race, it would be like visualizing crossing the finish line and celebrating the achievement. If I were a basketball player, I would visualize stopping, posting up, shooting the ball, seeing it go into the basket, and winning the game. Before heading into a business meeting, I would visualize the conclusion of the meeting where we shook hands and agreed to work together. This same technique can be used in every aspect of your life.

Once you have this mindset, couple it with your belief system, a set of principles that help interpret the reality of situations. This informs how you would conduct yourself and what actions you would take in various circumstances.

In my life, creating my mindset to focus on the outcomes and visualization of scenarios has been very important to my success. One experience happened when I was eight years old. I always loved listening to music, and I gravitated to percussion sounds, tapping to the music and keeping a beat. Of course, I wanted to make louder sounds, so I started banging away on metal garbage can lids in the garage. My dad would yell at me to stop, but I continued undeterred until I dented all the lids, much to my dad's disappointment. I then moved to pots and pans in the kitchen, which I couldn't damage, but the noise drove my dad from the house every time. (I also perfected using butter knives as drumsticks, which I am still known to do with a set of knives at dinners, parties, and events, much to the amusement of friends and colleagues.) As a family, we enjoyed going to flea markets where I would break away and stop in all the booths to find random ephemera, gadgets, etc., and would ask the dealers to tell me the story of what they were used for. One day I happened to see a Ludwig antique drum set in a dealer's booth. Of course, I smiled ear to ear. My first visualization was me sitting behind this drum set and playing to music. My parents came walking by and saw me looking at the drum set. I remember my mom and dad having a conversation, and I overheard my dad say something like "over my dead body." My mom's response was, "don't squelch his creativity." For the next month leading up to my 8th birthday, every single day, I visualized seeing the drum set in our house and my sitting behind it and playing the drums. My birthday came, and I received the best present I could ever receive; the drum set! I visualized this happening, and it did! Of course, it was against my dad's wishes, but mom won this time, and so did I. Fast forward to recent times, I had set an intention and visualized myself playing on stage at the House of Blues in Boston, Massachusetts. A few years ago, I was thrilled to be invited up to play on stage with two different bands at the House of Blues. Once again, my vision became a reality.

In health, I experienced a near-death moment when I believe having the right mindset going into the situation was what pulled me through. I was diagnosed with Stage 3, advanced prostate cancer. While this news isn't the kind anyone wants to hear, my first reaction was, "I got this!" I was determined not to let cancer hold me back! Like others, I have had many life obstacles I have had to overcome, and this was the next one I needed to beat.

Early morning on October 23, 2018, I was off to the hospital for a "routine five-hour robotic surgery." When I signed the release, I even joked about the line: "this procedure could result in death." I would not think this was funny later.

As I was being prepped and given anesthesia, I joked with the doctors about wanting to see the maintenance records of the robot. I went under anesthesia smiling, laughing, and high-fiving the doctor. I was ready to own this surgery. I visualized a successful surgery, a quick recovery, and getting back on track with life. As I often say, "it was go time!"

Twenty-five hours later, I awoke from my five-hour surgery, which actually took 9 hours due to major complications. I remember looking around and thinking to myself, "this looks anything but routine." There were 10 people in my room, IVs of blood and machines beeping all around me. My lead doctor, the Chief of Urology, informed me that I had died on the operating table, and they brought me back. Imagine that! I couldn't grasp this at all. I thought, "How is this possible with a routine surgery and literally millions of these procedures performed each year?" As it was explained to me, a blood vessel burst, and because it was tucked up under my pelvic bone, they couldn't reach it to stop the bleeding. As I literally bled to death, I went into cardiac arrest and needed to be fully resuscitated while they replaced 120% of my blood to save my life.

When I went under anesthesia, I was happy, joking, ready, and confident. I was completely unconscious when I went into cardiac arrest, so I didn't see lights or hear angels singing (or devils cheering).

While it was indescribably tough to go through a 10-week recovery after the trauma, I had to make a choice. I could either let it bring me down, own me and define me or stay strong and fight. I chose the latter and treated cancer like I do with other challenges in life; just another obstacle that I needed to tackle and kick to the curb.

I believe someone (she) up there decided it wasn't time for me to go. I feel I was brought back to continue my journey and empower others, so I don't take one minute for granted. My mindset played an important role in my overcoming all that happened.

I can't finish this story without a PSA Announcement for PSA tests. Guys, get your PSA tests done, and don't put them off. While there are different schools of thought about PSA testing, I'm glad I did it because an early diagnosis can be managed.

In business, I had an experience that I am not sure I would have the guts to do today. I was in my senior year at Syracuse University School of Management. We used a case study while in a marketing class on a hot computer company called Prime Computer in Boston, Massachusetts. I was living in New Jersey at the time, but with my mom being from Boston, since I was young, I often said how I was going to move to Boston one day and visualized my doing so. After learning about this company, Prime Computer, I said that I wanted to work for them. I called the corporate office in Boston and asked to speak to the head of worldwide Sales & Marketing. As a senior in college, who in their right mind would call a senior executive at a major corporation to ask for a job? Me, that's who. I called and was connected with an executive assistant for Mr. Kirby. I asked to speak to him, and after stating my reason for the call was to talk about being hired for a job for Prime Computer, I was told by his executive assistant that they only hire people with a minimum of 5-10 years of experience. I didn't want to accept this response as I thought they would be missing a big opportunity hiring right out of college. I was kind but persistent in trying to speak to him.

After many attempts and becoming friendly with his assistant, I finally got a 30-minute meet-and- greet (because they weren't hiring right out of college). I visualized our meeting and Mr. Kirby shaking my hand to offer me a job. After 4 visits from New Jersey to Boston for interviews with the entire executive team over a 2-month period, I was hired to be the first recent college graduate hired by Prime Computer. My confidence in achieving this outcome carried me through this process. I was asked to join the training department to attend all the current trainings, see what resonated with me as a recent college graduate and what else was needed to build a curriculum for others to follow.

At the completion of the first year, I was the company's "Rookie of the Year," outperforming all first-year new hires. I was also one of the top company performers overall, reaching over 130% of my annual goal. From there, Prime went on to hire 80-100 recent college graduates annually, and I was asked to speak at all the follow-on new hire training programs.

In life, health, and business, having the right mindset/way of thinking coupled with the right belief systems can help you achieve the outcomes you desire. There will be many times when we feel like David and face an insurmountable opponent in others or even within ourselves. If we consciously prepare, are resourceful, and draw from our experiences or those from whom we seek counsel, we can overcome many of life's challenges.

ALEC STERN

"America's Startup Success Expert"

Alec Stern is an entrepreneur, speaker, mentor, and investor. He has become known as "America's Startup Success Expert" for performing hundreds of keynote speeches worldwide and for his popular sessions at top conferences.

He's been a co-founder or founding team member of 8 startups with 5 exits—2 IPOs and 3 acquisitions. As a primary member of Constant Contact's founding team Alec was one of the original 3 who started the company in an attic. Alec was with the company for 18 years from start-up, to IPO, to a $1.1 Billion-dollar acquisition.

Recently, Alec was selected to the *Influence 100 Authority* List by *Influence Magazine* and was recognized as The World Authority for Entrepreneurship by The Credible Source. In 2020, Alec was a 2-time Visionary Award and a Legend Award winner for his success as an entrepreneur and for his work helping startups and entrepreneurs. In 2021, Alec was 2-time Award of Excellence – Keynote Speaker recipient at top conferences.

One of the Northeast's most accomplished entrepreneurs, he is a limited partner in Boston-based G20 Ventures, which provides early traction capital for East Coast enterprise tech startups. Alec is also an angel investor and mentor in a number of rising startups in various industries. Today Alec is innovating in a variety of industries like SaaS, Technology, Web 3.0, Metaverse, Crypto, Medical Devices and Cannabis.

Alec is passionate about small business, entrepreneurship and innovation. Working within the inner cities, or as he calls it, "urban innovation" is near and dear to his heart.

Only a sideman when it comes to music, Alec is an accomplished drummer and has had the honor of sitting in with a number of musicians including Toby Keith's house band in Vegas.

www.AlecSpeaks.com
www.ThePrinciplesofDavidandGoliath.com

Cynthia Kersey

THE GIFT OF GIVING

Who knew that when my husband of 20 years and I separated in December 1999, my pain would open the door to my greatest purpose?

We had planned on spending the holidays with my parents in Florida. Now, my son and I were going alone. I felt devastated and overwhelmed, but somehow in the midst of my pain, I made a promise to myself that the next Christmas would not find me at my parents' house, feeling sorry for myself. I would instead dedicate myself to doing something for someone else.

As soon as I got home, I called my mentor and friend Millard Fuller, the founder of Habitat for Humanity International, asking him for advice. I met him while interviewing him for my first book, *Unstoppable*. He said, "Cynthia, when you have a great pain in your life, you need a greater purpose." He told me about his recent visit to Nepal, one of the poorest nations in the world, and suggested that building a house for a Nepalese family in need could be a great project for me.

As I sat with his suggestion, I thought, "How many houses would I need to build that would be bigger than this pain in my life?" Even though I had never built one house in my life, it wasn't until I got to the number "100 houses" that it felt bigger than my pain.

That was a crazy audacious goal that I had no idea how to make happen! Each house would cost $2,000. I was a single mom, living on a $14.95 book. I had no big community of potential donors to draw from and didn't even know exactly where Nepal was! But I had a purpose that was bigger than my pain and was invigorated by my newfound project. Plus, I was grateful to have something to focus on besides my problems.

Throughout that year, while grieving the loss of my marriage, there were times when I felt so depressed that I didn't even want to get out of bed. At that moment, I'd think about the Nepalese families who didn't even have a decent place to sleep at night. That thought got me up and moving forward.

One year after separating from my husband and subsequent phone call to Millard, I had raised my goal of $200,000 simply by asking everyone I came in contact with to donate. I brought a team of 18 people to Nepal over the New Year's holiday, and we built the first three of the 100 houses that would subsequently be built over the following year.

I'll never forget the connection I formed with one of the women receiving a home that we funded. Chandra was also a single woman supporting seven family members, including her parents, brothers, and sisters. They all lived together in a tiny one-bedroom shack.

Although Chandra diligently saved money each week for 18 years from her job at a biscuit factory, she would never be able to save enough money to build a home without the help of our project. Her gratitude was apparent in her constant smile. Even though we didn't speak the same language, our hearts were connected. When it was time for me to leave, both of us were in tears, and she begged me never to forget her. As we hugged goodbye, I thought, "Forget you? How could I ever forget you? You were the purpose that got me through the most difficult year of my life!"

That experience changed my life forever. It was the first time I had really experienced the transformational power of giving. When I started this project, I thought I was doing something great for these families. What I hadn't expected was how this project would change my life!

I also experienced something else firsthand: the Law of Giving and Receiving. Unexpectedly, that year I earned more money speaking and selling my $14.95 book than I had earned in a very successful corporate sales career, earning a six-figure income. I was starting to understand the spiritual axiom, "Give, and it shall be given unto you." The Scripture doesn't say wait until you GET something, whether it's getting more money, more time, more love, more support, or more resources. It says GIVE.

The law of receiving is activated by giving. When we wait for something in the future to change before we give, it puts us in a congested state. Stopping the circulation of giving is like stopping the flow of blood. Whenever blood stops flowing, our cells begin to die, and our body ceases to function.

I began to see how when we give, we become a channel for the universe to work through. And this channel is activated through giving. That experience fundamentally changed how I ran my business. With every new book or project that I launched, I attached a philanthropic project to each one. This ignited a deep passion in my heart and brought great joy and meaning to my business.

In 2005, my 2nd book, *Unstoppable Women*, came out, and I was looking for my next philanthropic project. I received an invitation "out of the blue" to attend the first-ever Rural African Women's Conference. The only thing I knew about this conference was that women from rural Kenya were going to meet with us and share their stories. While my schedule was full, I knew I needed to say yes. So, I booked my flight and flew halfway around the world.

Forty other women from North America said yes, and we all flew to the Nairobi airport for the next step of our journey.

Picture this:

We're on a crowded, uncomfortable bus, and the shock absorbers are definitely not working. What's worse, it's hot and muggy, and I am crammed on a bus with women I didn't even know ten minutes before. It's been 12 *LONG* hours. With each bump in the road, I was feeling more and more uncomfortable and getting crankier by the minute.

I had a moment when I thought, "God, please help me get over my little self so that I don't miss why I was called to fly halfway around the world."

An hour later, we drove around a corner, and I could see our destination in the distance. It was a very modest college campus where the women's conference was going to be held.

A couple of hundred women were standing in the driveway, and as we got closer, I could see them smiling and waving. I thought, "Wow, they must be here for us!"

As I walked off the bus, a woman took my hand and pulled me into the middle of this large group of women, and we all began singing and dancing, and the last 12 hours had disappeared. I was in heaven!

The next morning at 8:00 am, I walked into the auditorium, and 400 women were waiting to take the stage. I found out later that many of the women had never left their small village before in their lives and yet they had walked miles, many of them for days, to meet with me and the 40 other women on this journey.

Over the next five days, each woman stood up and, through an interpreter, told their heart-wrenching story. The first woman shared how her youngest daughter got malaria, and the nearest medical clinic was 20 miles away. She had no choice but to carry her daughter on foot to the clinic. On the way, her precious daughter died in her arms before reaching help. And what made her death even more heartbreaking is that she could have been saved with medicine costing the price of a cup of coffee.

The next woman told us that she and her eight-year-old daughter spend 4-6 hours every day fetching water and firewood to keep their family alive.

The third woman told us that her family frequently goes without food for days because they have no way to preserve fruits and veggies, and it's even worse in times of drought.

And their greatest hope and greatest concern was, "How can we get our children an education? Because without it, "nothing will ever change." These women weren't there to complain. They were looking for solutions to create a better life for their children and families.

And as I listened to these women, I first felt sad and great compassion for things they had to endure that I couldn't even imagine. Then I started to feel outraged that simply by virtue of where they were born meant they'd have to live a life of back-breaking poverty with little way out.

As clear as a bell, a voice in my head said, "Cynthia, you've got to do something about this!" And immediately, I heard another even louder voice that said, "This problem is so big and has been going on for so long. What difference could you really make?" Feeling overwhelmed, I decided to ignore both voices and just be present for the experience I was having.

Five days later, it was time to get back on that bus. As we were saying our goodbyes, I hugged these women whom I have since fallen in love with, and they were pleading with me in a language I didn't understand. I turned to my interpreter and asked, "What are they saying"? And she said they're saying, "Please don't forget us."

Something welled up inside of me, and I couldn't ignore their pleas, and I promised them that I would do something to help them.

On the 12-hour bus ride back to Nairobi, my mind was racing with the question of, "what am I going to do about this? I made a promise; where do I even start?"

I was visiting my friend Debbie Ford over Thanksgiving, and she told me that her son Beau did the most wonderful thing for his bar mitzvah. Instead of the customary tradition of receiving gifts and cash, he wanted to do something meaningful. Instead of giving gifts, he asked people to donate money to build a school in Uganda.

It was as if the light bulb had come on. I knew at that moment what I was going to do to make good on that promise I made to those women.

I was turning 50 in a few months, and I would turn that birthday into a fundraiser. I wanted to build a school in East Africa just like Beau had done.

We booked the Shanghai Reds Restaurant in Marina Del Rey, California, and I invited all of my friends to attend. But I gave them a specific request. Instead of giving me a present, I wanted their help to give children in East Africa a present: the gift of an education.

One hundred people attended, and it was standing room only. Afterward, something happened that I hadn't anticipated. People were thanking me for giving them the opportunity to make a difference and change the lives of hundreds of children around the world.

That night we raised $80,000! It was an incredible evening, and I thought, "If I could do this in one night, what could I do if I really put my time and energy into it?"

I was 100% committed and started the Unstoppable Foundation. After doing some research, I discovered something that shocked me.

There were too many well-intended organizations building schools in developing countries, and in five years, many of those schools were empty.

Why were they empty?

- Because you can build a school…

- But if girls don't have access to clean water, they're spending hours every day fetching water and aren't able to attend school.

- If children don't have access to basic medical treatment, they're often sick and can't attend school.

- If children don't have nutritious food, they're hungry and malnourished.

- And if parents can't generate an income, how can the project sustain itself? It can't! I had an epiphany.

If this is going to work, we don't just need to build schools.

We also need to provide the children with access to clean water, healthcare, nutritious food, and training for the parents to earn an income, so the entire project is self-sustaining.

That became my marching orders to find an organization that would help me implement all five pillars. I was fortunate to find a partner on the ground in Kenya who had just started implementing these services, and together we created a program called Sponsor a Village.

It wasn't charity in the traditional sense. It was empowerment!

So, I began asking people to join me in this vision. And what I discovered is that people really care. They care about others, whether they're in their own communities or halfway around the world. They just need a vehicle that they trust to get behind.

And so they gave. They had fundraisers. Their children had fundraisers. They asked their friends and community to write checks. They used their birthdays as fundraisers.

And the results have been amazing.

Because of our generous supporters, we have impacted over 100,000 men, women, and children in the Maasai Mara alone with our five-pillar model.

Entire communities are now thriving with the tools to lift themselves out of poverty.

And people continue to thank us for the great opportunity to give and experience the blessings that come from that act of generosity.

What began in 1999 as a philanthropic project designed to provide a purpose that was bigger than my pain has grown into a lifetime commitment.

The joy of working with dear friends like Bob Proctor, Mary Morrissey, and other generous supporters on this mission has been one of the greatest gifts of all. As my mentor, Millard Fuller, always said, "I feel like the richest person on the planet."

To learn how you can be a part of this important mission, go to *UnstoppableFoundation.org* for more info.

CYNTHIA KERSEY

Cynthia Kersey is the Founder & Chief Executive Officer of the Unstoppable Foundation whose mission is to ensure that every child on the planet receives access to the life-long gift of education.

Cynthia is a leader in the transformational industry. She's the bestselling author of two books, *"Unstoppable"* and *"Unstoppable Women,"* a collection of powerful stories and strategies from people who through perseverance and consistent action turned obstacles into personal triumph. These books have motivated countless readers with over 500,000 copies sold worldwide in 17 languages.

Cynthia is also an inspiring speaker, entrepreneur, national columnist and contributing editor to Success Magazine, and was a featured guest on the Oprah Winfrey Show when Oprah launched the Angel Network.

Cynthia is a member of the Transformational Leadership Council—an organization made up of internationally known thought leaders and educators including founder Jack Canfield, creator of the mega best-selling "Chicken Soup for the Soul" series.

As an organization, they impact millions of people worldwide and through a rigid vetting process awarded the Unstoppable Foundation as their designated humanitarian organization to support in 2012.

Cynthia's passion is showing how each of us can solve the world's most seemingly impossible challenges through simple individual actions.

www.UnstoppableFoundation.org
www.ThePrinciplesofDavidandGoliath.com

Rob Angel

PICTURE THIS!

Everybody has a David and Goliath story, whether it's being an underdog, one of the misunderstood, a person who had the most significant challenges, or the most extraordinary battles to face. Those experiences are unique to each of us. Little did I know that my David and Goliath story would result in such a positive way in the creation of one of the world's most successful board games of all time—PICTIONARY!

Given my background and our business circumstances, when I decided to create Pictionary and launch it, there wasn't access to production, distribution, or even capital like there is today. I don't want to come across as sour grapes, but my two partners and I were up against the world while launching this game. When we physically put the game together, we didn't have, just one company; nine different companies supplied pieces to the game and we put them together by hand. We decided to sell the game locally in Seattle, The top retail big box stores, Toys R

Us, TB Toys, etc. were wrapped up so tightly with policies and procedures that we didn't have access to any of those stores because we were so small. We had to make up our own rules and develop our own unique disruptive distribution channels. We had to make up our selling techniques that were against the norm. The industry standards were to sell to only independent toy stores and big-box game stores. We did give the standard procedures in the industry a try, but there was only three independent toy stores in Seattle at the time. The more prominent game stores took up everything else in the market.

We couldn't survive on just selling to the small stores in Seattle. So we had to improvise and innovate new sales techniques and channels to make our success, including department stores, which had never been done before by other game companies. Of course, the bookstores, knickknacks stores, and all different types of stores were open to us so we could still compete with the big boys.

Challenges have always energized me. I love them, and I was never an oh-woe-is-me guy that I can't play with the big boys, or I can't do necessarily what I thought I was going to be able to do. It was just a challenge that I loved. It was exciting to wake up every day and ask myself, "What will I do today to succeed? What am I going to do today to be different? I will have to rise to the challenge." It was invigorating and exhilarating, and nothing was too big or small of a challenge. When things went right, and they did, it was awesome. And when things went wrong, it was also fantastic.

So it was very much the mindset that I had at the time was to risk everything and just go for it. I have nothing to lose. I love my product. I love my partners. We're going to make this work, no matter what.

When faced with adversities and challenges, what you do says a lot about you. Your mindset should always be that of gobbling up the challenges. No matter your background, status, or upbringing, how you reponed to challenges, and they will come, will define you and your business.

The Power of Naivety

Naivety truly helped me face the Goliaths in this industry. I never doubted we could do it, so I found a way around the obstacles before us. Back then, challenges were just things that had to be confronted. So, I didn't take anything, policies, or circumstances personally. I didn't take the fact that we couldn't get distribution personally or that we weren't getting sales in the big box stores personally. All I knew and cared about was getting it done. That has always been a big part of my character and the makeup of who I am Naivety was more of a wanderlust kind of thing, where it was just a got-to-get-it-done mindset. It's just part of who I am.

It's More than Just a Game

As Pictionary took off and got into bigger stores throughout the country, some of the greatest triumphs of the journey included me landing my first big break and sale. We got a big sale with Nordstrom department stores. They didn't have a game department. Nordstrom had never sold anything outside of clothing shoes, handbags, and jewelry, so my naivety and valiant attempts won us some big wins. I figured, "Why not? They should be selling Pictionary. Everybody should be selling Pictionary because it's an emotional experience, not just a game."

That was a big belief for us. We weren't only selling a game—we were selling an experience. People collaborated, had fun, forgot their troubles, and had precious moments while playing Pictionary. Growing up, playing board games was a simple opportunity to be present and have fun. So I just thought that they should be selling out at Nordstrom, even though they didn't have a game department.

When I went to pitch Nordstrom, I offered them the moon and the stars. I'd take the games back that they didn't sell. I would do demonstrations and personally sell all the Games they bought. I would restock their shelves. I would even go as far as to tell their employees how to play the game. All this so Nordstrom could make more money and us more sales.

But that way, I gained a foothold in this enterprise called Nordstrom, which turned out to be a pivotal moment for us. They are such a great retailer and have such an excellent reputation. We were getting traction and awareness by other stores just by being there. That was a huge win. It turned out to be a pivotal moment and not just because of the sales.

The excitement of Pictionary traveled amongst the managers and stores along the west coast. This excitement gave us a strong foothold outside the Seattle market. That is precisely why I'm sitting here today—our most enormous Goliath was our success. We became so popular because of the hard work that we were doing.

We were very successful in Seattle, where we did all our sales and marketing and kept tabs on the product. By the time we needed to distribute it on a national scale, we didn't have the resources, Weirdly, if we weren't successful as quickly as we were, we could have just bootstrapped it and kept plugging along We were clever, but demand was too strong, so without help, we could have very well failed because of our success. Hence our success was our most significant challenge and Goliath. We had to find other means to scale the product and the business.

I recently wrote a book called *Game Changer* about my Pictionary experience and am currently working to turn that into a documentary, a master class, and possibly even a movie. I'm currently working on keeping up the momentum while preserving the Pictionary legacy. It's gone just fine, without me in the ownership seat, but it is my story. It intertwines with everything in my life.

Pictionary Is My Cosmic Gravy

The stories of creating Pictionary are cosmic. They make up the theory of the universe in which I live. The game is my meat and potatoes, which ultimately created my livelihood. However, playing Pictionary created memories and experiences stories that people share with me everywhere. Those stories are my gravy.

I hear stories constantly. I call them unintended consequences. Their reports on the game's influence on their homes and families have changed their lives dramatically. Who would have ever thought any of this was possible just because I created a silly little game? I never knew what Pictionary would amount to as we knocked on doors of departments stores.

It was not a silly little game, it was a very powerful game, and it was a compelling catalyst for change, for raising the planet's vibration. Throughout the earth, over a billion people have played Pictionary. That's a lot of people with many stories, laughter, and memories created by a game. There's a lot of excitement and fun that has changed the world.

My advice to you, the reader of this extraordinary book, is to have a why-not mindset regarding your dreams. If you can be feel and believe in the outcome of your dreams without overcomplicating your journey, you'll find yourself climbing mountains, facing giants, and even having a bit of fun along the way. I recommend a game of Pictionary; it may just change your life.

ROB ANGEL

In 1985, Rob Angel was a 26-year-old waiter from Seattle. Using a few simple tools, a Webster's paperback dictionary, a No.2 pencil, and a yellow legal pad, he created the phenomenally successful and iconic board game Pictionary®. With no manual to turn to, he made his own rules by relying on his intuition, hard work, and unwavering entrepreneurial spirit to build Pictionary into a global powerhouse. Putting together the first 1000 games by hand in his tiny apartment, Angel mastered all the needed business skills, including sales, marketing, and distribution. For the next 17 years, Rob shepherded Pictionary to sales of 38,000,000 Pictionary games sold worldwide in over 60 countries.

Rob Angel is also the author of *GAME CHANGER: The Story of Pictionary and How I Turned a Simple Idea into the Bestselling Board Game in the World (Amplify/June 2020)*. Pictionary® is a registered trademark of Mattel, Inc.

Today, Rob is an entrepreneur, explorer, investor, philanthropist, and sought-after speaker on a mission to help people create their own success and best life by encouraging them to have the confidence to take their first small step. From running with the bulls to swimming with sharks, Rob is always OPEN to new and exciting adventures.

www.RobAngel.com
www.ThePrinciplesofDavidandGoliath.com

Adrienne Micali

TRUST WHAT COMES INTO YOUR LIFE

It's imperative to be open. I have a saying on my wall that says, "Have a mind that is open to everything and attached to nothing." That philosophy has led me on many adventures in my life. I may debate choices in my mind from time to time, but I never refuse the ideas entirely. Before I say no, I always trust the natural process and try it.

Curiosity and Openness

Years ago, I was out with a friend and struck up a conversation with a stranger. The gentleman had been wearing one of those colored rubber bands around his wrist. Naturally, I wanted to know what it was for, so I asked him, "What's that wristband mean to you?" Surprised by my question and interest, he responded with a smile. At the time, I had no idea who he was. I only inquired because of my curiosity and dedication to being present in the moment. I later found out after that conversation that I was speaking to one of the wealthiest men in the country. At one point in our conversation, he said, "You're a breath of fresh air." I get that a lot.

I don't remember his name, but the exchange was one where I understood the importance of meeting someone new and just connecting with them. For me, it is always about the connection, not the clout. I hope to connect without anything in return. Pay it forward with genuineness without expectation of something in return. I am there for that reason, which is why I am the way I am.

Far too often, we connect with strategy or alternative. Whereas, if we only take micro-moments to be curious and open, we can build experiences that will fill our lives with years of cherished memories. When you connect solely to connect, people will feel your genuineness.

For me, curiosity strikes inquisitiveness where I internally ask myself if I align with something or not. Often, I have had incredible experiences and lessons. I follow that inclination by not refuting and choosing to go along with the natural flow and process of what is in front of me at the moment. It's ultimately how I found the Habitude Warrior Mastermind and Global Speakers Mastermind.

This mindset is a driving force in my life. We have no idea what the result will look like, yet we still move forward. And it becomes the experience of the timeline of beautiful historical events that can bring us to the present. Be open and recognize that your life and decisions require you to be in a constant phase of shifting. Trust what is in front of you.

Awareness

I was born an identical twin. I quite literally was born with a mirror image, which has allowed me the opportunity to consequently learn the lessons that I needed to, to make conscious choices that enhance MY life's story and experiences.

I grew up in a household that, at times, was very stressful. My older brother was in and out of the hospital for a rare medical condition until the age of 40. My parents were young and were adamant about finding the proper care for him. This was way before Google could get you the information in two seconds flat. It wasn't an easy feat. This allowed for some hectic times, so I always tried to be this kid who didn't cause trouble. I grew up living cautiously in a psychological and socially limited box. That box in my youth drove me to break those limitations and helped me to develop a hyperactive curiosity. As a teenager, I experimented with many things that could have gotten me into trouble, but I tried everything for myself, not for others. I learned a ton. It was easy to move on if it didn't feel right or resonate with me.

That mindset has taken me on a different journey of finding myself. If one door closed, I quickly looked for the next open one. I had some friends who were also adventurers. At 19, we started traveling the world, trusting that our journeys would guide us. In my travels, I had many amazing experiences. To name a few:

- The Pope blessed me while visiting the Vatican in Rome

- Danced with an Aboriginal while in Australia

- Experienced extreme sports in New Zealand

- Danced until sunrise on the Isles of Greece

- Laughed the hardest on an overnight train from Paris to Italy

- Caught a free concert where John Legend and The Black Eyed Peas performed by the Duomo in Milan

Each of these experiences was an incredible adventure. Although I'll most likely never see those people again, my exchange, time, openness, and curiosity have forever influenced my life and mindset. People are beautiful!

Take the Good and Tune It Up

Professionally, I've been in personal development training for quite some time. I've helped support others in many ways, and I've been told that I'm good at it because I have this keen sense of what's happening.

From all the years of self-development, I've learned that our VOICE matters. We all need to stand for something fulfilling. That's the cycle of development. I'm looking to show up differently in a more significant way so that people can see themselves in me.

And I'm in a place now where I currently take everything I've learned and am bestowing that on my children. But, although I feel fulfilled in many areas, I still have more dreams to achieve.

The Clarity Catalyst

I am certified in a mindfulness and emotional intelligence program that was developed by Dr. Michael Ray in 1979 and based on his work at Stanford University and in corporations. I have trained it in a pilot group and taught it to adults and tweens.

My ultimate goal and vision were to build a community with a space of various healing modalities for people. I've taught in groups virtually; however, I prefer an in-person environment—the energy is just different. I have this vision to have a physical space where anyone can come and get what they need to be healed mentally, physically, spiritually, and emotionally. Reiki, sound healing, coaching, and more alternative work would be welcomed. Much like the REC centers I used to have as a kid, but with a sole focus on gathering and growing, it would incorporate everything they don't teach you in school, like money mindset, mindfulness, peer groups, and accountability partnerships.

It's helped the kids I've worked with achieve outcomes and results that people desire to experience. Like David fighting Goliath, I believe that a shifting mindset can help anyone experience everything they were meant to and more so that they are adequately equipped to handle their various battles, giants, and challenges. Their toolbox will contain all they need to meet any challenge that may arise in the process of life.

I had the unique opportunity to see children go through the pilot program group, including my daughter and her friends. Although my daughter gave me the most pushback in this sequence, I got to see it work through her choices and in her life.

These concepts are not like math or English. Traditional schooling does not teach or equip us with any sense of emotional intelligence. For many of the kids in this proven program, it was all about feeling confident about their own ability to make decisions, learning about time management, using their unique gifts, and trusting the process of it all.

Trust the Process

'Trusting the process' could change the trajectory of someone's life. The process is simple. It is a flow and a belief. It allows you to see and experience the parts that accumulate to a fulfilling life of energy and hope. My goal is to have a lifetime of experiences, knowledge, and connections and then coach and transfer that belief system to others, so they too have those.

As I apply this belief in every aspect of my life, I find myself in these spaces where people say to me, "You're the only one who understands what I'm going through." I'm discovering that more and more people need and want to be understood.

It's time for me to teach and help people trust the process of life. I have been curious enough to live a life wholly. I connect with society, and my next step is figuring out how to perpetuate and duplicate my learnings to help people be understood and heard.

I actively seek clarity, results, and solutions for my life. I started yoga to control my thoughts and energy, and people laughed at me, even close friends and family. However, I learned to use that yoga practice in childbirth. Breathwork is profound and can heal the body and mind. I've always taken the pieces that work for me—I know my breathing helps me—take some deep breaths and let them run through you.

Rather than complaining, "Why is this happening to me," you should exclaim, "Who do I get to BE in this process?" There's no one answer for everyone. It's uniquely personal. However, there is always something for everyone to learn. We often get stuck in the way things look and forget that it's all part of the process.

When my daughter comes home after a hard day, I've learned to sit with her and hug her for as long as she needs. What they need most is to be held and heard. I hug her, that's it. It takes self-control not to react or give immediate feedback. Fortunately, I have the tools to shift out of that mindset.

Simplify Everything

Life is too exciting to overcomplicate things. Simplify it. It isn't complex. Make it simple and replicable for every area of your life. Our core qualities form our mindsets through the choices that we make.

One of my biggest challenges is watching my loved ones go through difficult stages in life. If things are hard, why can't they also be easy? It's all in your mindset. It wasn't hard for David to take down a giant, but for the entire army, it appeared too difficult of a task to complete. It's important to take immediate action rather than sit on something for too long. I don't wallow. Be in that moment and ready to shift. It's why I've been able to have these experiences because I take the next steps.

My desires have led me to travel, experience, and meet remarkable people. It's been a lot of fun, and it's not over. THERE IS ALWAYS A NEW SEASON IN LIFE. EACH SEASON LOOKS DIFFERENT.

Trust the process. Simplify your methods. Show up in your life.

ADRIENNE MICALI

About Adrienne Micali: Adrienne is a wife and mom of two beautiful souls currently living in Brooklyn, New York. As a certified life coach in Clarity Catalyst, a program based on a Stanford University Master's Degree course, she is skilled in helping clients achieve mental clarity by sharing formulas and tools needed to spark empowered self-growth.

Adrienne's passion to serve is an example of what is possible if you are willing to take a leap of faith, commit to the life you love, and make conscious choices. Her mission is to inspire and motivate those willing to grow and live the life of THEIR dreams.

Author's Website: *www.TheSwitchSpace.com*
www.ThePrinciplesofDavidandGoliath.com

Dr. Angela Harden-Mack

SLAY THE GIANT

You are great. You were created to do great works. You were blessed with great goodness. These great things are your destiny. They won't come to you automatically or without opposition. As a matter of fact, many of your great works and goodness, your big and bold dreams, will have giant obstacles blocking the path that leads to you. If you are to do the great works you are called to do and make your big, bold dreams a reality, you must overcome the giant obstacles. I will refer to the giant obstacles as giants. It would help if you had a positive mindset to overcome the obstacles. It's vital to have a positive mindset to slay your giants. You must think like a slayer. What does the mindset of the slayer include?

"I am an Awesome Achiever. I turn my dreams into reality. What my mind believes and conceives, I achieve. I am living my dreams!" This faith confession has served me well over 20 years. It is a part of my slayer mindset. This faith confession was created based on a positive mindset nurtured by parents who had positive mindsets. My parents taught me how to slay my giants. A positive mindset is needed to overcome the giant obstacles that exist as part of the life experience related to accomplishing big and bold goals.

Big, bold dreams require big, bold goals. My parents often told us we could be anything and do anything we wanted. My father would often say, "You need roots and wings. The roots to ground you and keep you strong and the wings to dream and soar." My roots and wings equipped me with the mindset to slay giants. As a young girl, I often dreamed of the life I wanted. I didn't hold back. I believed what my parents told me, that my dreams could come true. I conceived of plans to make my dreams come true. My parents taught us lessons such as faith, positivity, gratitude, kindness, humility, perseverance, and resilience, to name a few. My parents taught me to aim high, dream big, and work the plan until the dream became a reality. They taught me how to have the slayer mindset to slay my giants. I dreamed. I believed. I conceived. I slayed my giants. I received my dream. I AM LIVING MY DREAMS! I have what I have because I am a warrior with a slayer mindset.

Based on the mindset definition from dictionary.com, this is my working interpretation: "Mindset is the set of beliefs that determine how someone interprets and responds to circumstances." Think of it this way. Your mindset is about what you see and how you act about circumstances. If you have a positive mindset, you will have positive expectations and act or respond from overcoming and victory. If you have a negative mindset, you will have negative expectations and act or respond from oppression or defeat. The slayer mindset is positive. The slayer expects ALL things to work out for good for victory. The slayer sees past the giant to the great goodness behind the giant. The slayer says, "I can. I will. I must defeat the giant to claim what is MINE." The slayer aims for extraordinary and does not settle for ordinary. To walk away, allowing the giant to remain and continue to oppose the goodness, would be to settle for the ordinary. Not so for the slayer. "Greater is He in me than he in the world," says the slayer. No matter the type of giant obstacle, the slayer shows up.

Giant obstacles come in many forms. Some people report limiting beliefs as a giant obstacle. Some people report negative emotions, such as fear, as their giant obstacle. Some people report time as a giant obstacle. Commonly, many big dreams require significant preparation and time. Often, it's years and years to become a reality. My giant obstacle was time. At age 10, I set my sights on the dream to become a doctor. I dreamed, set my goal, created a plan, and worked on that plan for approximately 15 years. Fifteen years is a long time. At times I grew impatient with the timeline. A few times, I questioned if the dream was worth the sacrifices. The great news is that I didn't allow impatience and time to cause me to quit prematurely and miss my dream. The dream was worth the sacrifices. The slayer mindset equipped me, and I'm excited to report that I have been living my dream as Dr. Angela for more than 25 years! I maintained focus, resilience, and perseverance because of behaviors common to those with the slayer mindset. Those behaviors are to show up, speak up, and suit up.

What giant obstacles are you facing? What's standing in the path keeping you from your dreams? Do you have the positive mindset necessary to slay giants? Will people recognize you as a slayer? Are you ready to slay your giants?

You will recognize a giant slayer by his actions. It's battle time when the giants show up to oppose you and prevent you from your great goodness. Slaying the giants isn't merely saying to the giants, "Be gone." You have to show up to do battle. Engaging, confronting, and overcoming the giants blocking your path is necessary. You free your great works and great goodness. Slaying the giants requires participation, not observation. You cannot simultaneously stay on the sidelines watching and step out in the battle to engage the giants. There is a decision to make. It is the choice to be passive and be oppressed or be active and overcome. If you decide to be active, get out in front of the giant and conquer it. Giant slayers show up ready to overcome and triumph. The slayer knows that God is bigger than every obstacle. The slayers know that they have everything in Christ Jesus to overcome and triumph.

The giant slayer is a warrior. He shows up and suits up in the armor necessary for the battle. His armor is person- and battle-specific. Others may suggest the type of armor to use or offer their armor. The slayer, however, knows that he needs what is explicitly designed for him. If you are not triumphant in battle, perhaps you are in armor designed for someone else. The giant slayer is skilled in the weapons of his warfare. His skill and expertise will determine the tools that will result in his victory. The slayer mindset includes seeing what is not seen with the eye and does not look at his weapons with natural eyesight. The slayer walks by faith - not sight - and the weapons of his warfare are mighty. What appears to be a simple object is a mighty weapon in the hand of the slayer.

Giant slayers show up and speak up. Words have enormous power, and giant slayers speak with authority and power. Giant slayers know the importance of speaking the correct words at the right time to overcome their obstacles. The giant slayer knows that words have the creative power to build, tear down, pull up, root out, attract, and repel. The giant slayer releases into the atmosphere words that result in victory. The death of the giant obstacle and the life of the slayer's dream is in the slayer's speech. The slayer, with wisdom, declares and proclaims, prays, and recites power-filled words that set into motion actions that attract divine troops and repel troops of the enemy. The giant slayer speaks to the giant mountain so that it moves. The slayer shouts to the wall to bring it down. The slayer declares victory before launching the attack, resulting in the giant's defeat.

The mindset necessary to overcome opposition, make dreams reality and live great lives is in the positive mindset of the giant slayer. This mindset results in positive expectations, resilience, focus, and perseverance. You are great. You were created to do great works. You were blessed with great goodness. If you are bold enough to dream big, bold dreams giant obstacles will stand to oppose you. If you are a warrior and have a slayer mindset, you can overcome the giants. Will you suit up and speak up to fight and overcome every giant opposing and declare your victory?

DR. ANGELA HARDEN-MACK, MD

About Dr. Angela Harden-Mack, MD: Dr. Angela Harden-Mack wears many hats. Her unique skill set as physician, speaker, empowerment coach, author, and bible teacher has equipped her for a career inspiring and empowering people for more than 25 years. She reports feeling fortunate to use her experience and expertise to help people achieve wholeness and live great lives. It is her honor and joy to serve.

She is the CEO and Founder of Live Great Lives, LLC, Women's Empowerment Coaching. Live Great Lives serves the busy professional woman who feels undervalued and overloaded. As a result of the transformational coaching programs, the busy women served by Dr. Angela and Live Great Lives, show up feeling unapologetically awesome with power and intention. Dr.

Angela's engaging speaking style delivers messages that inspire the listeners to aim high, breakthrough limitations, and step out with boldness and intention to experience great living.

Dr. Angela is the author of a discipleship journal and a great living and visualization handbook.

She is a proud graduate of The Johns Hopkins University and a proud graduate of Wayne State University Medical School. She joyfully serves family and friends while enjoying fun time activities such as reading, traveling, and horseback riding.

Author's Website: *www.LiveGreatLives.com*
ThePrinciplesofDavidandGoliath.com

Angelika Ullsperger

MIND POWER

Since the beginning of time, people have turned to religion for moral guidance, faith, and community. Religious text has acted as a guide to teach us lessons and morals. Regardless of whether you believe in religion, anyone can benefit from reading these scriptures. All you must do is open your heart and your mind. Look to understand, not to judge, as we explore the principles of David and Goliath.

In the plains of Israel stood a man seemingly larger than life itself. Not a single person came anywhere close to him in size. He stood firm, covered in illustrious armor, and challenged any man to defeat him. Many brave men stepped up to the challenge, but not a single man survived. Not even the best soldiers could stand up to the tower of a man they called Goliath. Until one day, a young shepherd, his head held high with confidence, defeated a challenge every other person deemed impossible.

Even the strongest men lost, falling to the hand of Goliath. Yet David, who was only a shepherd, triumphed over the undefeatable giant with nothing but his knowledge, a slingshot, and a rock.

How did he do it? Every other man failed; something about David was different. The best rival of unmatchable physical strength is the power knowledge can lend.

All the power David used to defeat Goliath came from inside of him. It started with his mindset. With not a lick of experience in combat, David knew he did not have the skills or strength to compete. He did have the skills acquired from his time herding livestock paired with a passionate faith to fuel him. He did what everyone thought was impossible.

Part of David's mindset comes from his faith in himself & his abilities. David could have given any reason why he couldn't fight Goliath. But he didn't. He was smaller, weaker, and didn't have the experience. David remained courageous in himself and stepped up to the challenge. David was not focused on what he didn't have or couldn't do. He focused on finding the how. He doesn't just believe he can do it; he knows he can do it. As Henry Ford said, "Whether you believe you can do a thing or not, you are right." David believed he could conquer Goliath, so he defeated Goliath. Even when expressing their concerns for David and his abilities, he didn't waver. The faith he has in himself is so strong that David can overcome the opinions of those around him, but he canface and beat the biggest challenge of them all. A challenge so large everyone 'knew' it couldn't be done. David knew differently. He knew he could. He instead used his intelligence to think outside of the box to do something that everyone else thought was impossible.

As I learned from Sharon Lechter, what you want is achievable; sometimes, you need to re-adjust what you are doing to get there.

Every problem has a solution. It's not a matter of if; it's a matter of how. You can do anything you truly set in your mind.

People will try to get you to stop and do something else in life. These actions don't always come from a place of malice; they can come from love and fear. Some people are so terrified of you failing and suffering they will try to talk you out of your self-conviction. But when your mindset is strong enough, you *know* you will get there. It becomes no longer a conversation of 'ifs' but of 'how.'

Regardless of how skilled you are, if you don't have conviction in yourself and your abilities, you will struggle to overcome challenges.

Even though David was surrounded by people who doubted him, his mindset was so strong it didn't matter. If you're not at this point yet, it's okay. David didn't go to sleep without faith in himself and woke up the next day filled with conviction. Mindset is grown. If you can, surround yourself with others who have the mindset you want, people who will support you until you've forged a mindset of steel.

In most cases, the way our parents or caregivers speak to us growing up forms our inner voice. Sometimes the negative voice inside you isn't your doing; sometimes, it is. Regardless of where it came from, you can overcome it by rebuilding your mindset and altering your belief systems.

For me and many others, our most enormous Goliath is ourselves. Now, that's not your fault. We can control ourselves and how we react/perceive, but we can't control the forces around us. The voices in our minds form from how our parents and caregivers speak to us. So, for those of us who've spent time growing up around negative, cynical, abusive people, it will affect the way your mindset forms. Like many things, though, it can be changed through working on yourself. You can rewire your brain and upgrade your mindset. One way to begin this change is affirmations. For some, the idea is corny, and honestly, I thought the same for a while. The realization hit me strongly, why am I judging something so harshly when I've never even tried it? I was a hypocrite for someone who takes pride in not being judgmental. After trying it, to my surprise, it does work.

Everyone struggles and I am no exception. Things were rough.

I missed over 400 days of high school. It got to the point when people were surprised when I was in class. I eventually had to do weekend school, online school, and in-person private tutoring to graduate.

I had the idea after high school ended, things would be easier. On the night of my graduation, my grandfather's health deteriorated rapidly. I helped take care of him until he passed on. My Yiayia was left alone without her best friend. She didn't want to keep living, so she decided to pass on about a year later. A year later, I got into an abusive relationship. It destroyed me. It's hard to convey the psychological torture properly he put me through; all I can say is he broke me. I wish I could say things started to get better after that, but not really. They got worse. To help my mom feel safer, we let my friend move in. After allowing him to move in, he started to show his true colors. However, that is a story for another time.

Scott came into our lives out of the blue, but his humor, kindness, and creativity won us over quickly. Scott was a genuinely good human being. He was a true inspiration for me, but he was also having a rough time. One day I called 911 for assistance because he was not doing well.

The police came and shot him. They left him for hours to bleed out even though we live less than five minutes away from a fire station. Instead of doing anything to help him, they lied and said it was because there were hostages. We told them no one else was in the house. When I voiced how poorly everything was conducted, they tried to say I was on drugs. They made so many excuses, but that will never change the fact they took away a life unjustly.

I thought I was broken before, but that shattered me. I thought I slept a lot before, but now, all I did was sleep. The only time I got up was to move somewhere else to go back to sleep.

Year after year, I encountered traumatic events. The only thing that got me through was my mindset. My mind was set on the idea that everything would be okay; it was just a matter of time.

After suffering for so long and feeling so much pain, I didn't want anyone else to suffer in the way I did, but I also knew I couldn't help anyone unless I helped myself. I decided to wake up, and I turned the page to start a new journey.

People thought I wouldn't succeed, but their opinions never mattered. I knew I could do it, and now, I've been a featured co-author at a book-signing event at one of the #1 networking conferences in the nation. If I can overcome my battles, so can you.

With the rise of social media, it can seem more and more like everyone has a perfect life while you're struggling with challenges, but it's important to remember social media is a highlight reel of the lives of others. People only post what they want you to see, and for many, this means leaving out the struggles and focusing on, even exaggerating the positives.

Even though it may seem like it, you are never alone in your struggles. As big as they are, Goliaths come in many shapes and sizes. Everyone has them. Everyone faces a Goliath, but every Goliath has a weakness; you need to find it and find out what strategy works for *you*.

Think about every challenge you got through. There were times when you thought you couldn't get through it. But here you are. Right here, right now. Which means *you* made it. There hasn't been a day you haven't been able to get through, no matter how difficult.

Remember everything you have overcome the next time you encounter a Goliath-sized challenge. This means whatever obstacle you are facing; YOU can get through it. The journey can seem hazy when you run into a storm, but even when it rains, the sun still shines, and you can find what you want on the other side. It's always harder at the moment to imagine ourselves standing triumphantly on the other side but remember, up until this moment, you have survived every challenge you have ever faced, even the ones that seemed impossible. It may benefit you to keep this in mind when you feel like there is no end in sight. Remember every Goliath you've defeated when you feel like there is no end in sight. Remember, you CAN.

ANGELIKA ULLSPERGER

About Angelika Ullsperger: Angelika is a serial entrepreneur from Baltimore, Maryland. She is a fashion designer, model, artist, photographer, and musician. Angelika has extensive and well-rounded professional experience, having worked as a business owner, carpenter, chef, graphic designer, manager, event planner, sales and product specialist, marketer, and coach. Angelika is now a #1 Best-Selling Author in the *13 Steps To Riches* historical book series. She is a life-long learner with a sincere and genuine interest in all things of the world with a significant interest in the formal subject of abnormal psychology, neuroscience, and quantum physics.

Angelika prides herself as someone who has saved lives as a friend, first responder, EMT, and knowledgeable suicide prevention advocate. With a vast knowledge and experience in multiple professions, Angelika is also a proud honorable member of Phi Theta Kappa, The APA, the AAAS, and an FBLA (Future Business Leaders Association) Business Competition Finalist. She is Certified in basic coding and blockchain technology. Amongst her career and vast experience, Angelika is an adventurer and avid dog lover.

Her ultimate goals and dreams are to make a lasting positive impact in people's lives through her wealth of knowledge and skillsets.

Author's Website: *www.Angelika.world*
www.ThePrinciplesofDavidandGoliath.com

Anthony Manzon

SUCCESS STARTS WITH MINDSET

If you ask ten different people to define success, you will get ten different answers. The beauty in the word success is that success can be achieved at any scale, big or small. For some, success may be having the ability to live debt-free, or for someone relearning how to walk, their success may be taking an unattended step. Success is simply perception. Success is fluid and constantly changing. What you define as success today will not always be how you define success.

Despite the many definitions of success, the one common factor is that success starts with mindset.

Think of success like you are building a brick house. Each brick you lay represents one of your thoughts. Positive thoughts strengthen your house; negative thoughts weaken your house. These thoughts may be beliefs about yourself, what you are capable of, what you deserve, and so on. If you don't carefully choose which bricks to use, eventually, your house will come crashing down.

What you have today: the money in the bank, the quality of relationships, and even your current physique are in direct proportion to your mindset level. If you are not satisfied financially, spiritually, relationally, or physically, that's ok. However, understand that everything you look to achieve is above the current level of your mindset. If you want to change, your mindset must change.

If your mindset is weak and undisciplined, like mine when I first started, that's perfectly fine. Acknowledge it and commit to strengthening your mindset. Understand that a strong mindset is not developed overnight or completed after a weekend seminar. Think of your mind like a giant muscle. The more you exercise it, the stronger it becomes. No one ever went to the gym once and said, "there, my muscle is strong, and I never need to come back again." A strong mindset is created, strengthened, and crafted, one thought at a time. If there is one thing to remember from this chapter, it is this: you are one belief away from everything changing.

Today I am 32 years old and one of the top Realtors in San Diego. I was awarded the prestigious National Association of Realtors 30 Under 30 award. I have made over $100,000 in a single month 18 times, and I have even generated over 1 million dollars in a single year twice. I am most proud to share that I am married to my amazing wife, Regina, and we are parents to Cejay and Maya.

My life is more than I could ever dream of, and every day I am grateful for the strong brick house I have built. I assure you; I share my accomplishments as a servant and humble leader, and I am still on my journey to success. There are many lessons I have learned on my journey, but these are three key lessons I learned when I was a struggling, brand-new Realtor.

Lesson 1: Against all odds, believe in yourself.

If you don't believe in yourself, then who will? Success starts with you believing that the changes you desire are possible. The odds may be stacked against you; however, I assure you, there is someone who has accomplished your goal, and they were in a worse situation than you.

"Whether you think you can or you think you can't, you're right." - Henry Ford

When I got my real estate license at age 24, there were many reasons why I shouldn't have succeeded. I was too young. This was my first "real job," and I didn't even own a house; in fact, I was still living with my mom. Yet, against all odds, I chose to believe in myself and that I would accomplish my goal.

My motivation was being able to pay for my wedding, which was eight months away. To start the business, we completely diminished our wedding fund. I didn't even have money for a suit I needed for my business cards. However, this minor obstacle would not stop us! Regina was able to edit my head onto someone else's body wearing a suit! To this day, I save that business card in my office to remind myself where I came from.

It was either succeed in real estate or cancel the wedding. Canceling was not an option since we sent out 250 wedding invitations a year early. There was only one choice, and that was to succeed. When I passed my real estate test, and it was time to step up, I knew it was time to be great!

Against all odds, I believed in myself.

Lesson 2: Do what you say you are going to do

Nothing builds confidence or strengthens your mindset faster than doing exactly what you say you will do. It can be as simple as committing to waking up at 5 am and doing it, or it can be as challenging as becoming a vegetarian. When you do exactly what you say you will do, you build confidence and momentum, strengthening and disciplining your mindset.

Only commit to actions that are in alignment with your destination. Think of success like it's the destination on a map. Every time you take action that aligns with your goal, you are taking steps closer. Each time you take action that does not align with your goal, you take steps backward. To succeed, your actions in alignment with your goal must heavily outweigh your actions out of alignment.

On the day I received my real estate license, I committed to doing whatever it took to be the Rookie of the Year, which would allow me to pay for my wedding. The wedding was approaching quickly. The previous Rookie of The Year made

$120,000 in their first year, which was my goal. This was a massive stretch for me because I never made more than $3000 in a single year being a "breakdancer" who traveled and competed as a lifestyle. However, I believed that if I took the actions of someone who accomplished this goal, surely, I would too. After consulting with my coach, I needed to do five open houses a week, no questions asked. Whether I had an open house, and no one came, or 20 groups came, it didn't matter. I was doing what I said I was going to do. Not only did it build my confidence, but it also took me steps closer to my goal of Rookie of the Year and paying for my wedding.

Lesson 3: Never Give Up

Every worthwhile goal has a moment where you will question yourself. Being disciplined is no longer convenient, and the pain you are experiencing is too great to continue. DON'T GIVE UP!

If you push through, you will find your breakthrough. *There is always a breakdown before the breakthrough.*

The wedding was now three months away. I made three sales with roughly $1,000 in our bank accounts, and I was NOT on pace to pay for my wedding or be Rookie of the Year. It appeared hopeless, but I did not give up. At the end of the month, there was an eight-week training program designed to jumpstart an agent's production. The cost for the program was $800, and luckily the first class was FREE. I decided that I would only attend the FREE class because if I signed up, I would only be left with $200 in my bank account with our wedding just three months away. After the FREE day of training, I was so inspired that I knew the only way to accomplish the goal was to sign up. I rushed to call Regina, expecting her support, but I was immediately declined to my surprise. In her mind depleting our funds for training would take us further from our goal. I will never forget the internal struggle I faced that day.

Nevertheless, I committed to doing whatever it took to succeed, and I believed in myself, so I signed up anyway. I remember coming home to her, crying, because of our depleted bank accounts. I asked her to believe in me; I was ready to prove myself!

With the wedding three months away and $200 in our bank account, I had no choice but to succeed. I took each class intensely and did everything that our coach said. I showed up early and left late. I showed up in a way that would make my future self proud. Two weeks before our wedding, I am proud to share that I made enough sales to pay for our entire wedding, go on two honeymoons, and at the end of the year, I was awarded the Rookie of the Year award; making $113,000 in my first year! The momentum from that single decision, to believe in myself and never give up, changed my life's trajectory forever. That was the defining moment in my life.

Everything you desire to accomplish and attain in your life is achievable if you are willing to strengthen your mindset be disciplined. I hope that my story's lessons inspire you and act as a pivotal moment in your life on your journey to success. To achieve what you desire, start with your mindset. First, believe in yourself; second, do what you say you will; lastly, never give up.

ANTHONY MANZON

About Anthony Manzon: Anthony is a San Diego native who created success through selling real estate. He currently leads one of the top real estate teams in San Diego along with his wife Regina, and they have built their real estate team from the ground up.

Anthony started selling houses at age 24 and has consistently been one of the top agents in his company every year since. In 8 short years, he was awarded Rookie of the Year, National Association of Realtors 30 under 30, #1 producing agent in his office (2015-2020) just to name a few.

Before starting Anthony's real estate career, Anthony was a dancer who specialized in Breakin' aka "Break Dancing." He was always practicing, jamming and competing all around the United States. He is a proud husband, and father to his two kids Cejay and Maya.

The best way to contact him is through his Instagram @AnthonyManzon.

Author's Website: *www.TeamManzon.com*
www.ThePrinciplesofDavidandGoliath.com

Bonnie Lierse

NO TIME FOR FEAR

It is so easy to forget our accomplishments, mindset, dreams, passions, or even what we are capable of, "especially" during our challenges, low self-esteem times, as well as our failures! However, without those FAILURES, we can't succeed. I know I LEARNED from my FAILURES! But I also know that deep down, my mindset was to conquer any Fear! I / David was going to beat Goliath whenever possible!

I still remember people constantly telling me; you're too nice, too sweet, etc.! Really?

Or, in a bad situation, when I had personal success or perseverance, I was told it was me running away from my problems or burying my head in the sand. Maybe I was, but it contributed to many successes. Everything starts with our proper mindset. We must watch those naysayers who don't understand stages of success. I always considered myself an independent FREE THINKER, but most of all, I have a FEARLESS MINDSET and take risks! I never liked going the safe route! Would David?

I grew up in an apartment in Brooklyn, NY, in a pretty average middle-class family, my parents were warm and simple folks, and I went to a pretty crazy and dangerous high school! You betchya! You NEVER knew what to expect when you walked into the school building. That was Erasmus.

I remember a riot during a major concert on senior day. Instruments were flying off the stage, and other insane stuff. There was NO time for FEAR! My mindset was fearless always!

FEAR had to be suppressed to get out safely. We had to make sure we got our friends out safely, and I remember other friends getting me out safely. It was frightening, but someone had to be the David or the Goliath there. Very, very scary! I'm here to tell the story, so I got out safely. David came out of me that night!

I was also a twirler back in that same crazy, dangerous high school. I remember one game we went to at Boys High. The team was worried about a riot because our football team was winning. My desire to be a twirler was intense, and I always dreamed about supporting the school teams. It took priority over my fear of these or any situations. My mindset back then was to take some risks and then move forward. David did take victory! We did get out safely.

It started with a David and Goliath mindset.

There was a "Four Seasons" concert in Central Park, New York, New York.... just like you see on television. I remember going to that concert that evening. It was incredible! Spirits were flying. We went with friends from college. Being the crazy, fearless youth I was, my friend and I were determined to see the Four Seasons in person at their trailer. My friend and I wanted autographs too. We did it! We got to see them in person. We had a determined mindset. It was unbelievable. When we left the Four Season's trailer, it was extremely dark, very late, and everyone left Central Park. Yes, two young girls left alone. Two girls by themselves, in the middle of the park! Truth be told, our mindset and determination to see such fame in person conquered any fear for what would happen and being stranded there. Yes, we did get home safely finally, but it was scary! A risk we took and conquered that fear. All because of our "mindset and determination!" I believed we would get out safely!

I learned a lesson: I need a solid mindset to constantly better myself for David to beat Goliath! They're both in all of us and around us.

It takes remembering feeling "NO FEAR" at times in my life. My mindset was set!

One example: I was at a beautiful park by a lake with my significant other Tom at that time. As we were down by the lake, I saw someone from a distance, walking near our belongings on a blanket, snooping around, a distance from the lake! I took off like a crazy person after that suspicious character; I was running pretty fast, a quick whippersnapper, and chased them away! I startled them. Now, I can laugh about it, but I released any FEAR; my mindset was GET THAT DUDE and scared whoever that was by our stuff. I just ran up the hill and scared them away to protect our personal belongings.

I learned that sometimes we have to take impulsive risks in life and push away the FEAR. That was my mindset always!

Again, David beat Goliath.

Another time a friend called me; she was in serious trouble at her home and in danger. She had young children at home, and I didn't think twice that I needed to help her. Someone in her house, her spouse, frightened and threatened her big time. She was stunning, and he felt threatened by that. I learned the need to take RISKS again and put FEAR on the back burner (MY MINDSET) and just went to rescue her.

I know I stopped the dangerous situation just by showing up. It could have escalated big time! Instead, we do what we need to do and throw FEAR & RISK out the window when necessary. It starts with our mindset.

Another time, a friend found out her husband was cheating on her. She needed to know the truth. Putting any FEAR aside, we took a trip, in a snowstorm, into another state to find out the truth about his affair. We confronted the situation and went to the "girlfriend's" house. It was dangerous with him, probably alcohol involved (if looks could kill from him, oh yes). The situation was confronted. My friend moved on with her life and let go of him from then on. There was a significant "RISK" doing what we did! When you love someone, whether family, friend or someone else, you do what you have to do. I learned that RISKS come with any David and Goliath situation, especially if there is alcohol or drugs involved with the person you're up against.

I learned that I am a David when it comes to family or friends!

At the time, I was in an unhealthy marriage. You can love someone but know there are RISKS with someone who has personal issues.

I remember needing to protect my children from an unhealthy environment at the time. Incidents happened multiple times! Sometimes, we have to put our cape on and change who we are to protect our loved ones. You cannot be AFRAID, or you won't take the necessary RISKS to protect. It's MINDSET!

Yes, our David did win long-term.

I cannot explain it, but when David needs to beat Goliath, FEAR cannot exist in you!

I've learned that some people would say, "Are you crazy?" I say, "You have to trust your gut instincts!" You'll always know what's right and what to do at that moment.

One way I was Goliath was when I let people take advantage of me. I let others beat me down. Confidence and self-esteem were not my strong point. That was something I had to overcome in time.

Where do I start with this next part? I lost my dear husband two weeks ago. It has been painful and traumatic, a bit surreal. Voices in my head were battling each other, which brings me here. We all have a David and Goliath within ourselves.

Fighting and beating on each other. Pulling each other down. It's up to the David part of us to fight stronger and arm wrestle Goliath down until he's gone! Our brains play tricks on us, and all that self-talk can be positive or negative. We have a choice. We can be the David with strong mindset and be laser-focused, or we can be weak and be destroyed.

When you know you have to keep a roof over your head, you better believe David better win! Someone is not always there to protect you from Goliath. Do you agree and understand? I'm living through it now. My family is amazing and supportive, but this is my fight, and I have to believe and know in my heart that I WILL win! I will miss Tom Lierse to the universe and back, but he always believed I would be the David from when he met me in 1990. I know my protector is there for me in heaven, but this is my fight. It's ok when people help and support you. Say thank you, I love you and appreciate it. I don't take time or life for granted anymore! The rest is on you! Fight the fight! You got this; we got this together! We can all bring the Goliath in us down today! I'll keep you posted on what happens next!

This chapter is dedicated in loving memory of my husband Thomas Lierse. My best friend, soul mate and beloved husband passed away unexpectedly, November 23, 2021. I know his wings will protect and give love to those he left behind in his life! He was a very wise gent! Among many things, Tom loved our country having served in the U.S. Navy submarine division. Tom was a great writer, trumpet player, and enthusiastically loved participating in local theater productions.

Here's a Mindset reminder to all…. don't take TIME, MONEY, ANYONE or ANYTHING for granted! Say I love you often. Spend quality time together. Smell the roses on your way to success, and look into each other's eyes regularly. Time flies so use it well! Live life and pay it forward!

BONNIE LIERSE

About Bonnie Lierse: Bonnie Zaruches Lierse is extremely artistic and creative, with an entrepreneurial bent. Besides that, she is a seasoned agent with more than twenty years' experience in real estate in the New York/Long Island area. She relocated to Northern Virginia in 2012 and continued her real estate career there.

Another passion is creating leaders by working in business leadership development with *Leadership Team Development* (LTD), marketing products supplied by *Amway*. She was also a member of *The Screen Cartoonist Guild of Motion Pictures* for many years. Also, she did freelance for Sesame Street in New York City. In addition, she was a District Director for an interior accessory design company, as her own business.

Bonnie is blessed with five beautiful grandchildren and is very close with her children and family, some of whom are also in Virginia. Her missions are leadership, mentorship, paying it forward, and changing lives one at a time. Her motto is "<u>You</u> be the difference!"

Author's website: *www.Amway.com/MyShop/SplashFXEnterprises*
www.*ThePrinciplesofDavidandGoliath.com*

Bryce McKinley

UNCERTAINTY CREATES OPPORTUNITY

I am an underdog, from being raised in a cult to joining gangs. I have overcome more in my life than anyone should. That also includes significant shifts in my life, such as moving back into the corporate arena, losing my son and my wife, and then attempting to take my life, to name a few.

It's up to you. It's first of all mindset and belief systems. In the David and Goliath story, what went through David's experience and his choices showed up in the battle. Whether you relate yourself to David or Goliath, it doesn't matter; It's taking that perspective and asking yourself, "What is it exactly have I overcome?" Or maybe you ask yourself, "Have I had the faith to choose to do the right things in the eyes of God." Was it ridiculous or crazy, or were you the underdog, unprepared just as a shepherd in the field to take on the armies of Philistines? Just relate that to your life. You've got so many things that have shaped your life.

That's the angle, but this is to share at least one perspective, one David and Goliath story that may influence and help other people who read this.

In the Bible, 1 Samuel 17:45-47, David said of the Philistines:

> (45)"Then said David to the Philistine, Thou comest to me with a sword, and with a spear, and with a shield: but I come to thee in the name of the Lord of hosts, the God of the armies of Israel, whom thou hast defied."

(46) "This day will the Lord deliver thee into mine hand, and I will smite thee, and take thine head from thee, and I will give the carcasses of the host of the Philistines this day unto the fowls of the air, and to the wild beasts of the earth; that all the earth may know that there is a God in Israel."

(46) "And all this assembly shall know that the Lord saveth not with sword and spear: for the battle is the Lord's, and he will give you into our hands."

This passage is highly relatable to all business owners and entrepreneurs. When David's father asks him to deliver lunch to his brothers, he gets to the battlefield, and he sees Goliath and the Philistines harassing his brothers and the Israelites. It's like the Philistines were trash-talking to people of God. And the Israelites' response was a little cowardly. They were afraid to fight.

That example describes most entrepreneurs as many people who go into business are scared to take that next step. In the Bible, they were afraid to take responsibility and have true convictions for what they stood for, having a backbone and believing in their faith. They let their fear of a giant get in the way of their mindset for freedom and victory. But David wanted to handle this the right way. And so, when David goes to Saul and tells him, "I'm going to fight Goliath," Saul is first like, "Uh, no, get out of here." And David went back to him and said that God gave him this power and authority, so he had already fought this fight. David mentioned that he had fought lions and beasts in the fields. His mindset and belief system were founded on God's power, and he knew he was to become a conduit and modality for God's work.

David believed that he had already experienced the mountains and valleys, the highs and lows in his life. Therefore, he knew firsthand that not only was the battle ahead of him already won, but he was capable of so much more.

Martin Luther said, "Faith is a living, daring competence in God's grace, so sure and certain that a man could stick his life on it 1000 times." That unshakable confidence in your belief systems allowed David to say to Goliath, "You come to me that the sword and spear and javelin, but I come to you in the name of the Lord, and the God of the armies of Israel."

David's faith in God's belief and trust is so absolute and pure that he staked his life on it. And that's true faith. And I think that the most significant difference between the Davids and the Goliaths in business and entrepreneurship is that David sets out against Goliath with faith as the assurance of things hoped for, but the conviction of things not seen.

This is hard for us as humans. We want to see with our eyes; we want tangible proof even though it is hard to place our faith in something or someone we can't see. We can't see the money we desire in the bank. We can't see the brick-and-mortar business we strive to obtain. We can't even see the 200, 2,000, or 10,000 employees ten years from now that we dreamed. But we shouldn't build our faith on our imagination or the conjurer of what we think of God. Instead, we must develop our faith in what we know is true. And this is why we need to be in our word and study our Bibles rather than relying on the books and philosophies of men and women about other people's testimonies. Our Bibles are written testimonies by God of His power and faithfulness to carry you through those dips, hills, and valleys in your business. That should be your fuel.

Take On Your Giants

There is a saying that "uncertainty creates opportunities." As you step out in faith, take on the Goliath-size armor for confidence. If you have a David-size business and Goliath-size responsibilities, those uncertain times create uncertain opportunities. We have to know one thing in those opportunities, faith does not work on feelings. So when you remove your emotions from something and look at the facts, they will help you put one step in front of the other and makes progress. Whether you're taking running bounds some days or taking baby steps down the path, there's no emotion in business, and there's no emotion in faith. It's a simple action, one step at a time, reach out, but whatever you do, don't do nothing.

I'm on a mission. I'm just taking one step at a time. I feel like David right now. I've got a much higher calling and mission in my life. I encourage you all to seek that same mission and take one step toward the uncertainty. God has already won the battle for you, and he needs you to put your faith in him and leap forward in his direction.

BRYCE MCKINLEY

About Bryce McKinley: Bryce is an International Best-Selling Author and one of the Top 5 Sales Trainers in The World! With over 20 years of working with various Fortune 500 companies, including but not limited to the likes of Ford, Nissan, Tyco, and ADT. Helping each of them transform their sales process to focus on better conversations and building better relationships.

Over 8,000 transactions in Real estate later, Bryce is one of the leading experts in wholesaling houses with his 5 Hour Flip method and has been able to close almost every deal over the phone, only ever walking five properties.

Author's Website: *www.5HourFlip.com*
www.ThePrinciplesofDavidandGoliath.com

Charlson Gaines

FREEDOM TO CHOOSE

The very famous story of David and Goliath is one in which there are two opposing fighters, and one of them seems to have an overwhelming advantage over the other. The problem with this story is that so many people view it as a story to provide entertainment. They do not believe they can apply this to their own lives.

This is because they cannot identify a Goliath in their lives. A Goliath is a singular enemy with a specific weakness to exploit for victory. Unfortunately, our current society seems to be the source of not just one Goliath but countless adversaries. If only we could identify our Goliath and find our slingshot, we may have a shot at being victorious.

Well, there's good news, and there's bad news. The bad news is that you can't escape Goliath. The good news is that you can't escape Goliath because you are your own Goliath. We can choose our enemies and choose our means of defeating them. However, what we tend to do is to identify our enemies and then just ruminate on them, allowing them to harness the power or our own thoughts and beliefs to get us to defeat ourselves.

However, the key to all of this is to recognize that those thoughts and beliefs are our own, and we have the power to defeat them. The truth is you can defeat Goliath even easier than David did. All you have to do to conquer your Goliath is to choose to win. Auschwitz survivor and best-selling author Dr. Viktor Frankl once wrote, "Everything can be taken from a man but one thing: the last of the human freedoms—to choose one's attitude in any given set of circumstances, to choose one's own way." This is the power of David that we each have inside of us also to defeat that internal enemy we've chosen to perceive as Goliath when, in reality, it is no Goliath at all. It is merely our failure to choose at the moment, within these circumstances, that there is no Goliath at all.

I realize this is easier said than done. We've all faced adversity, and some of us labeled struggles as Goliaths and proceeded to lose to them. But there are other times when we've battled and fought in unwinnable battles and won them anyway. Let's acknowledge those times. Let's recognize those times when you chose to be the David in the story, and you decided to win.

My personal story begins with the worst week of my life as of 2012. I was on active duty in the US Air Force. I was supposed to go to Afghanistan. I was behind in my deployment prep. If I wasn't ready on the day of departure, it could crush my career. I was struggling for a variety of reasons. The stress was crushing me. Then it got worse.

My mother called and told me that she could not feel one side of her face. She might have had a mini-stroke. I had one week to get all of my pre-deployment processing done, and instead, I went to see my mom. I immediately took her to the emergency room, and she was admitted. The doctor from my home station told me that I needed to get my vitals checked to fill in some boxes on a checklist for my deployment. So, I went to the military clinic on Ft Bragg, NC, to get this done. This was the day after my mother was admitted. The plan was to get this done and then visit her where she was staying. Well, I couldn't. My blood pressure was 172/126. The doctor wouldn't let me leave. She was a military doctor, and if I left, I'd be disobeying a direct order. They drew blood and discovered my kidneys were failing. I was unable to see my mom that day. I lied to her about why. Every day I had to go back and have my kidneys checked. Every day they were worse.

They were in free fall. My mother spent 12 years on dialysis due to failed kidneys before getting a transplant. Now, as she's in one hospital, I'm getting the same kidney diagnosis in another

They ruled out a stroke for my mom. They did an MRI and found a growth on her brain stem. They said it could be cancer. I told her that I had kidney disease. On that one day, I thought my mom could be battling brain cancer as I transitioned to dialysis. Dialysis is a process where you're hooked up to a machine for four hours, three times a week, to run all of your blood through this machine so it can do what your kidneys no longer could. You either do it, or you die.

My kidneys stabilized, and I took my mom back to Colorado with me. We identified the cause of my kidney disease. It's an autoimmune disorder. My immune system was attacking my kidneys. My mom caught pneumonia, and they gave her antibiotics. Within a week, I saw a kidney specialist, and my mom's growth was shrinking. The doctors believe it was an infection, and the antibiotics to treat her pneumonia killed the infection and growth on her brain stem. As I began managing my kidney disease, my deployment was canceled. So I was able to oversee my mom's recovery and implement a plan to manage my illness as well.

Here in 2022, ten years later, the 2nd anniversary of my kidney transplant is coming up on March 30th. My mom also had a kidney transplant. Although she passed away in 2019, she showed me how to manage living as a transplant patient. I received my new kidney on what would have been her 67th birthday.

I did not earn or deserve a new kidney. I did not do anything to make me need it more than other people on the transplant list. Yet, I was given a second lease on life. This is because someone, prior to passing away, decided to be an organ donor. So, I live every day of my life with purpose and gratitude because this life that I have is one I did not earn. This life is a gift. Just being able to live it motivates me to make the most of it.

We must fully understand that each day is a gift. Our responsibility is to ensure we show this day the respect it deserves. There are so many people who were availed of yesterday, but not today. By respecting today and our opportunities to do so much with today, we ensure that our lives have meaning and purpose. Dr. Viktor Frankl said, "Those who have a 'why' to live can bear with almost any 'how.'" I know my why. What is yours?

Understand that you have the freedom to choose your purpose. People often ask, "What is the meaning of life?" Do not ask that question of others. The choice is yours. Ask it of yourself. The meaning of your life is whatever you say it is. You choose if you are going to serve others. You choose your values. You choose to align those same values with your thoughts, actions, intent, and behaviors. What you need to do to maximize this one life that you have is to choose your mindset.

Let me tell you about mine. Gratitude is the foundation of my every day. The mindset I have chosen is the KOPE Life mindset. Kindness, Optimism, Positivity, and Empathy. On any given day, you can find misery. People all over the world are more miserable, lonely, angry, and in pain than we've been in decades. What do they need from us? What do they need from me? We each can give painkillers. We each can provide the same advice and quotes from the internet. But the KOPE Life mindset that you choose to bring is uniquely yours. When you are hurting, you often want a specific kind of empathy from a very specific person. People need kindness. They need empathy. They need to know you care. They need to know that they matter, have value, and deserve happiness. And when I say "they," that includes you and me. You deserve to be happy.

Happiness is a choice. Choosing a KOPE Life mindset empowers you to elevate your happiness and the happiness of others around you. Don't believe me? Go hang around five happy people all day and see how you feel in the evening. Happiness is a choice. Happiness is contagious. Once you adopt that mindset, your beliefs must align with it. You have to believe you deserve to be happy to take action to elevate your own happiness. This is a must, not a should. Because if you do not believe that you deserve to be happy, you will find it difficult to do what is necessary to be happy because it opposes what you believe.

So, it would help if you believe that you deserve to be happy. It is a must. Then you adopt the mindset to be happier without obstacles, without a self-constructed Goliath. Then you can empower yourself to be happy, which you must do because you deserve to be happy.

CHARLSON GAINES

About Charlson Gaines: Charlson Gaines teaches people to replace misery with happiness. He is a disabled US Air Force veteran who served in Iraq, Afghanistan, Qatar, Kosovo, Korea and many other locations worldwide. He is a Health Psychology Ph.D. candidate, holds two Master's Degrees, and is a 1st degree black belt in Kuk Sool Won. Charlson is a professional speaker, emotional intelligence life coach, and hosts the KOPE Life Podcast. He has provided dynamic presentations on real and virtual stages over 50 times to over 6,000 people including the National Air and Space Intelligence Center and US Southern Command. He was a featured panelist at the 2022 Department of the Air Force Women's Air and Space Power Symposium. He also delivered outstanding presentations at the 26th Annual Institute of Violence, Abuse and Trauma San Diego Summit and the 29th and 30th Annual Safety and Environmental Professional Development Symposiums hosted by the US Navy.

Author's Website: *www.CharlsonGaines.com*
www.ThePrinciplesofDavidandGoliath.com

Crystal Lindsey

REJECTED

My David and Goliath story started when I was born.

My mother never seemed to love me. She liked my older sister, but she never wanted to look me in the eyes or hug me. I knew I was treated differently. I got more beatings and less food. My sister got her share of beatings, too, but my treatment seemed to be different. I was scolded and mocked, while my sister was not.

I was constantly told that I would never be anything in this world. My mother's slogan for me was, "What do you think you are, special?" Or perhaps the lovely, "If I knew you were a girl, I would have aborted you." She already had two other girls by two men and wanted a son. Apparently, the ultrasound's misreading saved my life.

I was an outsider in my own family. My own mother rejected me. Little did I know this was the greatest gift someone could give me. My whole belief system about why I was treated this way was about to change in one afternoon when I was nine years old.

My mom arrived to pick me up after school crying. The tears must have blocked her vision because she was swerving all over the road. I could tell something was brewing. She seemed hysterical, and I was terrified. Finally, she pulled over and parked the car.

My heart raced as she spun her head around to look at me in the back seat. She yelled through her tearful eyes, "Your father is not your father, and your sister is not your sister. Your auntie is not your auntie. Your dad doesn't care about you. That's why he left you! He never wanted you." Then, she seemed to pull herself together and drive somewhat normally. The tears had ended after she had said what she needed to say.

I sat there stunned in the back seat of the car. Oddly, I don't remember any real emotions coming over me. I guess I didn't know what to think. I just stared out the window until we arrived home, where I could finally lay on my bunk bed. I began to sort it out. "Well," I thought, "I always knew I was different...." My mind trailed off into the million and one ways my sister and my mother rejected me. I could see now that I really was different.

I decided this was good news. My heart started to sing, and my feelings of confusion lifted. Finally, I had figured it all out! If my dad was why I was so different, then he must be really powerful! I just knew he was an alien from outer space with special powers that would rescue me. He would come back to get me. He had to, right? Wrong.

My dad never did decide to come to rescue me. He didn't have superpowers. Spoiler alert: he also wasn't an alien. But that didn't matter.

I had already changed my expectation about my future, and thus I had altered my MINDSET and belief in myself. Suddenly I didn't spend my time wondering why my mother didn't seem to love me. I quit wondering why I was not enough. I stopped having feelings of despair. Now I had new thoughts of what my future would be like with my new family.

I thought of my new future with my dad so much that I even had a recurring dream about it. In the dream, my dad, an alien from outer space, would come bursting out of the attic on a motorcycle and swoop me up. He would take me away with our hair flapping in the wind. I was finally free. In this dream, I would laugh in joy and amazement. The moment had come; my dad was here to take me away from the suffering. Then I would wake up.

The problem is he never came. Instead, the abuse continued to escalate after my older sister had run away. At eleven years old, my mother attacked me, ripping my shirt off me and hitting me with an icepick handle. I ran away and was placed into the shelter for foster care children.

One day, the people who worked at the shelter sat me down. I remember they were clearly trying to say something difficult to me, but they couldn't get it out. "Come on," I told them. "You can tell me," I said with the most bravado I could muster at eleven. One finally blurted out, "Your mother left in the middle of the night, and we don't know where she went." I was shocked. I made them take me to the apartment I had lived in with my mom just last week.

The apartment was empty. She had taken every single item I owned.

Yet again, I went back to my bunk bed to lay down and sort it all out. See, I have always been committed to living a life of greatness. I remember telling my sister, "When I get older, I am going to make a lot of money. And the only thing I am going to buy you is an education!" This only got more intense after I learned about my dad not being the same as my sister's dad. I was different, and I knew it. That knowledge was power.

I decided I would be the victor, not the victim in the situation. And now, again, I lay on my bed and had to commit myself. I affirmed that "I was destined for greatness," and this was a gift. My MINDSET shifted. It was me and me now. That's it. With every ounce of my soul, I promised myself that I would take good care of myself. And that I did.

Now I am launching a whole new department for a digital marketing agency. I am also a proud accountability coach, artist, best-selling author, entrepreneur, and former college professor. I earned two master's degrees and continue to earn six figures with joy in my heart

Now, I have bigger dreams to do even more!

I have shifted my mindset from making six figures to making seven figures. Now I am becoming a multi-millionaire from foster care. My multi-millionaire empire will create a legacy I can pass down to help other foster youth when I am gone. Every day, I want to commit my life to helping people change the way they think to become who they are meant to be in this world.

How did I do it? That is for the next book. I will give you the exact strategy formula that I used to create the building blocks of my success. Right now, I want you to understand that I used what could have been the two biggest traumas of my childhood and turned them into my greatest turning points. The key to my future was my ability to shift my thinking about rejection.

Like how David had to shift his mindset to conquer Goliath, I had to change how I perceived myself without my mother's belief in me. David was rejected and dismissed as an unequal foe because of his diminished appearance. Likewise, I was rejected by my mother because my father left. However, like David, I believed in myself and committed to doing my best based on a belief I had from God.

I had to change my mindset. I knew that the rejection I felt was real, but I also knew I could decide what I believed. And I believed that I was going to be OK. I committed that I would always take great care of myself. I believed I had value in this world.

I was unprepared before birth to go up against a giant like Goliath. Then, as a child, I learned I was different. This knowledge allowed me to create a mindset that I was special and destined for greatness. I suddenly believed in myself even when all of the odds were stacked against me, and no one believed in me.

I could not have created this mindset shift without the gift of rejection. God used rejection to allow me to take down the giant even while being woefully unprepared.

Let me clarify: you can only thrive out of trauma when you choose not to be a victim but the victor. You must see everything that has happened to you as a gift. So, if you are out there struggling with hardships, I want you to know you can change your life at any given moment by choosing to live intentionally and change what the trauma means.

I have news for you: your Goliath, your challenge, will always be there. Life will always throw you a curveball, even after you "make it." However, you can change other people's lives by changing what hardship means. In addition, this slight shift in your story will change your belief in yourself.

Remember, you change your beliefs and mindset by changing how you define your life circumstances. You can overcome poverty, rejection, fear, disappointment, or even loneliness by deciding you are worthy. You can change your mindset by speaking positive belief systems into your existence. You can change the meaning of your story. It is up to you. No one needs to give you permission.

Only you can do it, but first, you have to decide you can.

Please reach out to me at crystaljlindsey.com to let me know how you are changing the story of your lives. I would love to hear. Truly!

CRYSTAL LINDSEY

About Crystal Lindsey: Crystal Lindsey, MBA learned how to overcome "Goliath" when she was abandoned into the foster care system and disowned by her family at 11 years old. She raised herself and overcame "Goliath" alone.

Crystal went on to overcome tremendous odds and became a bestselling author, public speaker, college professor, artist and dynamic digital marketer.

Currently is known as @GratefulMarketer! She teaches business owners the exact biohacks and marketing hacks that she used to beat the odds. Crystal is currently the Digital Marketing Manager - Dallas for M. Roberts Digital.

Follow her on Facebook and Instagram @GratefulMarketer, to learn how to put yourself in a peak state, grow your business and leverage digital marketing.

Check out crystaljlindsey.com to learn more about her book, Grit & Gratitude: The Former Foster Youth's Playbook for Adulting.

Contact Crystal for Public Speaking, M.C. or Emcee, Corporate Trainer, Inspirational Speaker, Panel Guest, Marketing Consultant, Corporate Sales & Marketing Training.

Author's Website: *www.CrystalJLindsey.com*
www.ThePrinciplesofDavidandGoliath.com

Darrell David Stern

YOU ARE A GIFT TO THE WORLD

My David and Goliath story is about sheer willpower, perseverance, and using your gifts.

I'm Darrell DAVID Stern, the digital marketing Jedi, and I believe that YOU are a gift to the world, and the world needs your gifts. What YOU can teach, what you KNOW, and what you can DEMONSTRATE that you might take for granted IS your greatest digital marketing.

My story is about a local auto mechanic named Saul who went from fixing cars in front of his mom's house to running the largest single-location auto mechanic shop in the nation.

He beat the Goliath big luxury auto mechanic shops and dealerships by being determined to show how skilled he and his team were and to tell the TRUTH about luxury auto repair.

The HOW is where I come in.

In 2016 I met Saul, the auto mechanic who wanted to be the #1 mechanic in the entire world. Not only that, but he had the WILL to do ANYTHING it took to get there.

He hired my digital marketing agency to do just that.

The reason why this story is so inspiring is that this auto mechanic was still in his 20s, and instead of just WORKING as a mechanic, he already owned his own shop.

I will take you through, step-by-step, how Saul went from practically no internet presence to rising to become a leader in his industry, a millionaire, and an internationally known influencer in his field.

How?

Simply by showing the world how good he is at what he does. By SHOWING the world how knowledgeable, trustworthy, and just flat out KICK ASS he is at what he does.

I will point out that Saul is very talented at speaking. He is extremely articulate, and more than that, he is a great PERFORMER of his craft.

The Will To Succeed And The Vision To Do So Matters

I started visiting Saul's shop once a week. We would spend about two hours together looking at the cars and trucks he was fixing, and we would decide on three to five that had a really great story behind them.

Some stories would be about funny things like the time a woman had gummy bears stuck to her driveshaft, to major recalls of parts, to historical videos like the history of Jeeps.

The great thing about Saul is I would point my finger at him with my phone filming, and he would just go.

"Hi, I'm Saul over here at Saul's Automotive, and today we're talking about…"

Towards the end, I would raise my other hand to my ear like a phone to remind him to say… "We are open 365 days a year. Give us a call at 303 919 7769."

And that was all Saul had to do.

Tell a great informative story and let me video him. That's all HE had to do.

The rest was up to me.

It dawned on me that to crack open YouTube AND Google and SLAY Saul's SEO, I had to have each video TRANSCRIBED, so every word out of his mouth could be WRITTEN OUT as a blog article.

A blog article WITH a VIDEO on top of it as the "Featured Image."

Most great blog writers know that a blog feature in WordPress is to include a featured image.

Great featured images make a blog more enticing to read. They also show up on Facebook and other platforms when you POST the blog.

BUT you can also use a YouTube video to REPLACE that featured image, creating a blog article that plays a video at the top of it.

These videos also create what is called the blog GRID or the list of blogs on the blog PAGE of the website.

These both LOOK impressive and also create confidence at a glance in Saul and Saul's Automotive.

With the transcriptions, I did have to do a lot of editing as what you SAY sometimes does not look quite right printed out.

Although Saul nailed every one of these videos, I changed things like 'gonna' to 'going to' and so on.

Next, I really took a look at what statements Saul was saying were important and BOLD and marked them with an H3 tag.

(HTML is NOT a programming language, it is a MARKUP language. Just as your English teacher would mark up your paper with symbols indicating this, like "make this a new paragraph," HTML simply allows a web browser (Internet Explorer) to format text, so it is not just one big long run on one line of words going on and on and on making it very difficult and BORING for the reader to read.) << Did you see what I did there? HAHA>>

I will give you a simple example. Saul might say:

"Step one: I moved this brake pedal up." OR

"It is important to understand the Volkswagen auto group makes all of the parts for these vehicles." The first step is I would change this:

- Step one: I moved this brake pedal up.

To

- Step one in repairing your Mitsubishi eclipse that has bad brake rotors is to move the brake pedal up.

I am expanding what he said to include the primary keywords I want to rank for.

Next, I want to scan for keywords and phrases Saul says in this blog that he uses in others. Brakes, Suspension, Steering column, rotors, Ford, Honda, etc.

WordPress has an amazing LINKING tool. Here is how to use it right. Step one, copy the keyword or phrase you are going to link.

Step two, hit the link button.

Step three, paste in the keyword or phrase into the URL box. (It actually doubles as a SEARCH box, and this is one of the powers of WordPress)

WordPress will SHOW you a list of PAGES and other BLOGS that USE that keyword or phrase.

I will give you a ratio; if you repeat the same key phrase more than three times in your blog, you can link to your main PAGE or landing page, or anchor page at least TWICE in your blog. Then, link the rest to OTHER blogs that have that phrase.

Now keep looking for more SUB keywords or phrases. What do I mean? Well, FORD and SUSPENSION are main keywords, but a specific part or procedure Saul uses a lot.

This is the difference between SEO and in WordPress between your Categories and Tags. Categories are the main things that you do.

Tags are things like the WAYS you do it. Simple example:

Categories: Breakfast Lunch Dinner

Tags: Ham, Bacon, Spoon, Vitamin C

The tags like Ham could be in different categories, but they are a topic or keyword that appears across the spectrum of your content.

So, in the transcription, I am linking tag keywords and phrases as well as main category words and phrases to each other.

So, what if you are working on your FIRST video blogs? Create and launch 10, then go BACK and do your interlinking. Call To Action: EVERY page of your website and blog/ vlog blog article MUST have at least one call to action. I usually recommend THREE.

The first is a HARD SELL.

- Call us today, or Schedule Your Appointment.

The second is your softer sell.

- Download video lessons or a white paper.

The third can be your social media link.

- Join our conversation on Facebook, or for the latest industry news and advice from (your company), subscribe.

In Saul's case, we always used his PHONE NUMBER first.

(Jumping ahead, his phone number is in every Facebook post, tweet, and YouTube video description)

The second is his schedule link. The third is to his Facebook page.

We repeated this process over 250 times over four years.

Systems and processes can disrupt industries and make new Davids defeat old Goliaths.

Saul moved to a much larger shop the size of a football field; his site comes up # 1, 2, 3, 4, and 5 on Google for luxury car repair and was offered $100,000,000— one hundred million dollars by the Goliath luxury car dealerships to buy him out. He did not.

In upcoming volumes of this book series, I will delve deeper into the mindset and systems we used to create an influencer and blow up profits and revenue.

Remember, YOU are a gift to the world TOO!

Text stern to 602-726-3890 for more STERN marketing tips, and let's defeat Goliath together.

DARRELL DAVID STERN

About Darrell David Stern: Darrell DAVID Stern is known all around the world as the digital marketing Jedi. As a thought leader and philosopher, Mr. Stern has been teaching how marketing is just two things; giving people hope and proving that you can do it to audiences around the world since 1997.

From marketing a local auto mechanic to massive profits and influence to taking an international biohack franchise to exponential growth, Darrell and his Stern Storming methodology have enormous proof of concept.

Darrell believes that YOU are a gift to the world and the world needs your gifts. Darrell resides in beautiful sunny Scottsdale Arizona.

Author's Website: *www.Stern.Marketing*
www.ThePrinciplesofDavidandGoliath.com

Dawnese Openshaw

FASTBALLS AND FACING FEARS

Out of the corner of my eye, I caught a glimpse of a 90-plus-mile-an-hour fastball coming my way as it tipped off the top of my dad's catcher's mitt. With little time to respond, I simply stood there and watched as if the ball was going in slow motion, and I took it straight to the gut. I'm just glad it wasn't to my forehead like David's stone which took down the giant, Goliath.

I was able to brush it off after a short time and carry on with my ball shagging duties. I honestly think my dad took a proverbial punch to the gut seeing me suffer. What I am indeed grateful for is that through that suffering, he knew what he did next would shape my thoughts about myself and my abilities. He realized how important it was that I didn't develop a fear around what happened and had me right back out shagging the balls before we left the field. He knew the value of keeping me "in the game" and not merely watching.

Because my dad believed in me at that moment (and in so many other moments throughout my life), I believed I could do anything.

Shagging baseballs with dad wasn't everyone in my family's favorite thing to do, but I loved being with him. I loved watching him in action as he coached a sport he loved and shaped the minds and lives of the young people he served. He was and still is my hero in so many ways. Watching him coaching baseball pitchers were some of the most impressionable moments of my life. My dad's coaching others to be and do their best on and off the field led me to know I wanted to coach too.

In the story of David and Goliath, David was merely a shepherd boy willing to go into a situation no one else was willing to venture into. He had the courage, and he also had the knowledge that he was chosen and had a divine mission to fulfill. His previous life experiences prepared him for this moment he would face Goliath and come off as the conqueror. He had confidence in himself and his ability. He believed he could do it even before the opportunity was in front of him.

In my youth, this powerful belief my dad had in me prepared me for the many Goliaths I would face. His faith in me led me to know that I, too, had a divine mission, and he supported me in learning how to have courage and show up in the face of fear.

My dad gave me my first leadership book to read, Dale Carnegie's *How to Win Friends and Influence People* when I was in 8th grade. I'm not exactly sure what he was trying to tell me, and he claims he doesn't remember. I am forever grateful he shared this with me because reading this book opened up possibilities for me and shaped how I saw myself as a leader. Seeing myself as a leader allowed me to surround myself with the influence of other powerful leaders, like my dad and my mom, who believed in me my entire life.

It wasn't long after reading Carnegie that I knew I was born to create a positive impact in the world. I felt called to bring love and light to the world around me. It was such an amazing feeling at 14 years of age to know my life had meaning. I was meant for more than shagging baseballs (though I enjoyed the time with my dad). I knew at that young age, just as David knew, I had something to do that would make the world a better place. However, I was also aware that great responsibility and sometimes unwelcome adversity came with this knowledge.

As a youth, just as I was filled with faith, I was also filled with fear and doubts that I've combatted authentically into adulthood. So, you could say, I have had my share of Goliaths to face.

Goliath = the giants you get to "overcome" in your life

My Goliaths have been self-doubt, perfectionism (in my DNA), not feeling worthy, and feeling like I had something to prove to the world so I could feel valued. It wasn't until recently, as I saw myself as a David in an imperfect slab of marble that I accepted who I truly am and the greatness I've had inside all along. I no longer have to prove anything to anyone, and I get to be authentically me, whatever that looks like.

In the past few years, I felt called to use my leadership to build and strengthen families. It is my privilege to support families now as a family empowerment coach. I've walked in their shoes and faced the giants of being a family in this day and time with so many distractions. I've also had some of my own battles as a mom, and supporting other moms to learn to accept and love themselves again is a gift.

I struggled with postpartum depression after my second child was born by emergency cesarean. Ten years later, I was diagnosed with PTSD soon after adopting my five-year-old daughter from foster care. Nothing like parenting a traumatized child to bring out all your childhood trauma.

We were blessed with two beautiful boys, both of whom were miracles. After about eight years of infertility, I was able to enroll my husband and myself into becoming foster and adoptive parents. It was something we both learned to embrace, and we acknowledge now that even though it's been full of many Goliath moments, we wouldn't trade it for anything. We have both learned so much about ourselves and have stretched beyond what we thought was humanly possible.

I wouldn't be who I am today without having the opportunities to face my own giants, especially as a mom.

Each of us in this human experience has the opportunity to face some type of Goliath(s). And we each have the power to choose how we will come to the "fight."

As a slinger, David knew how to choose the right stones. He went to the nearby brook and intentionally selected five smooth stones and placed them in his bag. Any one of these stones could have been the ONE to take down the giant. Armed with five stones and a slingshot of truth, he approached Goliath and ran towards him, facing his fear and doing it anyway. He had the courage, and he knew God was on his side.

If I were to choose five stones for the battles with my Goliaths, I would choose trust, love, integrity, divinity, and courage.

What five stones would you choose to face your Goliaths?

What core values and beliefs do you arm yourself with for your daily life?

I have come to know how much my stone of courage is used when I am faced with any sized challenge at home, in my business, or in the communities I serve. I have the power to choose how I will respond, and I have learned to arm myself with the five stones versus a body full of armor. As I hope you will, I have chosen to run towards adversity to learn and to grow in the face of fear. In these moments of courage, I have developed emotional resilience in my life, which I consider priceless.

My five stones (trust, love, integrity, divinity, and courage) have helped me be who I choose to be as I live with purpose and intention every day. I am intentional in what I am creating in my life. I am learning to live life on the skinny branches versus being on the ground and hugging the tree's trunk in fear or self-doubt.

I am running towards my Goliaths and welcoming the lessons I will learn, no matter the pain I may experience.

Every moment I live, I get to choose if I will fill that moment with my past, my stories/goliaths, or if I will fill that moment with what I was called to do, trusting in myself and God. I get to choose! We get to choose! You get to choose!

I choose to fill my life with fear or courage, hate or love, doubt or trust, dishonesty or integrity, with feelings of worthlessness or the power of my divinity.

Thomas Monson said, "The giant you face will not diminish in size or power or strength by your vain hoping, wishing, or waiting from him to do so…The battle must be fought. Victory cannot come by default. So, it is in the battles of life." Life doesn't just happen to us, it happens for us, and we get to choose how to respond to every Goliath (or baseball) that comes our way.

DAWNESE OPENSHAW

About Dawnese Openshaw: Dawnese Openshaw is a radically authentic John Maxwell certified leadership coach, trainer, and speaker. At the age of 14 her father had her read Dale Carnegie's *"How to Win Friends and Influence People"* and she has been a student of leadership ever since. With over 25 years of experience in small business and non-profit organizations creating and executing plans for growth, Dawnese offers marketing and strategy coaching for small businesses and training for non-profit boards.

Dawnese Openshaw Coaching expanded in 2020 to include families—supporting emotional regulation, communication, and relationship building. She combines her passion for leadership and commitment with strengthening families as a family empowerment coach, primarily serving families with teens. Dawnese empowers families to heal individually and as a unit, creating harmony in their home. She supports frustrated parents to love their kids again and not just like them.

She has been married to her husband, Scott for 26 years and they are the parents of three amazing children (Randy, Thaniel, and Olivia) and one doodle (Tigger).

Author's Website: *www.DawneseOpenshaw.com*
www.ThePrinciplesofDavidandGoliath.com

Derika & Christopher Faamausili

POWERS INSIDE YOU
BEYOND YOUR BELIEF

All I could think about was getting off my feet as I floated from room to room, mingling with friends and family and picking at the food each time I passed the kitchen table. It was a sunny California day in the summer of 2009, I was eight months into my first pregnancy, and we were throwing a baby shower to celebrate.

After several laps carrying the weight of my huge belly, I finally found an open spot on the couch and plopped down when I heard something that caught me off guard.

"I think you're crazy for wanting to deliver your baby at home!"

I looked and realized it was Jane (not her real name), a friend and mother of two. Maybe it was the pain in my back and feet, but my flash reaction was: "I think you were crazy for delivering your babies in a hospital!"

Upon discovering I was pregnant with our first child, Solen, a strong desire was born in us to give him a better life than we had, starting with a healthy birth.

We explored the benefits of water delivery and learned about natural birthing without pain medications. In addition, we studied Elimination Communication techniques for allowing the baby to use a potty toilet rather than diapers.

We read books about cleansing our bodies and avoiding toxic chemicals in the food and products we consumed so they didn't pass to him through my milk.

Though interesting and exciting, this information challenged our belief systems and way of life. As a result, we soon realized that we would need to change everything about ourselves if we were to succeed.

Just imagine, if this stuff was new and strange to us, it was the same for our family and friends. So many struggled to support us, especially when our views opposed theirs openly. Some called us "hippies," while others said we were "hoity-toity" as if we thought we were better than everyone else.

Jane's comment was not a surprise. From the beginning of our relationship, Chris and I pushed boundaries that challenged those around us, and the further we ventured into the unknown, the bigger the distance between them and us grew.

Fortunately, we had a doctor who did his best to accommodate our wishes though they were outside his scope and comfort zone.

Seven months in, all was going well until he informed us the hospital could not meet our requirements due to their policies. To make it worse, my insurance wouldn't cover us delivering at another hospital.

We were devastated. You see, this wasn't just about us trying to be "different." It was about us empowering ourselves and changing our family's destiny. Our dream would have failed if we didn't do this birth on our own terms.

Chris researched other options and discovered we could deliver at home, with a midwife, but there was just one problem: we had to pay $5,000 out of pocket, which was an incredible amount of money back then.

We quickly sold everything we didn't absolutely need and cut back expenses but, in the end, we only raised $3,000. This sent us into a new emotional low.

Finding the rest of the money seemed impossible, and we discussed just giving up when Chris suddenly had an idea: "Let's throw a baby shower and ask for money instead of gifts!"

"Yes, that's perfect!" I thought as if our problems were solved." But will people want to contribute to us?

Despite differences, some gave graciously, and we are eternally grateful to them.

At this point, we hired the midwife, and we were knee-deep into the unknown with only each other to depend on. And though it seemed like every step thus far was met by Goliath, nothing could prepare us for his next move.

The emotions I felt holding my son were indescribable. Any fear or pain was long gone and replaced with pure joy as I'd ever known. All I could do was cry.

Chris kissed me, and I never felt so bonded with anyone in my life. I smiled at him and said, "we did it!"

We stared at our son with such love and amazement. He was living proof that we succeeded. The new life we always dreamed was possible is now here, and the journey has only just begun.

~Derika Faamausili

You desire to be, do, and have more deep down inside. This desire is so intertwined into every strand of your DNA and so embedded into the very fabric of your soul that it literally screams 24/7.

Imagine this desire as a basketball floating on top of the water. Now place your hand over the ball, push it under as deep as you can and hold it there.

What's it doing?

It's relentlessly seeking its way back to the top. Well, like the ball endlessly seeking to be where it wants to be, above the water, your desires are constantly seeking to be where they want to be— fulfilled. However, chances are, they are being suppressed.

When you desire something you don't have, it must be created. We wanted a new way of life for our family and started creating it by learning and doing new things in line with our desire.

Think of the act of creating as expanding beyond your boundaries and into the unknown. For many, this is a scary place. But why?

This is where Goliath enters. He is a tyrant who seeks to suppress your desires and stop them by any means. If that's true, how do some desires slip past him and get fulfilled?

This is where David enters. He's a brave warrior that protects your desires while seeking fulfillment in the unknown.

I remember the night clearly. I was putting a new tire on my bicycle in the garage when Derika opened the door with a concerned look. "I think my water just popped!"

Calmly, I grabbed our birthing instructions. The first line said: "Don't call the midwife until contractions are five minutes apart." Using Derika's phone, we counted her contractions, and they were twenty minutes apart, which gave us time to prepare.

Despite being 100% in the unknown, we remained focused on our mission.

As contractions grew closer together, Derika began doing something strange. She would disconnect from me for long periods and go into a kind of trance without communicating.

I looked around the room at one point, and the reality hit me that we were alone. Fear rushed through my body as I struggled to stay composed.

Twenty hours later, our midwife was with us, and Derika was in the tub experiencing unbelievable pain. Then, with the contractions only seconds apart, Goliath launched an attack that tested us both to the core of our souls.

As the pushing began, Derika suddenly came out of trance and screamed in terror. "I can't do this! It hurts too bad! I'm so scared!"

She looked at me in tears pleading in desperation to take her to the hospital.

At that moment, I realized Goliath had infiltrated her and was working to divide us, and not even comfort from the midwife could penetrate his hold.

"Is this the end?" I thought. "After all we've been through, do we give up now?" I felt alone, afraid, and wanted to run away from making that decision when something happened to me that could only be described as miraculous.

David stepped in and said, "Chris, she's alone and afraid too. You must find your courage, and she will find hers."

With unshakeable conviction, I became resolute in seeing this through. Words of power and certainty flowed through me and into her ear.

Her breathing began to slow, and her body became relaxed. As her panic subsided, I realized she had found her David.

When the next contraction hit, the energy in the room was different. Silently gritting her teeth, she pushed with fierce determination. Then, suddenly, a small patch of baby hair became visible through the water.

She caught her breath, paused, and pushed again a few minutes later.

Exhausted, she momentarily dropped her head to muster every bit of strength left. Then, with one final push, she roared so loud the whole neighborhood could hear it.

Suddenly, I saw the midwife quickly lift our baby out of the water and place him on Derika's chest as if in slow motion.

Deep down inside, you desire to be, do, or have more. Your journey to success will lead you into the unknown, where Goliath will be waiting. And should you persist, your courage will be challenged in unimaginable ways. But rest assured that David is also waiting, and he will reveal powers inside you beyond your belief.

After defeating Goliath, Derika and I felt unstoppable. We created bigger dreams and rushed towards them with unprecedented confidence. But little did we know, just a few short years later, he would return with a vengeance.

~Chris Faamausili

CHRIS AND DERIKA FAAMAUSILI

About Chris and Derika Faamausili: Chris and Derika are small business entrepreneurs specializing in mindset coaching and residential care facilities for the elderly. As a husband and wife team they began their journey together over 12 years ago. Having both come from broken homes and troubled childhoods, they vowed to turn their back on their pasts and create the happy and healthy life of their dreams. As parents to five children (and one on the way), they exemplify what it takes to make a marriage, family and business successful.

As founder of Wholesome Hypnotherapy, Transformation Coach and Hypnotherapist Derika coaches clients from around the world, helping them achieve goals in all aspects of their life. She has a wonderful gift of insight into what people need to help them break through what's blocking their happiness and success.

As founder of Wholesome Elderly Care Homes, Chris manages the business and operations of their assisted living facilities. With a natural talent in envisioning and innovating systems, he loves imagining the big picture then putting all the pieces together to bring it to reality.

Together, they form a unique mastermind and share it with the world to help others create their dream life.

Author's Website: *www.WholesomeHypnotherapy.com*
www.ThePrinciplesofDavidandGoliath.com

Diana Smith

LIFE AT THE BACK OF THE ROOM

This is how my life unfolded for me, and this is my story of overcoming the Goliaths in my life. I was not a particularly attractive child, but I knew as a Child of God, I trusted Him to guide me and he had a plan for me.

Some kids sit at the back of the room, and there is a reason for that. They hate their lives. I was one of those kids. Life at home sucked, and you don't always know what acceptable behavior in the outside world is when it seems like you don't do anything right at home. You want to hide in your room or be away from those who treat you wrong. Disappearing from the world would be ideal. Rejection has to be the main reason for low self-esteem and low self-confidence. Self-hate follows if a person doesn't feel loved, so why love yourself?

From birth, I was not wanted by my real dad. He told Mama, "That is not my child." Actually, I was, but his girlfriend of two-plus years didn't want him to have me either. They didn't want to pay child support for three kids, so they moved away and took my two older brothers, leaving me alone with a heartbroken mother.

They divorced, and seven months after my birth, she remarried and moved to the east coast. Daddy's sisters always referred to me as "Al's stepdaughter" while we lived near them. That was MY label. One by one, they came, a total of four siblings within ten years, girl, boy, girl, girl, and they are my truest best friends in the world. I was the only child in this family with a different last name, Dye. Diana Kay Dye. Everyone else was a Smith. I was the odd one out.

Each became favored by Daddy's sisters for their own special reasons and would be showered with love and gifts. One relative did prefer me by showing me THINGS THAT CHILDREN SHOULD NEVER KNOW OR DO. I was only five years old. However, it was our secret, and I was not to tell anyone. My parents wanted to know where I was getting my quarters from, and I told them. If I was not favored before, it really went downhill from that point in my life.

I learned a lot from my parents. Daddy taught me how to cut down pine trees in our yard and saw them into chunks to create the firewood to keep our concrete block home warm and toasty. Living right next to the national forest allowed for tons of recreational snake burning two to three times per year. These poisonous snakes could be found in the chicken coops, rabbit hutches, pig pens, and horse troughs. It was my job to help feed the livestock, and I learned to scream like a banshee when I encountered a snake.

Mama, on the other hand, was crafty and created my love for sewing. Cooking was not her forte, as most of her meals were black in color. One year, Mama blew a huge hole in the kitchen ceiling while canning food for the winter. Mama was a big gardener, and I mean big. Every garden was at least a quarter acre, and I was the lucky one to get to pull weeds. Snakes would end up there, too, and I learned to scream in order not to have to pull weeds all the time.

Somehow, my parents became very frustrated with me or life in general. Punishment for me was switches or the belt. I got a lot of punishment. My sister, just two years younger than me, was never punished like me due to severe burns on her legs. My brother was the only boy and could do no wrong; he was too cute. The younger sisters were too little to really receive any similar punishments.

We moved to Missouri to Smith Valley in my eleventh summer of life. Mama had contacted my natural father to see if I could spend some time with them before we moved there. This seemed like a dream because it would be a change and a chance to maybe fit in with people with the same last name as me. Unfortunately, it turned into a nightmare for me. My stepmother was not my friend and did not like me and neither did her daughter, my half-sister. The only good that came out of that visit was meeting my two older brothers and half-brother.

The only three places where I found solace were school, church, and the woods. I was a good speller and loved to read and write stories. Science and history were not joys in life, but I did my best to pass all my classes. The biggest problem for me in school was gym class. In the locker room, I discovered other girls with big boobies and felt like I was not normal like the other girls. I did not even have bumps; I was as flat-chested as they come.

My family was poor, and I mean below the poverty-line poor. I wanted to be like everyone else, so I stole a pair of jeans from a girl. Everyone knew I did it, but I still denied it. I got the beating of a lifetime from Daddy. One of my teachers felt bad for me and bought me the prettiest dress in the world. I arrived at home with the dress on, and Daddy was furious. He demanded the return of the dress back to the teacher and said, "We are not a charity case." Another beating was at hand.

We were Mormons living in the backwoods and would travel long distances to be at church for hours on end. I loved to sing and bang on the piano. One Sunday, I was chasing the bishop's son around in the parking lot and said, "Come here, you little bastard." I did not know what the word meant but I still got a royal beating for using the word.

The woods were my favorite place to visit for peace. I would screech to my heart's content, and I found a friend there. Larry the Racoon would hang on the screen door and wait for me to come out of the house. He was my little furry friend.

The beatings became horrific. Mama would clasp my wrist and swing in circles beating me with belts until she became tired. One time, Daddy kicked me on my tail bone and told me to get up. I could not walk; I crawled to my room.

My grandparents came to visit one year. They were both friendly and brought gifts for everyone. My grandfather favored me, and I soon learned why. He had spent time in prison for raping his own daughters and did not learn his lesson well enough. I learned how to keep our secret of touchy-feely times.

I started high school in Indianapolis. I was a country girl thrown into a school where girls did not wear bras and boys had long hair, and everyone smelled funny from marijuana. I learned to adapt quite well, and my grades did not suffer. I loved modern rock 'n roll music on the radio and being alive.

One of our many moves put us in the country near one of my grandfather's cousins who like to touchy-feel with young girls too. He was my last molester, and I later heard he had committed suicide. It did not really bother me at all. He chose his fate.

I graduated from a small high school and soon got pregnant with my first child. The father of my child wanted nothing to do with me and our baby. My dad kicked me out, and I lived alone for a while. Finally, one of his sisters took me in and took care of me. Later came a healthy baby girl and I named her Araminta.

My grandfather died, and Mama, me, and my baby went to his funeral. I needed to say goodbye and wish him well in hell. My older brother found me and said dad wanted me to move to Texas, so I did. My stepmother still did not like me. I moved there and, within a few months, had to put my child into a foster home. My step-grandmother was coming to visit and "did not want an unwed mother with an illegitimate child in the same house as her."

I married the first guy that came along and got my child back. Then, at the age of twenty, I was pregnant again and had another baby girl named Lilly.

I did have some fun times as a kid, but I became wary of most people. Trust and love are sacred parts of life. Being poor is not bad; just believe there are better roads ahead and trust God will lead the way.

Don't be afraid to live. Give it all you got to make memories and be a David! Trust your instincts and move forward in your life regardless of the dark journeys and confusing paths.

What did I learn through my young years? Not all parents are caring and loving. Not all adults can be trusted. Sit in the back of a room, keep your head down and watch your back.

DIANA SMITH

About Diana Smith: Diana suffered many abuses in her childhood, this left her unsure about her own adulthood and trusting others in her life. By 1979, she had two biological daughters. Poverty stricken and nowhere to go, she learned to survive in a world of doubt and desperation. In 2011, Diana's youngest child was killed by a drunk driver on her birthday. Diana suffered grief and severe depression for seven long years.

Diana researched mental health to understand the effects of her own mental well-being. She is writing a memoir of her loss and a book on parenting called *If My Brain Had Wheels*. She is a motivational speaker on mental health regarding depression and childhood abuses.

Diana met and married a wonderful man after her move to Colorado. Together, they have five children, four grandchildren and one great grandson. Life has gotten much better for her.

Author's Website: *www.TheFWord.biz*
www.ThePrinciplesofDavidandGoliath.com

Eileen E. Galbraith

LIVE YOUR DREAMS

It was the summer of 1966; we won't know whether the operation was a success or not for a few weeks. Fear, anxiety, and frustration swirl through my thoughts as I lay in my hospital bed. All of the 'what ifs' start to creep in.

As a nine-year-old, these are not what I should be thinking.

I want to be outside playing with my friends, I want to be in school learning my lessons, but that will not happen for most of the school year.

Imagine your doctor telling your parents that if Eileen is ever hit in the head, she may go totally blind in both eyes.

As an infant, I was diagnosed with whooping cough, which caused the muscles of my right eye to loosen, resulting in my eye becoming crossed, and the eyesight never developed, leaving me one sighted

Learning at such an early age that any possible injury to my head could cause total blindness led me to be fearful, shy, awkward, and with very low self-esteem, as I was bullied and left to feel worthless. Sports were out of the question! As you can imagine, I hated gym class!

So, I grew up as a very fearful child. I was not allowed to do anything adventurous for fear it might ruin my sight and life. I was afraid of my own shadow—so much that I developed an ulcer at age 14.

Bullying truly affects you. I have always feared trying something new throughout my entire life. In many ways, it was the opinions of others that created these limitations for me, and the fear was my incarceration.

Moving forward and throughout my life, I stayed in my lane. I enjoyed the jobs that I had. I became good at what I did, but my fear would never let me go that extra mile to make something happen. It wasn't until I went through a traumatic experience with a divorce that I wondered why I was even on this earth; what was the purpose of it all anyway? The depression was so great that my thoughts led to committing suicide.

I was in my car inside the garage with the doors closed and the engine running, which could have ended it all for me. But something stopped me from going through with it. I realized that I'm a pretty awesome person. I have a lot of talents and gifts that are God-given. I have learned a lot of things over the years. This was later in my fourth decade of being on this earth. I know I have the greatness to bring out, and people love me. My personality always showed up before I did because people love the person I am. People take a shine to me for whatever reason. And despite my many fears, I love people. I love being around people, and I always make people feel very comfortable around me.

"Someone's perception of you is not your reality." ~ Les Brown

While in my car, lying there on my passenger seat, was a book by Les Brown called *Live Your Dreams*. Les Brown was one of my favorite authors and motivational speakers. I have listened to Les Brown audiobooks and speeches ever since my youth. He had a way of motivating me even though the world terrified me. I picked up the book off of the passenger seat and started reading. I turned off the car and continued reading. He saved my life, although he didn't know it yet.

Everything came at me at once. While sitting in my car and thinking of the negative, I remembered the trauma from my youth. Things like being afraid of doing anything, a turning point came, and I said to myself, "What if…what if I actually could do something and achieve greatness? What if I could be good at something?"

I had excellent grades in school, but doing physical things was a giant leap of faith as it was the stuff I would never do. That was the turning point in my life. My fear was my Goliath, and I felt unprepared and inadequate to defeat it. I'm sure David didn't feel fully prepared, but it was his faith in God that he believed in more than the opinions of others.

My greatest epiphany was, why would I want to end a life that the world would miss? I genuinely believe that at that moment in time, I had a lot of "greatness within me," as Les Brown would say, and I needed to get out into the world to make that happen.

After this experience, I learned something about myself that other people need to know. I now had in my possession knowledge of how to overcome the limiting fears within ourselves, and I felt a personal responsibility from God to help people overcome similar challenges in their lives.

Our limiting beliefs challenge our self-worth. The feeling of not being good enough, or being fearful of everything getting in our way, are two of the significant feelings that crippled me. However, if we can have faith, believe, and trust in the existence and meaning of our lives, we can overcome that significant obstacle and reframe that limiting belief to move so much further in our lives. I did that, and the transformations started happening in my mind, body, profession, and relationships.

If I could go back in time and counsel my younger self, I would say, "Stop worrying about the worst-case scenarios and ask yourself what if all those things did happen." Even my dialogue crippled my sense of adventure and imagination.

The thought of, "I can't do this because I may go blind" debilitated my mind and heart. I couldn't do anything because I feared going blind. However, what if I could ask myself, what if it didn't happen? What if I was successful at something? What if I could play basketball and put that ball in the hoop? What if I could take a bat and hit a ball? What if I could do these physical activities that I was told I should never do? Coming to that realization was so freeing and liberating. I felt so free. Eventually, I said, "Screw it; let's see if any of it will happen." And so, I did.

The 3 Secrets to Living Your Dreams

Because I was bullied so much as a child, I collected a lot of nicknames that I believed were true. Names like Ella, the Elephant, and Four Eyes were many. Those unkind words form your identity as a young person. A few years ago, I started reframing how I looked at myself, and even today, every morning, the first thing I do when I get out of bed with a big smile on my face. Then, I look in the mirror and say **positive affirmations** to myself, such as, "you are fabulous. You are a wonderful human being, and the world would miss you if you were not here." I start every day on a very positive note. Just like the bullying affected me, so has the positive self-talk.

It's all about how you start your morning and end your days. Everything else will be the beauty of what you created for that day. Always make a conscious effort to wake up happy.

People used to ask me how I was doing when I was working a J O B, and I would say, "I'm fabulous. I woke up this morning being fabulous." It would be best to appreciate that you have another day to positively impact the world and improve your own life.

The second thing you must do to overcome fears and gain more confidence in your life is to **write things down**. I used to hate writing things down because there was that fear of what people would think of me while writing them down and if they ever read what I was writing.

So, I write in a journal every morning. First, I write the three things I am most grateful for from the day before. I also write three things I want to accomplish each day. Then, I write three things I can do to serve people around me—I was to help improve people's lives. I always believe I can do that by being present and actively engaged.

The third thing is that in the evenings, I always go back to that journal, **write down my successes** of the day, who I served, how I helped them, what the results were, and then prepare myself for the next day.

For me, it's all about gratitude. I get to serve people. I get to help someone change their life because I was so down and out, and I, other than having that book sitting there, really didn't have anybody telling me how fabulous I am. I had to go inside myself and realize the world would be no better off if I were gone, it would be a much better place with me being here.

> "You've got to be HUNGRY," ~ Les Brown.

I remind myself every day that the world is better with me here. Growing up, it was always about what people thought of me, whether I was good enough or said something wrong.

Go and live your dreams. That one book changed my life. Let that encouraging phrase influence yours as well.

EILEEN E GALBRAITH

About Eileen E Galbraith: As a Financial Architect for Business, Entrepreneurs hire Eileen to build their Influence and Scale their Profits because most lack essential methods and channels to create success, lack Funding Opportunities, and may face continuous struggles resulting in business disarray. So, Eileen helps them define, align, and design a visible, credible, and sustaining business. Financial Disarray is a precursor to failure, do not let that happen to your business!

Eileen is a Certified FICO Pro, International Best-Selling Author and Speaker, a sought-after Business Success Coach, and the Founder of Renewed Abundance and Credit Knowhow.

She has run multi-million-dollar businesses throughout her career and increased cash flow and profitability throughout her markets. Recognized as a professional Business Coach, Eileen positions her clients toward optimal possibilities, such as optimizing their Personal Credit to position themselves to build Credit in the name of their business. This all-important step opens the doors to Financial Creditability, Fundability, and Business Growth. Eileen has a high-energy, no-nonsense approach and loves supporting people with their goals. Just look for the Dancing Queen, and you will find Eileen!

Author's Website: www.RenewedAbundance.com
www.ThePrinciplesofDavidandGoliath.com

Erin Ley

CONQUERING SELF-DOUBT WITH SELF-CONFIDENCE

Malcolm Gladwell brilliantly stated in his book, *David and Goliath,* "We are, all of us, not merely liable to fear, we are also prone to be afraid of being afraid, and the conquering of fear produces exhilaration. The contrast between the previous apprehension and the present relief and feeling of security promotes a self-confidence that is the very father and mother of courage."

When asked to contribute to this book series, I thought long and hard about which tremendous obstacle in my life I would choose to write about. Then I examined the common thread through all of them and decided that my "Goliath" throughout all the challenges I have experienced have been self-doubt. Self-doubt, for me, constantly stemmed from uncertainty, which always landed me in some form of fear.

One example of this was when I went through a shocking and lethal cancer diagnosis in May 1991. Very few people survived non-Hodgkin's lymphoblastic lymphoma. If the cancer wasn't the demise, then the egregious two-and-a-half-year protocol of aggressive chemotherapy and radiation was. I experienced massive self-doubt because of the confusion. I did not understand why this was happening to me, and my mind became riddled with fear. This lasted for a few months. Then, the uncertainty, self-doubt, and fear began to dissipate as I stepped into courage and began to take control of my life mentally, physically, and spiritually, finally filling my entire being with self- confidence – my David.

I was twenty-five years old when informed of the diagnosis. Before this, the deepest I went with my relationship with myself and my relationship with others was incredibly superficial. It was all about what I saw in the mirror and what the outer world thought of me. I took on everyone else's opinion of who I was as my own beliefs. I looked to others to tell me how pretty I was, how smart I was, and how successful I would be. I did not understand the power I had regarding my mindset until I began to tap into what was previously unknown. Mind over matter is more than a cliché; it is a lifesaver.

When lying in the hospital bed in Memorial Sloan-Kettering Cancer Center in Manhattan, I began to read an incredible number of books. In addition, I consumed a tremendous amount of cassette tapes on personal development. I craved learning more and going deeper within, learning more and more about the whole inner world. The more I tapped into the depth of my faith, courage, strength, and compassion for myself and others, the stronger I became mentally, physically, and spiritually. I was able to reprogram my subconscious and rid myself of all the former beliefs that were no longer serving me. Instead, I replaced them with empowering beliefs that have significantly impacted my life.

Before long, I was defying all the odds. When the doctors would enter my room with news such as, "I'm sorry. You will not make it out of the hospital. Please get your things in order. We will call your parents to come to the hospital as soon as possible", I reminded the doctors of how I learned there was a lot I could do for myself that they were unable to do. I was going to walk out of the hospital despite their opinion, and shortly after that, breathing the fresh air of the outdoors came to be my reality. My mindset became stronger than any worldly issue.

Once I lost the self-doubt by making the firm decision to intentionally stay grateful for every little thing every moment of every day, the courage surfaced, and eventually, self-confidence filled my being. The self-confidence I experienced at that time in knowing I was more powerful than I ever imagined changed the trajectory of my life forever.

After the two-and-a-half-year protocol was over, and the doctors were shocked I survived, I went on to have three perfectly healthy children the doctors swore would never happen. Yet, I believed that I would have my own children with every fiber of my being.

I was challenged, however, once again after my first son was born. The doctors were so happy and relieved to see I could conceive. Nevertheless, I had three miscarriages in-between my first and second son. I was devastated. The mental pain I felt during that time is indescribable. Once again, the self-doubt crept in. Then the fear and frustration quickly followed. I became angry and knew that was not the space to create anything. Finally, I decided to go to church. My faith is incredibly strong, and at the time, I wanted to feel the peace my church provided me and the calming presence of God. I cried a cathartic cry all the way home. I felt like a huge burden had been lifted.

Once I shifted my energy from the fear, lack, and scarcity, into gratitude and faith, I conceived my second son shortly thereafter, and my daughter was conceived four months after my second son was born. I knew I had to do what I did with the cancer and tap into my faith and the self-confidence in knowing that we can create what we want from a place of gratitude and appreciation. I had to negate the self-limiting beliefs, self-doubt, and any form of fear, including anger and frustration.

The doctors at Memorial Sloan-Kettering Cancer Center saw what I could accomplish and began to have their patients call me at home. They could not explain what I was doing; however, they knew I could. And I did. This is how I began Life Coaching in the 1990s. I coached cancer patients for free for years as my way of giving back and sharing with patients around the world the insight I acquired that brought about miracle after miracle. As time went on, I began to coach individuals and business owners. The same MINDSET principles applied, whether it was personal or professional. As an Empowerment and Success Coach, I love walking the journey with my clients as they go from feeling the fear, lack, and scarcity to experiencing the focus, fearlessness, and excitement for life and business on what I call the "soul-ular" level—such a better feeling! And from that space, amazing things are created.

I believe that everything begins and ends with mindset and having the right belief system in place. What we choose to take on as beliefs, good or bad, is up to every one of us. We must be conscientious with how we speak to ourselves, verbally and non-verbally—words matter. We must guard our thoughts carefully. Thoughts truly become things. Our mind is the breeding ground for creation. Many people are living in fear, lack, and scarcity constantly. Cortisol is flying. The only thing created with that mindset and the self-limiting beliefs that go with it is more of the same and dis-ease. We attract people, places, and things to us based on our thoughts and the feelings that go with those thoughts. Choose your thoughts wisely and grow your life so that all your dreams come true. You, and only you, can control your thoughts once they enter your mind. Will you continue to entertain negative thoughts and perpetuate negativity in your life? Or will you be diligent in quickly switching your mindset from negativity to gratitude and stay focused on what is right with your life? This is a choice we have all day, every day. Choose gratitude and appreciation, and walk enveloped in faith as you do.

I invite you to examine how you speak to yourself and the feelings you allow yourself to feel. Are you experiencing amazing things in your life? If so, you have developed the habits and attitude of a leader, attracting the appropriate people, places, and things to you so that your goals can be met and your life continues to grow. On the other hand, if you are experiencing fear, lack, scarcity, or maybe even overwhelm and distraction, then you need to analyze your self-talk and reevaluate your mindset. Self-doubt is a dream crusher.

Mindset determines a great deal in our lives. If you have the mindset of abundance, fearlessness, and joy coupled with the belief of living from a heart-centered place committed to serving others, then your cup will runneth over.

Celebrate life, and you'll have a life worth celebrating! When you have thoughts of gratitude, love, joy, and inner peace, they bring up feelings of celebration and more reasons to be grateful. This is the mindset that brings about miracles. I always say miracles are normal when you have the right mindset and belief system in place.

ERIN LEY

About Erin Ley: As Founder and CEO of Onward Productions, Inc., Erin Ley has spent the last 30 years as an Author, Professional Speaker, Personal and Professional Empowerment and Success Coach predominantly around mindset, Vision and Decision. Founder of many influential summits, including "Life On Track," Erin is also the host of the upcoming online streaming T.V. Show *"Life On Track with Erin Ley,"* which is all about helping you get into the driver's seat of your own life.

They call Erin "The Miracle Maker!" As a cancer survivor at age 25, single mom of 3 at age 47, successful Entrepreneur at age 50, Erin has shown thousands upon thousands across the globe how to become victorious by being focused, fearless, and excited about life and your future! Erin says, "Celebrate life and you'll have a life worth celebrating!"

To see more about Erin and the release of her 4th book *"WorkLuv: A Love Story"* along with her "Life On Track" Course & Coaching Programs, please visit her website.

Author's Website: *www.ErinLey.com*
www.ThePrinciplesofDavidandGoliath.com

Fabiola Gonzalez

ACHIEVE ALL THAT YOU VISUALIZE

I always thought we were rich! We lived in one of the poorest neighborhoods in Tijuana, Mexico.

Our house was made of wood walls, and it was only two rooms; one was the bedroom, and one was the kitchen and shower area. The kitchen was missing one-half of a wall, and my parents used to cover it with a piece of wood at night. The bathroom was outside, and it was a spooky dark little room that smelled really bad. We used to shower in the kitchen with a bucket of water and a plastic cup.

Yet I always thought we were rich. How is that possible? I remember I was around seven years old, and my mom and my dad both had cars. However, most people in the neighborhood did not have cars, and their houses were even smaller than ours. So could that be why I thought we were rich?

When it rained, the dirt streets were not walkable as huge ruts used to open up on the dirt streets, and big rocks used to show up in the river like streams that ran down the streets.

My dad used to send us to pick up rocks. He used them to build the cement walls constructed on the side of the house to stop the dirt from the lot next to us from flooding our yard.

Most neighbors did not have a fence; we did.

When I became an adult, one of my sisters sent me a picture of us when we were little. I saw our outfits and our shoes. It was then that I realized we were actually poor when we were little.

But how come I never felt poor or needy?

It was my mindset—the amazing mindset I was born with.

I used to focus on all the things we had that others didn't instead of focusing on what we did not have. That focus came from feeling gratitude, not superiority, and I think that was the key to a joyful childhood.

We moved to the United States since we had a permanent residence from having a grandpa that was a US citizen. My mom rented a little apartment in San Ysidro, CA. Kids used to pick on us for not speaking English. However, I managed to make friends with some of the most popular girls in the school. Somehow my confidence helped.

One day, one of the girls asked if I wanted to come to her house; she said she had too many clothes and wanted to give me some. So I walked to her house after school, and she opened the door to a closet full of clothes piled up on the floor. She said I could take whatever I wanted from there.

I still remember what I felt. "Wow, she must really like me; she really wants to be my friend; she can see how cool all these clothes will look on me." So I took as much as I could carry.

As I got older, I figured it out: She could see I wore the same thing over and over again and wanted to help me. She liked me, but she could see my need. I did not see it.

This positive mindset would help me so many times in my life with the challenges I was going to be faced with. See, I believe we come to this life with the traits we will need to overcome every obstacle and genuinely enjoy this life as we learn more and experience life.

As a kid, I also loved to journal all my thoughts and feelings in a diary. I always felt I was having a conversation with God, my guardian angel, or someone up in heaven. Even though I was Catholic, I was not so sure about who was really the creator of this world, but I knew someone was watching over me and there to help me out whenever I needed help. I used to write down and imagine what I wanted, and I found out that most of what I wrote I wanted and visualized came true. Now I know those were affirmations and visualizations.

But how did my mindset help me in my adult life?

I went to college but did not graduate. I wanted to be a teacher, so I started taking classes for that major, but I soon realized that I was not enjoying what I was learning. I spent too much time crying during some of the classes when they talked about child abuse, so I decided to take business management classes instead since I worked in retail at the factory outlet in San Ysidro.

I loved sales and customer service. It did not feel like work. I loved being part of a team and loved to help others grow. They made me a store manager very quick. I found my passion: helping others! I loved finding our clients the right product. I loved helping the employees grow. I loved helping the company make money too, it was a win-win.

I married at a very young age, and by the time I was 27, I had two boys and was separated. I wanted to come live in the US again since I lived in Tijuana with my husband, and I used to cross the border daily. I did not want my kids to experience long lines and just an overall stressful situation when they started school. I wanted to buy a house but was living on a single income, supporting two boys by myself.

I saw and posted on the side of the road that read, "Buy a house with no down payment and a low monthly payment." I called. My credit was horrible, and I had too much debt to qualify. I worked on that for one year, and I was determined to buy a house. I did not focus on the negative aspects of what I was trying to achieve or that most of my friends all were renters and did not qualify to buy with a similar income to mine. I focused on what I wanted—owning a house.

I was introduced to an agent that had first-time buyers programs, and I bought my condo in National City all by myself! When I look back, all the odds were against me, or so it seems. Yet I had my mind set to owning a house, and life found a way; I just had to take action and enter the doorways that were opening up.

My oldest son was diagnosed with ADD when he was in kindergarten. It was very hard for him to focus and sit still in class, and we had so many issues at school due to his behavior. It was really hard for both of us. For him because he struggled so much at school and for me because I had to leave work to go pick him up many times, which was affecting my job.

I started writing in my journal:

- I want a new job where I make more money and have a flexible schedule so I can leave whenever I need to.

- I also want to move to Eastlake so my son can benefit from their amazing school district and programs.

I used that affirmation over and over again every time my district manager had an issue with me leaving early. I would just say in my head, "Don't worry; you will find that job that you dream of."

One day a broker came into my store; I helped him and his wife get some lotions and body products and a bubble bath for their Jacuzzi. Then, as they were paying, she said, "You should sell bigger things, you are such an excellent salesperson, and you do it in a way that feels that you are just helping, not selling." "That is because I really am just trying to help you find what you really need," I replied.

She said, "Well, come work with my husband and sell houses!" I remember laughing. "Me? Sell houses? I don't know how to do that." She said her husband would help me. I told her my dream of moving to Eastlake, and she said, "Well, that is where my husband has his office." To make this story short, he helped me get my Real Estate license, and I became a very successful real estate agent making three times what I was making in retail the very first year.

I am living proof that you can overcome any obstacle and achieve all that you can visualize and affirm with confidence, faith, and gratitude with the right mindset and belief system. When you do things with the mindset of helping others, life just gives you more so you can help more.

FABIOLA GONZALEZ

About Fabiola Gonzalez: Faby was born in Tijuana, BC, Mexico and was raised in San Diego California. Mother of two sons, with a career in Real Estate and former Retail management, Faby has spent most of her life in the Customer Service sales industry. She loves helping people!

She raised her boys on her own and that experience helped her wake up early in life to a more spiritual and fulfilling life. Her positive approach to life and its challenges, her way of overcoming and facing her fears, her way of living life by faith and finding true joy… has made her a great leader not only for her team but for her circle of friends and followers on social media.

She loves the beach and dreams of living beachfront in the near future so she can wake up to the sound of the waves.

Author's Website: *www.FabyGonzalez.com*
www.ThePrinciplesofDavidandGoliath.com

Fred Moskowitz

SECRETS TO DEVELOPING AN UNSHAKEABLE MINDSET

Research has shown that our mindset begins to take shape around the age of three. This is because the environment children are in and the way they are nurtured have such a profound impact on mindset and the development of beliefs.

In her book *Mindset: The New Psychology of Success,* author and psychologist Dr. Carol Dweck presents the concept of two types of mindsets. A person can have a Fixed mindset, or they can have a Growth mindset.

With a Fixed mindset, the person believes that their qualities and capabilities are what they are.

People having a fixed mindset feel that their capacities are carved in stone, perhaps even assigned at birth. Nevertheless, it is the hand they were dealt in the game of life. This reminds me of that classic tune by artist Bruce Hornsby - "That's just the way it is… some things will never change…."

There is the belief that they will never be able to change, and it is often accompanied by the constant need to prove themselves to others. A person embracing a fixed mindset has sentenced themself to live a life of mediocrity. Unfortunately, the reality is that this is often the only way they know how to live.

Unfortunately, there are so many people that have become disabled and are severely held back by these limiting beliefs, limiting beliefs that were often formed early in life as a child. These ideas were impressed upon the child by what they heard from the people around them—limiting beliefs formed from what was told to them by a teacher, a family member, coach, or another authority figure in that person's life. As a person grows up, they then continue to perpetuate these beliefs through self-talk and what is known as "The Story That You Tell Yourself," and they often will share this story enthusiastically with others. You will see this expressed as an excuse or a crutch to justify living a life of limitations.

How often have you heard someone say something like this:

- "I'm terrible at math…."
- "I am such a clumsy person…."
- "I am such an idiot, that's just like me, I always do that."
- "What was I thinking? I will never be able to do [activity].."
- "I am not worthy of being loved…."
- "I am not smart/pretty/talented enough…."
- "I am too old/too young to accomplish…."
- "I'm not good with handling money…."

The words that we use when we talk about ourselves are extremely powerful, which can work negatively or positively. Therefore, it is imperative to constantly monitor the words we use in our self-talk and express ourselves to others.

I have personally witnessed people successfully overcome all kinds of limiting beliefs, often under the guidance of an experienced coach or training facilitator. Fortunately, there are many coaches and experiential workshops that focus on helping people break through limiting beliefs that were self-imposed or imposed upon them when they were a child.

Let's look at the other mindset, which is the Growth mindset. The Growth mindset is all about believing that your qualities can grow and expand through your own efforts. All it takes is the desire to set the intention and then put in the hard work.

Those with a Growth mindset tend to come from constant learning and are focused on continually growing and expanding. And this can be accomplished by growing through your own efforts and strategies. However, growth can also be accomplished through collaboration with others, and this underscores the importance of surrounding yourself with the right growth-minded people. These environments include public speaking groups, workshops and seminars, marathon or triathlon training groups, and mastermind groups.

Be aware that each and every one of us has so much more influence over our state and our mindset than we realize. Once we understand this, we can then leverage this influence in a very beneficial way.

I want to share a personal story about coming face to face with this exact concept. When I was a young engineering student in college, I met with a professor assigned to be my "academic advisor." He briefly looked at my grades and made a cavalier remark that I will never forget. Looking back, I know that it was one of those defining moments in life that I can replay over and over again in my mind.

He asked the question, "Have you ever thought of changing your major to another discipline? Perhaps you might be better suited to taking up a different major other than engineering."

There I was, thinking that I was consulting with one of the "experts" that could provide guidance and direction, and I was in quite a bit of shock when I realized that this was where the conversation was heading.

I left that meeting to contemplate and get in some "thinking time." All sorts of thoughts and emotions were racing through my mind. It was right at that moment that I decided that I was not going to let this advisor define such an important outcome for my life. In fact, he barely knew anything about me or who I was!

After some deep reflection, I started to gather my thoughts together to answer the questions, "Now what? What's next?" It was up to me to either let this define me or leverage this experience. I then used the outcome of that brief encounter to fuel a significant fire under me, to motivate me to work extra hard with my studies. Was it an easy road? Certainly not. Sometimes, it felt like I had to put in twice the amount of work just to get through some of the more challenging courses. Yet, I was successful, and I did it in the end.

To this day, I feel nothing but gratitude for that advisor, who unknowingly provided me with the inspiration that I needed to complete my studies and earn my engineering degree.

When it comes to mindset, let this be something you are constantly working on. Having a growth-oriented mindset with the belief that you can always improve your qualities through your efforts and strategies will serve you very well. Imagine how far you could go if you simply focused on improving yourself by 1% every day. Small amounts of growth, consistently over time, will always yield amazing results.

In summary, let me share with you some of the qualities of a winning mindset that I often observe:

- The attitude that "life happens for you, instead of to you." This is the idea of directly taking on challenges and obstacles in life, seeing them instead as opportunities, and seeking from them the lesson that can help us grow.

- Living in gratitude every day.

- Striving to be a lifelong learner. The pursuit of constant growth and personal development.

- Participating in new experiences, hobbies, activities, and skills.

I have a friend that purposefully sets out to learn something new each year. What a great way to approach life! This idea has inspired me so much that I have also adopted this practice in my own life. At the beginning of each year, I spend some time choosing what will be the new thing that I will be learning throughout the coming year.

I will leave you with the following actionable steps that you can begin implementing today that will put you on the path to further developing a winning mindset.

- Read books, articles, and blog posts about developing your mindset.

- Listen to an audio program, podcast, or watch a video about the topic of mindset. There are countless hours of programming available for you to consume and benefit from. Some of my personal favorites? Jim Rohn, Dennis Waitley, Napoleon Hill, and Earl Nightingale.

- Join a group where you will find other like-minded individuals who will uplift and uplevel each other.

- Learn a new skill or hobby. Enroll in a class or workshop.

I encourage you to adopt a growth mindset and watch what amazing changes will come about in your own life.

FRED MOSKOWITZ

About Fred Moskowitz: Fred Moskowitz is a best-selling author, investment fund manager, and speaker who is on a personal mission to teach people about the power of investing in alternative asset classes, such as real estate and mortgage notes, showing them the way to diversify their capital into investments that are uncorrelated from Wall Street and the stock markets.

Through his body of work, he is teaching investors the strategies to build passive income and cash flow streams designed to flow into their bank accounts. He's a frequent event speaker and contributor to investment podcasts.

Fred is the author of *The Little Green Book Of Note Investing: A Practical Guide For Getting Started With Investing In Mortgage Notes* and contributing author in *1 Habit To Thrive in a Post-Covid World.*

Author's Website: *www.FredMoskowitz.com*
www.ThePrinciplesofDavidandGoliath.com

Gigi Sabbat

RESILIENCE DEFEATS THE GIANTS

As God's servants, we are called to serve His people.

Always remember, no matter what you go through during this lifetime, you can overcome it. This is because all things are possible with God first.

As God's servants, we need to make sure our cup is filled to serve His people because, as the old saying goes, "You cannot serve from an empty cup."

Therefore, mindset is crucial, so you serve the way God needs you to serve.

It is essential to have a positive mindset, but also, you need to maintain a resilient mindset.

A resilient mindset is your ability to bounce back after a significant challenge or tribulation has occurred in your life.

Remember to get back up and keep up the good fight when you get knocked down in this lifetime. A resilient mindset is the mindset David needed to have to defeat Goliath in "David and Goliath."

Each individual has faced a major challenge in their life, in which they needed to have a resilient mindset like David in "David and Goliath" to overcome it.

In 2018, I almost lost my life death by strangulation in a domestic violence relationship while in law school. Strangulation is the number-one cause of death in domestic violence relationships.

I'll never forget, one day I had just finished studying. Then I was on the couch on a phone call with a colleague from the Student Bar Association because I was the Student Bar Association President. As I was sitting on the couch and speaking to my colleague on the phone, the abuser charged at me, beat me, threw my phone across the room, and when I tried to get back up to get my phone, I fell flat like a vegetable. At the time, I didn't understand why, but the domestic violence advocates told me that I had lost oxygen to the brain. Therefore, the fact that I can utilize my skills and knowledge is a blessing. After this occurred, I got baptized again as an adult, and I reread the Bible again as an adult.

Also, shortly after the domestic violence, while I was still recovering from the abuse, I was taken by a man, and I was sexually assaulted while out on a work function. I was sexually assaulted when I was eight; therefore, this was the second time I was sexually assaulted in my life. Keep in mind that I took all of the precautions you can think of to avoid this from happening again.

Overcoming is a journey, and everyone's healing process is unique. Some folks take longer than others to recover, and that's okay, do what works for you. However, also remember you are not alone.

I kept a resilient mindset regarding the mindset David needed to defeat Goliath. A "resilient mindset" is the mindset individuals need to have in general to overcome challenges they face in their lives.

Joshua 1:9 "Haven't I commanded you be strong and courageous, do not be afraid or discouraged, for your Lord your God is with you wherever you go."

God does not want His children to handle their battles alone.

Give your battles to Him. I gave the Lord my battles concerning domestic violence and sexual assault.

Never give up and keep God first in your life.

You are not the trials/tribulations or challenges you have faced. You can overcome.

Always remember, forgiveness truly matters. The Bible states, "father please forgive them for they do not know what they are doing." Always give your battles to the Lord. Forgive and move forward with your life and continue to serve His people with a resilient mindset! God First!

Hold on to faith.

REGELINE "GIGI" SABBAT

About Regeline "Gigi" Sabbat: Gigi Sabbat, also known as Gigi, is the CEO and Founder of Life Service Center of America, LLC, Motivational Keynote Speaker, 5x BestSelling Author of the *"Walk With Me"* and *"God First"* books that have been endorsed by Les Brown. Gigi is also the Co-Author for several best-selling book collaborations, and she is a Life Coach and Confidence Coach. First generation Haitian American, Financial Expert, Florida Chapter Leader for World Women Conference & Awards, the host of Walk With Me Podcast on JRQTV, Domestic Violence Advocate, Sexual Assault Advocate, Breast Cancer Advocate, Human Trafficking Advocate, and Mental Health Advocate, etc. She is an experienced leader who has adopted a traditional approach to help people grow spiritually, financially, professionally and/or personally. She does this by setting clear and measurable goals for those that are ready to take action and experience life growth and transformation. She also helps people get unstuck financially.

As far as focusing and transformation goes, Regeline truly believes multi-skilled individuals make great leaders. It's not about focusing on so many things at once, but it is about utilizing all of your skills for the greater good and overall fulfilling God's purpose for our lives and to serve His people.

Author's Website: *www.LifeServiceCenterofAmericaLLC.com*
www.ThePrinciplesofDavidandGoliath.com

Gwen Mitchell

HOW CAN YOU MASTER
YOUR INTERNAL GOLIATH?

When I was a little girl, I loved to hear the words "Once upon a Time" as it served as the prelude to a beautiful fairy tale or story that would be inspiring. I lived in my little village in a small town where my family ran its bakery for many years. The family business was a foundational catalyst that would drive the formation of many of the assumptions, methods, and philosophies for my life.

We would wake early every morning at the crack before dawn, at 4 am to start the day with prayers of gratitude followed by daily chores, then work until all orders were complete and everything cleanly put in its proper place. Those days filled with hard work, tests, and laughter, built our character. Then the day came for me to go to school. My siblings and I would stop work at 7 am to get ready for school to catch the yellow school bus, which picked us up at the end of the lane.

As I reflect on my life-changing first day of school, its memory, along with many others, provides imprints into what I now refer to as the "real world." I remember stepping onto the bus with excitement, ready to meet new friends and have new adventures. However, as the bus continued to pick up other students, it became apparent that no one resembled my family. Upon arriving at school, my siblings and I separated into different school buildings where the pattern I noticed rang louder. Once in my homeroom, I began to introduce myself to who I thought were all the new friends that my mother had shared with us as part of our bedtime ritual leading up to this day.

To my surprise, I learned that my hands were dirty, and no one wanted to touch me because they did not want their hands to look like mine. My ponytail hairstyle was ugly, and I didn't know children were allowed to say such mean things without getting their mouths washed out with soap. I must admit many of the words spoken that day I had never heard! Then came recess, where for 20 minutes I was trapped in a game of run for my life, which concluded with my pretty white dress and hair bows in disarray. The final bell rang, indicating school was over; Mrs. White, my first-grade teacher, guided us to our bus for home. As my siblings and I connected eyes, the joy resonated, it appeared they shared similar adventures.

As the bus door sprung open, we dashed for home; I was relieved to see the burgundy Pontiac Bonneville still park in its spot, which meant Mr. Cleveland Grover Hardman, standing about 6'3, a giant to me, was still here. As I approached this distinguished dark majestic gentleman whose nature oozed a calm, quiet, peacemaker spirit – he opened his arms, and I ran in. Somehow, he could sense before any words that I had not had an excellent first day. My Granddiddy and I had a special connection; he got me. On that day and many that followed, he shared his wisdom that would stand the test of time beyond his taking flight from this earth; his words hold timeless truth. I can still hear his voice and words ringing in my ear, delivering a deeper level of clarity in many life situations. That day set forth my seeing the world anew, forming beliefs, thoughts, and feelings that would determine many of my actions. After explaining some of the words hurled at me earlier in the day, he shared how words can be powerful, but only I can choose to give or not give them energy. I remember him saying learn to see every situation as a gift of opportunity.

A gift of opportunity - what did this mean? Granddiddy clarified by stating that you can use every outcome or circumstance to your advantage in life. I quickly realized that he must be referring to another lesson that he had gleaned from his avid love for chess, which served as a metaphor for the "real world." Let me share what I know about wisdom; it is often apparent to the person providing since it has been solidifying with their experiences. The funny thing is that it usually takes you to try it before you can appreciate its relevance which frequently comes with a few bumps and bruises before it sticks. My siblings and I devised a few strategies in preparation for the next day. First, we would educate our opponents on the true meanings of words when used carelessly. Then be slow when turning the other cheek, as referenced in the Great Book. Finally, adopt the queen's mobility by stopping running, standing firm, and selectively picking targets to fight. This approach resulted in after-school detentions, which opened the door to knowing the opponents. Before long, name-calling shifted to being told that we were "one of them now." I realize that the intent was to be a compliment; however, accepting a person for their differences is how you make a difference.

Those early days I will always hold as my fondest memories. Over the years of life circumstances, my studies in neuroscience and psychology congealing with ancestral wisdom allowed me to grow. The quest to expand upon challenging old notions, assumptions, and limiting beliefs require looking within. My studies had unearthed new philosophies that gave additional meaning to my early life experiences. During our formative years as children, the environment in which we find ourselves has influence. During this time, within each person, our internal judge is developing. Our inner judge finds fault with self, others, and circumstances. This internal judge is known as our master saboteur and is the cause of our disappointment, anger, regret, guilt, shame, and anxiety. In addition, it has the power to activate accomplices' saboteurs. These accomplices' saboteurs start by being valuable assets to help you survive in your current habitat but quickly become a hindrance as you grow because they become blind spots that hide from your conscious awareness.

The journey to discovering how to master my internal Goliath, aka my inner judge, is a daily process that starts with self-awareness, becoming entuned with whom I am to be, acknowledging judgment, and owning my feelings at that moment. In learning to see every outcome or circumstance as an advantage, I recognize that there are three gifts from which to choose:

- The gift of knowledge – seeks the answer of what wisdom would I need to gain at this moment so that the payoff in the future could be more significant than what this is costing me now?

- The gift of power – is the ability to take and see the current problem like a weight in the gym and ask yourself which mental muscle must grow to handle this?

- The gift of inspiration – is acting by committing to something you wouldn't have done if this "bad" thing hadn't happened.

The opportunity of chose is a gift in every situation. When you are vigilant in selecting the strategy, which best fits the circumstances, upon its implementation, you grow your mindset into a better version of yourself that is the authentic gift.

You can employ strategies; the first step is beginning with learning to love yourself. If you are tired of being the slave to your anger, regret, guilt, shame, and anxiety, then let me show you how to master your inner Goliath. Please continue to read as I show you how to discover and use your internal powers to activate your self-command to tame the beast that lies within, which no longer serves your best interest. The journey to conquering any worthy opponent will not be easy. Still, if you act, the results will show up in relationships, shifts in your mindset, and, more importantly, how you feel about yourself.

GWEN MITCHELL

About Gwen Mitchell: Gwen Mitchell is the visionary founder and managing partner of 3rd I Business Solutions. Additionally, she is a certified Global Team Coach Practitioner, motivational speaker, and author. Her mission is to provide businesses with the structure needed to empower performance excellence, bringing clarity to the chaos. In other words, she is a Change Coach: Promoting changes in the way you think, listen, speak, problem solve, and do business… changes that not only affect the corporate bottom line but also how you conduct yourself in life. The goal is to evolve into the best version of "you."

The cornerstone of her process is communication - creating safe environments for all voices, an inclusive feeling, and critically listening skills. By implementing her proven techniques, people who work for the same entity become team players with a united goal working in unison for the company's overall success.

Everyone has a job to perform, and every ones job is essential to the business' accomplishments. With a commitment to inclusion and mentorship, Gwen develops and assists organizations in implementing processes that maximize the talents of their workforce. Her techniques and style are innovative, inspirational, time-efficient, and measurable, with strategies that bring people together and make them want to achieve because they feel they are integral to the organization's success.

During Ms. Mitchell's corporate career, she has developed a reputation for her ability to utilize resources judiciously streamline roles and responsibilities in multi-million-dollar projects. For over 20 years, her work and experience have directly benefited customers, vendors, contractors, and employees of client organizations.

Author's Website: *www.GwenKMitchell.com*
www.ThePrinciplesofDavidandGoliath.com

Jen Du Plessis

THE EMPTY SPACE

Sometimes Nowhere is Better Than Somewhere

Somewhere, something incredible is waiting to be known.
- Blaise Pascal

I've spent a lifetime seeking the answers to life's many problems and challenges, and over my years, the better I've been at answering them.

This is why I help high-achieving professionals who are missing something in their lives to uncover what fulfills them deep down. Helping them discover what it is to live a life of luxury truly. No, not the kind we all think about – with fancy cars, enormous homes, private jets, and incredible vacations. Instead, living a life of luxury is the emotional intelligence and awareness of choosing the luxury of spending time with loved ones, reading a great book, doing activities that were once put on hold, and living in genuine comfort of who we are or want to become.

Often, our belief systems are focused on the right answers to achieve our dreams and success, when they should be focused on the right questions. But unfortunately, the old answers don't work anymore. The world is changing. It's time for new questions.

Those who can let go, seek new experiences, and find themselves reborn, regenerated, and ready to take on anything life brings them will thrive.

Many may find these thoughts counter-intuitive. The more we know, the less we want to change our minds and lean into the unknown. We all run the danger of having too much knowledge. We know so much we become close-minded and stagnant. We overestimate what we think we 'understand' and underestimate what we do not know. In time, we become less and less receptive to new ideas or hearing those who share new knowledge with us; thus, stunting our personal growth.

We come to believe we know. The surprise is, we rarely do.

The empty space elevates the value of not knowing and promotes embracing the three most important words in our human language: I don't know. These words are the sounds from an empty space called Nowhere.

Sometimes new beliefs enter us, a whisper on the wind, a stranger in the crowd. At first, we retreat. The new thing lives and breathes in our midst. Everything in us pulls away, leaving behind an intoxicating, sacred silence. Then the discomfort of uncertainty falls away with three words and a chuckle, the realization, "I don't know."

If you believe in new ideas and are open to exploring new beliefs, then come with me. Come with me to Nowhere.

Nowhere On A Map

Nowhere is the land in between knowing and not knowing. It's liminal. It is the land where the tried and true has been abandoned but not replaced. So it is when you find yourself between what you recognize as familiar and any possible new thought.

There is no need to rush your visit to Nowhere. Much as you might like to move on, you can't hurry the journey. It will take as long as it takes.

Nowhere is a land of waiting, and you may arrive for any number of reasons. Perhaps a particular event or circumstance has interrupted the task at hand. Maybe something unfolding around you will significantly impact your next steps, but you have no control over its origin or timing.

Or perhaps, you are clear about your next steps yet somehow sense that now is not the time. But, of course, you don't know when the time will come, only that right now isn't it.

Passing through Nowhere, we might find ourselves face-to-face with our inner fears. Who we are, our responsibilities, the self we see in the mirror. We may be rethinking how we show up in the world, doubt our strengths and concerns about our vulnerabilities, and compare our victories to our losses. The transparency of Nowhere can cause us to question our beliefs and challenge our thoughts to the core.

It shakes us out of our habitual life and draws us out of what we have known yet does not allow us to understand what is coming next, nor when. Nevertheless, the message will soon become more apparent. Change is coming.

Nowhere extends an open invitation to surrender – an invitation to give over to something larger than our individual "self" and hope we will find whatever we need from outside ourselves. Those who are best able to draw from past experiences and explore change, be present, and anticipate; will be critical in today's world.

In Nowhere, transformation only happens when we are not in charge. When we are shaken loose from our foundations, we become open to something much bigger. It's the place where new realities and opportunities are born. It's a land where we can finally let go of an approach, a way of being, a role, an identity, and a way of thinking. This allows something new and explosive to be created.

A visit to Nowhere is essential for our personal transformation, evolution, and the growth of our culture and businesses from time to time. Although it may not be evident at first, Nowhere has an agenda for us. This usually involves letting something go. Old patterns dissolve so that we can discover the next iteration of our lives and the new work that awaits there.

People passing through Nowhere have described the land as insane, crazy, even psychotic. That can certainly be the case if there is a lack of understanding of Nowhere. But if one is willing to listen, sense, and feel what awaits - let go of control and surrender to a greater potential – the shifts in awareness, personal transformation, and business can be enormous.

I've been there more often than I can count. It requires focus and intention. The more I trust the flow and evolution of my own life, the more I understand the magic of the empty space.

An Observation About The Noise

In February of 2020, we lived in a land I will call Before. The Pandemic had just entered our consciousness, barely. It appeared that its effects would be contained.

Thirty days later, we woke in the land called After. The world began to shut down. Our lives froze. Everything locked down. We were immobilized.

The noise of the Pandemic accelerated changes in our global culture and thinking in ways previously inconceivable, changing our world in an instant.

Add in new sustainability, new values, and new lifestyles – now we had a tsunami hitting us with full force. Everyone and everything, everywhere, was impacted. Old behaviors were questioned and re-evaluated. What used to yield good results has become ineffective. Successful models and strategies are being abandoned, several lives and companies are crumbling.

We struggle to adapt and re-invent our mindsets and mechanics to meet the changing demands. We may think the pace of change is high now but buckle up; it will never be this slow again.

We need to leave some wiggle room for exploring potential variations or rethinking steps in the middle of a process if we want to succeed.

People have realized for some time that the "business as usual" model was for another time. Doing nothing is not an option. Change has been replaced by a new, organic reality, which is adaptable, nimble, and innovative, possibly even disruptive. Making the world a better place requires change: Thought change.

Transformation is not something you can complete in a single iteration. Instead, it is a journey toward value-based thinking that focuses on meeting you where you are and encouraging you to begin the process of being present again to Somewhere.

In Nowhere, we hear the fundamental questions associated with the decision to embark on the journey of change: Why am I doing this? How do I matter? What beliefs do I have that are holding me back?

It is not enough to want to change. One must also have the courage to change themselves and look at what they truly want in their lives. Dare to raise questions, rethink assumptions and existing beliefs, and come up with new ideas, thoughts, and outlooks. The Middle of Nowhere involves creating a culture where all dare to bring themselves fully into the moment.

Counter-intuitive right? Not exactly. Creativity can slow down because traditional thinking stays the same. One must challenge themselves and get out of their comfort zone. In a world where change is happening exponentially, the frightening thing is not the difficult questions being asked; it's the questions that are not being asked.

True transformation is having all the options available, which is essential for adaptive action. This is why I lead high-end masterminds. People with different backgrounds, experience levels, personalities, and drives create a talent pool of solutions for a variety of problems. Differing perspectives help everyone increase their awareness of the tremendous advantages of stepping into Nowhere and then returning to Somewhere. Here is where they begin to live their life of luxury and find authentic success and happiness.

JEN DU PLESSIS

About Jen Du Plessis: She is known as America's Lifestyle Mastery Mentor. People most attracted to Jen are high-achieving professionals and entrepreneurs who are missing something. Through her masterminds she helps people increase the awareness of what's possible to multiply their results in record time, while having the courage to say yes to their personal lives.

She has been in the financial services industry for 4 decades and was listed in the Top 200 of nationally ranked mortgage originators and funded over $1 Billion in mortgage loans.

She is a 8X #1 Amazon best-selling author, host of two (2) top podcasts, and a TV Show Host.

An expert in Living a Life of Luxury, Priority and Time Management, Business Relationships, Business Scaling, Sales Management, and a Certified Mastermind Facilitator.

She is a charismatic speaker, sharing stages with such icons as Tony Robbins, Les Brown, Darren Hardy, Jeff Hoffman, Sharon Lechter and many more!

Jen provides consulting through her high-level Masterminds and Retreat to entrepreneurs who are serious about growing to their next level, alongside a community of strong like-minded individuals.

Jen believes that entrepreneurs can Live their Legacy while Building it, and it's time to start Living a Life of Luxury every day!

Author's Website: *www.JenDuPlessis.com*
www.ThePrinciplesofDavidandGoliath.com

Jessa Carter

OUR GREATEST ASSET

It was 1982, in a small town in the mountains of rural Virginia. An only child born to young parents. My father was a free-spirited coal miner. My mother was a fiery, strong, independent woman. Unfortunately, they divorced when I was young. According to societal expectations, I was not supposed to amount to much. Yet despite my humble beginnings, I had other plans. Inquisitive, intelligent, and intuitive, I have always marched to the beat of my own drum and was never keen on the status quo. From a very young age, I had a deep knowing I was meant to be wealthy and do big things in the world, yet the how or what eluded me for decades. Fortunately, my mother did a phenomenal job reinforcing my intelligence and instilled these beliefs in me: The sky is the limit. You can be anything you want to be.

A stint of childhood seizures established my fascination with the brain and the mind from age four. Since academia was the only path my mother knew to ensure a better life for me than she had for herself, it also became the only path I knew. My mom was strategic and worked hard to guarantee my first four years of college tuition. Yet, when it came to my decision to attend grad school, she scoffed at me, "How are you going to pay for that?" My reply was, "They are called student loans, Mom." She believed student loans would haunt you, reflecting her fears regarding money and debt. At that time, I had a bachelor's degree but was barely making ends meet. It was not the life I imagined for myself. Thankfully,

I did not allow her doubts or fears to stop me. I went on to earn a Master of Medical Science and a 10-year career as a Neurosurgical Physician Assistant.

I achieved an impressive, reputable career, a fancy title with several letters behind my name, and the coveted six-figure salary. According to my mom and the societal definition of success, I was successful. Or was I?

The truth is, I was hiding behind my perceived success. I was working 60-80 hours a week, beyond stressed, mentally and physically drained, short-tempered, entitled, unfulfilled, and emotionally unavailable with a divorce and the death of an incredible boyfriend under my belt. The mental walls I had built around my heart would put Fort Knox to shame. I was incapable of being vulnerable. I would not allow myself to ask for nor receive support. I believed I had to do everything alone.

Notice I never mentioned being unhappy. I was happy, within my limited scope of what happiness could be at the time. Caught up in the societal-driven perception of success, I was completely unaware of how long I had been denying myself the meaningful relationship, love, wealth, and lifestyle I deserved.

In 2017, I reached my breaking point. I had an overwhelming sense of "What am I doing? This isn't life. This isn't Living." I came home after an eight-day work stretch, fell to my knees in tears, and in prayer with my significant other who had passed, I said, "These are the times I wish you were still here. I know my life is supposed to be going in a different direction. I need your help. I need your guidance."

Within 48 hours, I received the guidance I sought. I took a leap of faith, made a career shift, and moved across the country, affording me fourteen days off every month plus a hefty pay increase. I adopted the concept of "Life by Design" and became determined to figure out how to make it my reality. The first year, I used my newfound freedom to travel, dance, read, and live life to the fullest. The second year, it was time to get back to pursuing my dream of becoming an entrepreneur. Through further intellectual, personal and spiritual growth, my passion, purpose, and mission in the world became fully transparent. The courage and mental fortitude I gained along the way to jump from job security into the waters of entrepreneurship blows me away.

Be relentless in the pursuit of your dreams. You are not your circumstances, you are not your thoughts, and you are not your feelings. You are a Magnificent Divine Being designed for creation. Your mind and body both hold intelligence and power beyond measure. If you can dream it, it is meant for you. Please, read that again. Let that concept sink in. The potential to attain anything you desire already exists in the Universe, waiting for you to become the version of you who already has it, the version of you that you are meant to be.

Each event in your life since the day you were born is a piece of the puzzle. Your entire life is a perpetual, strategic plot in the pursuit of your greatness. The trials, tribulations, and triumphs you experience are intentional. The people you meet, you are meant to meet. Whether you know them for a season or a lifetime, it is precisely the time you are meant to spend together. There are no accidents in the Universe. Think about it, if one little thing in your entire trajectory were different, you would be different. So feel free to pause here and take some time to truly reflect.

When I reflect upon my journey, I distinctly remember the moment in my mid-twenties when I realized the only person who could create change in my life was me. Today, I see crystal clear how every little detail from day one, good or bad, big or small, formed the woman I have become and continue to become every day.

The mind can facilitate our paradise, or it can be our prison. It is undeniably our most precious, powerful, and valuable asset. As we become more conscious and aware, we understand that our thoughts, feelings, and beliefs play a vital role in shaping our reality and how it unfolds. Please note the nuance of a "vital role" versus control. When we attempt to control things, we eliminate the potential for the Universe to give us something greater. For example, supreme clarity of the outcome you desire is imperative to bring it into your reality; however, you want to release the who, what, when, where, and the how. This allows space for your subconscious mind's intelligence and the Universe to step in and give you something more significant than you ever imagined.

"When you change the way you look at things, the things you look at change." - Wayne Dyer.

Perspective is an integral component of the mind. If you perceive obstacles as obstacles, they will remain obstacles. If you choose to perceive obstacles as opportunities, they will become opportunities. You are constantly being given feedback from your body and external environment. Then you are left with choices. For example, if you believe you can, you can. If you think you can't, you can't. Either way, you are correct. Our perspective influences our beliefs, and what we believe is extremely powerful.

Another valuable perspective we can adopt is that life is happening for me, not to me. Everything happens for a reason, and that reason is there to serve me, even if I cannot see it right now." This is what I call an "Open Perspective," which is particularly valuable because it allows space for your subconscious mind to reveal the how and the direction meant for you. You may not receive guidance immediately, but it will arrive. See this as an opportunity to learn to trust divine guidance and divine timing.

Anything you decide or choose becomes attainable when you live through a lens of self-discovery and growth. Use your sovereignty to determine what is right for you. Decide mediocrity is for someone else. Go beyond societal norms, beyond the status quo, and beyond the perceived limitations in your mind. The only person stopping you is you. Gain the self-awareness to know when you are getting in your own way. Acquire the courage to drop your pride and join arms with someone who can elevate and accelerate your journey. No one became who they are or attained their position in life alone. Although I attempted life from that lens for years, it was not effective or fun.

In the famous words of Sir Richard Branson, "If your dreams don't scare you, they aren't big enough."

Are you scared yet?

Challenge yourself to reduce the number of ORs in your life and pursue more ANDs.

You can have a Dynamic career/business AND Extraordinary Relationships (Professional, Social, AND Romantic) AND Exceptional Health, AND a Lifestyle that sets your heart and soul on fire. You can have it all and feel exquisite along the way. Dare. Dare to Dream Big. Dare to Live Boldly. Dare to Love Deeply. Dare to Laugh Always.

JESSA CARTER

About Jessa Carter: Neuro Finesse Expert, Jessa Carter, is the most highly sought Intuitive Visionary and Life Strategist for High Achieving Leaders and Entrepreneurs who are missing fulfillment, joy, and passion in life despite their massive outward success. As the founder and CEO of Divine Heart Dynasty™, she excels in re-defining and re-inventing yourself, your life, your business, and your relationships to soaring heights that defy logic so that your time on earth is by Intentional Design, never by default.

A Certified Physician Assistant with a Master of Medical Science degree and a 10-year career in Neurosurgery, she went on to become a Quantum Energy Practitioner, Master Coach, Holistic Health Practitioner, and Certified ThetaHealer®. Her expansive expertise integrates powerful personal, professional, and spiritual development to unlock the unlimited potential within the subconscious mind.

Working with Jessa is an experiential, bespoke playground where the worlds of science, energy, and spirituality collide to entice depths of the mind, heart & soul's intelligence often left untouched. Jessa is a beacon of light illuminating a disruptive path beyond societal norms, beyond the status quo & beyond limitation. She is your unwavering constant, your cheerleader, and your advocate for feeling exceptional while co-creating a life and legacy beyond your wildest dreams.

"It is the plunge deep within the ocean of self that expands one's capacity to experience the vast depths of others and the world around us." ~ Jessa Carter

Author's Website: *www.DivineHeartDynasty.com*
www.ThePrinciplesofDavidandGoliath.com

Jessica Bojorquez

THE WOUNDED WOMAN

I think we all know by now, especially if you're reading this book, that life comes with challenges, trials, and tribulations. So, how does a single mother go from weighing over 209 lbs and having to start her life over again - to being in the best shape of her life, physically, emotionally, mentally, spiritually, and financially?

It was Fall 2016, which doesn't mean much for Phoenix as the temperatures are still in the low 100s until mid-late October. Typically, you can find Phoenicians running back into an AC chilled room or pool. However, the room I was in was heated at 110 degrees with 75% humidity. I was standing in a room with about twenty-five other sweaty yogis as the instructor cued the next pose. With sweat pouring down my face, I tried to listen to the next cue and focus on my breathing. At the same time, I was trying not to pay too much attention to my reflection in the mirror or the other distractions in the room.

The instructor cues us to stand straight and face the mirror to look at ourselves. I looked straight between my own eyes before scanning myself. I saw a woman with a very swollen face, hair sticking to her red, inflamed cheeks. With eyes filled with despair, her expressions looked like she was seeking the answers to end her grief. With my body weight nearly double the size of my normal weight, I stared back at the woman standing in front of me, almost unrecognizable.

At the time, I was in the middle of ending a 12-year relationship. I was blindsided by the breakup that left me completely shattered and heartbroken. I'd given myself to my relationship and family, spent my entire adulthood with my sole provider, and had no control over the final decision to split. The upheaval of having to move my son and I back home put me into a state of depression and anxiety. Not to mention, I was standing at my heaviest weight of 209 lbs. I felt like I was in the shell of someone I once knew.

As I stood looking at the person before me, wondering if I would ever be happy again. I heard the instructor talk about self-acceptance. "True yoga is about accepting who you are, as you are," she said to the room as her voice echoed off the mirrored walls and into my ears as I processed the words and redirected my thoughts. I took another look at the woman I saw in the mirror, and I had an epiphany. At that moment, I thought, "ENOUGH."

I was thirty-two at the time, and I found myself in a situation I never wanted to be in again. Starting my life over from being a stay-at-home mom with everything I needed and wanted. If I did not have it, I would order it on a limitless credit card. Until one day, the relationship ended out of the blue. My life as I knew it was taken away, and I had to start over again. While having to go back to work in society, I found myself in very unfamiliar territory. At that moment, I knew I had to make a choice. I chose myself.

This would not be the first story of great perseverance from my family lineage. I come from an extensive line of incredibly strong women. My background and family history in Arizona go through multiple generations. I am a granddaughter to a decedent of one of Arizona's original pioneers, King Woolsey and Lucy Martinez. There is a famous story behind the involvement of the two. One that has made Arizona history and earned Lucy Martinez an induction to the Arizona Women's Hall of Fame.

King and Lucy were domestic partners in the 1800s, back when biracial marriage was still prohibited. With two children and one on the way. King came home one night with his new wife. Woolsey, a ranching pioneer and an Arizona politician having land and money, decided he wanted full custody of their children. Lucy, a Yaqui Indian woman, was very young when Apache Indians slaughtered her family in northern Arizona. As Lucy was well-versed in fighting for her livelihood, she went to various courthouses to regain custody of her children.

On June 30, 1879, King died of a heart attack, allowing Lucy to win the verdict in court and regain custody of her children. Her courage to fight the courthouse in the 1800s as a 'colored' woman, with no money, won the case. This form of relentless bravery has later earned her induction into the Arizona Women's Hall of Fame. The story of Lucy and myself had many similarities. We both got our worlds turned upside down, and we had to dig through the trenches of hell to find our way out. Luckily for me, I was able to get through using the power of forgiveness.

Investments can sometimes be hard to make. We go through life having to make decisions and commitments to investments, but we have the hardest time committing when it comes to investing in ourselves. Why?

The moment I saw myself sweaty, trying to focus while pushing myself beyond my own physical limits. I knew there was a commitment I needed to make for myself. I was tired of looking at the person I barely recognized. I knew I had to go deeper. I had to do extensive soul searching for someone I never knew. For the first time in my adult life, I would do what it took to find the best version of myself. The commitment I made that day has led me to making the best decision I have ever made.

I wish there were a magic pill and an easy way to get through such obstacles in life. As the saying goes, "The only way out of hell is through it." There is an inner knowing we must face each day. A knowing of acceptance no matter where we are, and the peace of mind as each day passes. I have created a structure for myself that was self-taught and didn't come naturally.

I practiced hot yoga at least three days per week during the rest of the season, which developed into daily devotional practice. Over time, I connected into a community of like-minded, like-hearted people, which led me to earn my teaching certification. I started implementing other daily activities, such as meditation and hiking, which later turned into trail running. Although yoga wasn't how I physically got fit, it was a gateway and opening to connecting movements with my breath.

The pivotal moments in our lives are usually during times of great uncertainty. But the truth is, we can change our direction at any given moment. The hardest part is staying on track and motivated even while we're the only ones who can see the goals we're trying to accomplish.

By developing a committed daily routine of self-care and meditation, I have started and grown my real estate company as a solo agent. I've produced Millions in sales and have developed a virtual home tour marketing brand and platform called Virtual Tour Tuesday. My channel's high-quality videos and segments routinely receive tens of thousands of views. By marketing mine and other available luxury listings, I've connected and collaborated with some of the most influential people in the world. I've also curated my marketing strategies and now teach other realtors to scale their busing using video marketing on YouTube. By committing to myself, I not only found myself, but I've ultimately reprogrammed my entire subconscious to become the best version of myself.

When circumstances bring us a life-altering challenge, we must decide where we want to go and who we want to become. It requires courage, faith, and a shit load of trust in our abilities to push out of our disbeliefs and generational patterns to obtain our highest goals. Progression may not be instant, and if the results are meant to last, then it shouldn't be. True change starts from where we are and our commitment to take even the smallest steps towards becoming a better version of ourselves.

It took great strength to come out of the darkness I held on to; it was years before I fully recovered. Life presented me with one of the greatest obstacles that turned into the biggest blessing of my life. To heal my own heart and create a life of love and abundance takes great skill, a skill anyone can acquire. If you can follow the rules of the process and let go of attachments, you too can develop such a great place of love, beauty, and grace. But you'll have to wait for the next book to learn more!

JESSICA BOJORQUEZ

About Jessica Bojorquez: Jessica Bojorquez is an entrepreneur, and realtor, with eXp Realty. Jessica specializes in video marketing and selling luxury real estate.

Jessica believes in the quality of presentation and creating elevated experiences for her clients. Not only matching her clients with their dream home but telling the story of the home to match its dream family.

Jessica has created a marketing platform to showcase available luxury homes and give potential clients and viewers information through elevated story telling with levity. Her charismatic tenacity has caught the attention of highly influential thought leaders and is now in the process of teaching her strategies to other Realtors and Business Owners.

Jessica is a certified realtor and yoga teacher, certified with NAR, SAAR, and in the process of getting her MWBE certification.

Jessica is self-taught through the teachings of several mentors and teachers of a greater purpose and knowing our life's path begins with our beliefs. In order to elevate your life, you must first elevate your thoughts. "Welcome Home!"

Author's Website: *www.JessicaBojorquez.EXPRealty.com*
www.ThePrinciplesofDavidandGoliath.com

Jon Kovach Jr.

STONES TO A SWORD FIGHT

Since I was a young boy, I've had an entrepreneurial spirit. I knew how to work hard and hustle from food drives to lemonade stands.

When I was 12 years old, I helped my mom with a candy and snack vending business. At age 14, my brother and I ran the neighborhood lawn mowing business and landed a corporate job. At age 16, I started a DJ business so that the local school and church dances had better music. At age 18, I planned a Battle of the Bands event for our school, which raised enough funds to bring our student government out of debt and saved our senior prom budget. At age 21, I worked with my dad to sponsor a family in the Philippines with a micro-financing project. But when it came to college, I got caught up in job chasing and a fixed mindset.

In college, it is their curriculum and motivation to get you placed in a job after college to improve their stats as a compelling state college. It's a worthy goal, and Utah Valley University had programs and resources that landed me some of the most excellent internships and jobs. My first ever internship was for a start-up outdoor retailer company called Cotopaxi. They made bags and technical gear for hiking and outdoor adventures. I worked on the event team, where we marketed a 24-hour scavenger hunt challenge that attracted over 5,000 people and 500+ groups and progressed to over 12 cities across the US.

My second internship landed me a job with one of the top PR & communications firms, Spectrum Science Communications, in Washington, DC. I learned the corporate culture of big business and big pharma. Daily, I helped pitch newsworthy announcements to *The Washington Post, The New York Times, The Economist, The Hill, The Washington Business Journal,* etc. That experience awarded me great connections and raving testimonials from my supervisors.

These experiences and a few not mentioned ultimately helped me get the PR Assistant and Publicist role at Coldwell Banker Commercial Advisors, the largest commercial real estate branch in Salt Lake City, Utah, led by the real-estate mogul Brandon Fugal. This job was a corporate dream come true. It came with benefits, insurance, a 401K, unlimited drinks and snacks, annual corporate galas and holiday parties and surrounded me with the state's most influential business, economic, and government leaders. I met the entire governor's cabinet and team, the president and founder of the Utah World Trade Centers, and so many more powerful people. I always joked to friends and family about how beautiful the office I worked in was, saying it was so clean you could eat spaghetti off the floors. That's how nice Class A office space is, a standard fit for Mr. Fugal.

Despite the perfect job conditions, the environment that would become my career, and the routine that had me in by 9 AM and out by 5 PM, something was burning inside me that I denied until my breaking point.

I parked my new Land Rover Discovery Sport in the lot. As I entered the building, I whistled the tune of the last song on my radio. The sound of dress shoes clicked as I paced to catch the elevator with my colleagues. I broke the silence with a pleasant joke and exited the elevator on the A suite floor. Just as the doors opened, an uproar of laughter burst out of the elevator doors. I made my rounds saying hi to all the staff. Then rounded the corner to greet Mr. Fugal and the other executives in the board room. Finally, I found my desk, a small cubicle in the corner just outside the CEO's office. I unbuttoned my suit, loosened my tie, and sat down to a stack of manilla folders and papers. In my head, I said, "This is the dream," as I shuffled through those papers.

While shuffling through the papers, I accidentally knocked one of my favorite corporate pens off my desk onto the floor, which rolled clear under my desk. I couldn't lose my favorite pen, so I scooted my chair back, climbed down on all fours, still wearing my corporate suit, and crawled deep under my desk. It might have been a cave because my pen rolled clear to the back corner of my L-shaped desk. It was nice, dark, and quiet under there, and I felt like I could think clearly for once without the clickety sounds of the printing room or chatter from co-worker conversations in the mailroom. I took my sweet time inching closer to my fallen pen in this moment of clarity. Then, I reached for the pen, and under my breath came out the words my subconscious was thinking and feeling—I said, "I wish I could hide under here all day."

This moment of honesty shocked me! I recognized the truth in these words. Like the prodigal son, it came to me in a flash of memory and desire that my dream wasn't to be a publicist. I was supposed to be a leader, business owner, a motivational speaker from stages, where I'd help and inspire people to achieve their goals. I guess I got so caught up in the job hunt and living this life of corporate structure that I had forgotten my true dreams and passions. I knew that if I picked up that pen and returned to my desk work, I would be ignoring this epiphany. At that very moment, I promised myself that if I picked up this pen, I needed to take the next step in my journey to become a motivational speaker.

Devoted to my true aspirations, I grasped the pen with bravery and optimistically returned to my desk, where I immediately began to carve out a letter to my supervisors about my two weeks' notice and resignation. I didn't have a job lined up just yet, but I planned my leap with faith and submitted the letter to my boss.

Sticks and Stones

In the famous biblical David and Goliath story, we know that David of Israel believed God was with him and he could have the courage to fight and defeat the giant Philistine Goliath of Gath. David convinced Saul that he could face Goliath without any armor but to go to battle with his sling and staff. Moments before facing the giant, David went to a nearby stream.

In 1 Samuel chapter 17, verse 40 reads: *And he (David) took his staff in his hand, and chose him five smooth stones out of the brook... and his sling was in his hand: and he drew near to the Philistine (Goliath).*

David was so brave that he fought off bears and lions while taking care of sheep. He believed in his strength and mission that he could defeat Goliath.

David mocked the giant and said, "You come to me with a sword, but I come to you with the Lord Almighty." He believed that God was more powerful than anything. David then took a stone, put it in a sling, and slung it right into the forehead of Goliath.

David grabbed five stones before his battle with Goliath. I call these The 5 Stones of Mindset, which represent vital elements of conquering your enormous challenges in life.

The 5 Stones of Mindset consist of the following:

1. Devotion
2. Bravery
3. Clarity
4. Belief
5. Intuition

I relate my pen story to The 5 Stones of Mindset, as I know many people reading this now struggle with fulfilling their dreams and life missions because you may have settled for something that you convinced yourself of being a good thing. Like my corporate job was a good thing, I needed to face my giants of comfort and defeat my most significant challenge of self-deception. I needed to leap with faith and strength.

1. **Devotion**

   I devoted enough to my purpose to recognize my truth, which happened to be that I was a motivational speaker and not in a cubicle.

2. **Bravery**

   Without hesitation, I decided to do the right thing without dwelling on the consequences of my actions.

3. **Clarity**

   In the quiet space under my desk, I gathered my thoughts and the tools I would use to face my Goliath.

4. **Belief**

   In my mind, I could do no wrong. I believed this was a clear path to success, and I knew I must take it.

5. **Intuition**

   Despite the advice and mentorship of supervisors, professors, and leaders, the only source of knowledge that knows what is best for you is YOU! Follow your gut and trust your intuition.

I challenge you to take immediate action and equip yourself with your Stones of Mindset. Though you may feel that stones are not appropriate for the sword fights and battles ahead, be devoted to your purpose, be brave, seek clarity, trust your beliefs and faith, and follow your intuition. I can promise you that these stones empowered David and helped millions of people who have taken on their challenges.

JON KOVACH JR.

About Jon Kovach Jr.: Jon is an award-winning and international motivational speaker and global mastermind leader. Jon has helped multi-billion-dollar corporations, including Coldwell Banker Commercial, Outdoor Retailer Cotopaxi, and the Public Relations Student Society of America, exceed their annual sales goals. In his work as an accountability coach and mastermind facilitator, Jon has helped thousands of professionals overcome their challenges and achieve their goals by implementing his accountability strategies and Irrefutable Laws of High Performance.

Jon is the Founder and Chairman of Champion Circle, a networking association that combines high-performance-based networking activities and recreational fun to create connection capital and increase prosperity for professionals.

Jon is the Mastermind Facilitator and Team Lead of the Habitude Warrior Mastermind and the Global Speakers Mastermind & Masterclass founded by Speaker Erik "Mr. Awesome" Swanson.

Jon speaks on a number of topics, including accountability, The Irrefutable Laws of High Performance, and The Power of Mastermind Methodologies. He is a #1 Best-Selling Author and was recently featured on SpeakUp TV, an Amazon Prime TV series, with his keynote speech titled, Getting Unstuck. He stars in over 100 speaking stages, podcasts, and live international summits on an annual basis.

Author's website: *www.JonKovachJr.com*
www.ThePrinciplesofDavidandGoliath.com

Kearn Cherry

SOMETIMES A GIANT MUST FALL

Sometimes you just don't win at the moment. As a person creating events, it was always easy to get people to attend. You just have to create the right environment and connect with the right partners. But there are times when it's just not that simple.

I was always looking for ways to educate my clients and help them make decisions earlier. You see, the clients I was focused on were the elderly. They enjoy getting out and meeting people. For years, I hosted events that drew thousands of seniors. I knew we needed to offer more and improve our visibility.

One of my friends in the senior care industry and I decided we needed to target the caregivers. The caregivers really determine who's going to serve their loved ones and the types of services that are required. Most of them are unaware of what's available. I'm always creating events that provide solutions to a problem. We decided to create a conference that would do exactly that.

The caregiver conference had over 600 caregivers, seniors, healthcare providers, and other professionals each year. It was the largest in the region for an in-person event. I knew that you must continue to change each year and bring in new partners who would contribute to getting more attendees and spreading the word.

Every year I would spend thousands of dollars on visibility. We were on tv, radio, and social media. We would send mailers and e-blasts. So, when we were approached to partner with one of our local media companies, it was a "no brainer." I could now double my efforts with this media company, but my conference team members warned me not to bring them on board. We really didn't need them. She was correct, but I saw it as a growth opportunity and it could help with future events.

Sometimes, if your gut isn't telling you anything, you need to listen to your team members. You also need to find out what that partner hopes to gain if you are already paying them. Never assume that they will put your goals ahead of theirs. Media companies and others are concerned about their "bottom line," not yours. I was so focused on the prize that I didn't protect our interests.

Though I had been spending thousands of dollars with them for every event, I saw less media coverage that year. The organization decided either not to play my commercials or simply play them when no one would see them. It was them intentionally crippling our conference. It was definitely hard to watch. I decided that we would not use them at all the following year, but they had already created a plan to duplicate my conference after six years of success.

The next year was brutal. There was a new event for caregivers and seniors, and it was being brought to the community by my previous media partner. They broke all the rules and even hosted their event two weeks before mine the following year. This only created mass confusion, which was their goal. Everyone attended their conference. Friends and colleagues even told me that they thought it was our conference and of course, they were not attending another one. It was a major blow. My vendors were extremely upset and jumped ship the following year.

My friends suggested approaching their management team, but I knew that they supported the idea, if not encouraged it. It was a devastating blow to my ability to be seen as a successful conference producer. After all the years of pouring into senior events, to have it stolen was unthinkable! I pondered many strategies to repay the enemy, but there's no payment better than God's. Galatians 6:8 - "You reap what you sow."

I'm a conference producer, so it wasn't long before I decided to address another issue. But, you see, I was being set up by God for something much bigger. I would go on to create a Success Women's Conference with a new partner, becoming one of the largest in-person women's conferences. In the very first year, we had over 500 women to over 17,000 virtually.

As far as the previous conference and its owners, the event no longer exists, and the employees of that organization were all fired—all eighteen-plus of them. They probably assumed it was due to the industry changing, but I know they can't do evil and expect not to have consequences. Sometimes it may be a few years later, but watching from the sideline is always sweeter as God is the true Giant slayer. We are servants, like King David, who set the trap and take out the giants. Either way, He works all things out for our good!

There are times when it looks like the enemy is winning, and it seems unfair. You have given your all, and they just take so freely without a conscience. You don't realize there is a higher plan for you. Your purpose is unfolding right before your eyes. Sometimes you have to realize you could just be the person appointed as the giant slayer because there are times when a giant must fall.

KEARN CHERRY

About Kearn Cherry: Kearn Cherry is called the "Butts in the Seats Queen." She is a speaker, coach, entrepreneur, and 15 x #1 Bestselling author. She is the producer and creator of Power Up Summit and Level Up Summit. She is co-founder and director of Success Women's Conference with over 17,000 virtually and almost 1,500 in person. She is the owner of PRN Home Care for 25 years and KKonnections.

Mrs. Cherry is the visionary author of "*Make It Happen.*" She is also the visionary of "*Trailblazers Who Lead I & II.*" "*Undefeated*" is the next anthology featuring 100 women to share their secrets of winning. She has been featured twice in *Essence Magazine* as the "Comeback Queen," *Black Enterprise Magazine,* and others.

She often says, "When one door is closed, try the next one; if it's closed, go around to the back; if not, Create Your OWN, but never give up."

Author's Website: *www.KearnCherry.com*
www.ThePrinciplesofDavidandGoliath.com

Maris Segal & Ken Ashby

GOLIATHS HAPPEN, DAVID CHOOSES

Mindset, the Slingshot of Choice!

In the age-old biblical story of David and Goliath, David, a career shepherd, faces the giant Goliath and, against all odds, defeats him with a slingshot. Our world is a universe where Goliaths happen, and David chooses! We invite you to read on with curiosity, and a lens into your own life, as we explore Goliaths, monsters, obstacles, and demons, which occur in our personal and professional lives. We see two distinct categories of Goliaths: Human Driven Goliaths and Nature Driven Goliaths. We may be caught off-guard and find our faith and confidence shaken-to-the-core in both cases. These Goliath moments can be life-altering or, depending on our mindset and beliefs, and they can be life-affirming. When we stand up as David against Goliath, our greatest tool is the mindset of "choice." We can FACE (Freely Acknowledge Current Emotions) Goliath and choose to breakthrough with empowered action, or not.

The choice to FACE Goliath and how we view the situation can be the difference between thriving or just surviving. Conversely, we can choose overwhelm, fear, and avoidance, which is guaranteed to lead to defeat. Choice is the bridge between imprisoning or freeing ourselves. Science has proven that our brains can only process one of these choices at a time. Sometimes easier said than done!

Our business consulting and coaching work within the public and private sectors has taken us to twenty-seven countries, from classrooms to boardrooms and the world stage. We have experienced and supported friends, family, colleagues, and clients facing Goliaths wherever we have worked and played. The likelihood is extremely low that there is anyone on the planet who has not faced Goliath at least once in their life.

Human Driven Goliaths

As a couple, joyfully together over 18 years, and business partners for nearly that long, we know that Goliaths happen. From our childhood through adulthood, Goliaths have shown up as personal betrayals, financial collapse, loss of family members, daunting legal issues, abuse, alcoholism, divorce, earthquakes, hurricanes, mental illness, and acts of terrorism. You get the picture. Each created indelible moments, emotional memories, dramas, and traumas. These Goliaths also came with the opportunity to stand up as David.

For us, the emotions felt during and after facing each tangle with Goliath, ranged from embarrassment and shame, to anger, sadness, and fear. When we chose to freeze, lay down and surrender in those times, our will and confidence went AWOL. When we did choose to call upon our beliefs and convictions that the sun will shine again, we ended up as victors, not as victims! These painful David and Goliath moments shaped the purpose-driven life we lead today. When embodying David, we get to choose to FACE the giant creatively, exploring solutions, seeking support, and taking empowered action. With this mindset, we can break through the obstacles that vigorously threaten to shut us down.

There were also times when the Goliath in our path gained temporary power over us due to past experiences that built a seemingly insurmountable wall of fear. We chose to freeze, lay down and surrender. In those times, our will and confidence to stand up went AWOL. What we tell ourselves can limit the possibility of progress or empower us to prevail. In some cases, we rationalize that the monster is not our responsibility, that we do not have what it takes, or that those who marched before us tried everything and failed. That avoidance, resistance, and self-sabotage can wreak havoc on our jobs and our relationships.

The big lesson, what we resist persists, and we are often our own Goliath battling ourselves! How we feel inside is how we show up in all areas of our lives. Having worked through our own limiting beliefs, now, instead of feeling regret and failure around those memories, we recognize them as transformational opportunities.

Choosing Life

Ken: I was driving through the Rocky Mountains at night, hugging the dark highway winding over an even darker abyss just beyond the guard rail. Loudly ringing in my head, my self-doubts were careening me toward giving up and heading my vehicle over the cliff. I was at a point in my life when I felt I had lost everything, "why not just end it now." I was drowning in the past, stories of worthlessness and self-beat-up. One thought seeped into my awareness. If I did take that drastic action, I could endanger other people in the oncoming traffic. Thankfully, that thought awakened something in me, and I decided to stop and turn into a pull-out. With the engine off, I closed my eyes. At that moment, sitting in a calm space, I pulled myself out of the old recurring stories echoing in my head and embraced the present. Thankfully, I listened to the divine voice within me, and I chose life. I instantly understood that my past was not my present and that this Goliath would not define defeat me.

Nature Driven Goliaths

Nature Driven Goliaths surface in the form of natural disasters such as earthquakes, volcanos, storms, landslides, and pandemics. These Goliaths can strike without warning. In these moments, we struggle to understand why? Why do these destructive forces, these Nature Driven Goliaths, happen to us? These Goliaths threaten to permanently destroy the lives and all that we hold dear.

Maris: At 4:30 AM, I awoke to a loud tearing jolt, gas lines hissing and gas spewing into the air; our bedroom had split from the rest of the building by about twenty feet as our apartment building sunk into the newly liquified earth. Piercing screams that I could not recognize rose from the depths of my being. I was living in Sherman Oaks, CA, married just eleven months, with a great job, and loving life when the Northridge earthquake ripped through our apartment and every area of our life. At that moment, my first husband and I felt like marbles being tossed around in a shoebox, the noise unbearable. We clung to each other as the roof split and the stars revealed themselves against the damp cold night sky. We said, "I love you," certain in that moment that it would be our last!

The building collapsed—the neighbor's apartment beneath us crushed by ours. After pulling our neighbor to safety, we made our way to the street where cars were flattened as if in a junkyard. Standing among hundreds of people, now-and-forever connected by the wrath of this Goliath, we were overwhelmed with gratitude that there would be more tomorrows. As we began to put our lives back together in the following days, more Goliaths presented themselves one after the other. For months I was not sleeping at all, fearing that darkness brought no safety. I buried myself in my work, functioned as I always had, responsibly leading my team and with great control keeping it all together, so I thought! Then, my body began to shut down, I was yelling at everyone, and I came dangerously close to a nervous breakdown.

At every Goliath moment, I had a choice to make! Before that harrowing Goliath opportunity, I was never one to seek support; I have always been the "go-to" person. It took my getting beyond the breaking point to realize that I could not face this Goliath alone. From a place of courage and vulnerability, I began to accept support, and I saw my strength in a new light. I had come to a clarity that I was not done on this earth, and that mine was a life meant for using my gifts to serve and impact others. Gratitude, breathwork, and meditation became my source of profound peace and still our daily practice as a couple. The greatest corner turner for me was my mom's voice in my head, "Breathe and believe that what you need is inside of you."

With Nature Driven Goliaths, we can also engage with compassion in support of others. Our only innate ability is how we choose to respond as individuals and as a connected community. Our empathic and compassionate response through the outpouring of support, caring, and empowered action is crucial to our recovery. A fitting example of "being David" is the work of our amazing first responders globally. Even though they may have their own personal Goliaths to face during these disasters, they choose courage and put others first.

The impact of a Goliath in our lives depends on what we believe to be true about ourselves. When we say, "I can't," we never will, when we say "I will," we open the door of empowered action. What is the source of the false commentary inside our heads that can, in an instant, make a molehill into a mountain? Wisdom teachers explain it as an untrue narrative created by something that, of all living creatures on the earth, only we humans possess: ego! Each of us also can be Goliath, becoming the cause of pain and the obstacle that others must overcome. Choosing to be Goliath comes straight from our ego, needing to assert power, needing to be right. The choice to show up as a Goliath seldom ends well for anyone.

We love this quote from Pema Chödrön; "The ego seeks to divide and separate. Spirit seeks to unify and heal."

Mindset and belief systems are our greatest assets when dancing with difficulties and can be the difference between our empowered authority over an obstacle or our being overpowered by it. When our mindset opens to living in possibilities, we can do better than just slaying Goliath; we can evaporate the monster before it consumes us. We can choose to be David listening to the healing-trusted voice inside us that leads to freedom or we can become slaves to our egoic voice that always holds us back. Armed with the slingshot of a positive empowering mindset, we have the power to choose how we FACE the Goliaths at home and at work and the opportunity to live a thriving 360-degree life.

Reflections:

Recall moments in your life when you were David facing Goliath. Were you being courageous? What empowered actions did you take? Did you ask for and receive support?

Can you recall a time when you were Goliath, causing the pain? What triggered you to be Goliath? What was that impact on yourself and others?

KEN ASHBY & MARIS SEGAL

About Ken Ashby & Maris Segal: From Mindset to Marketing, Ken Ashby & Maris Segal, husband and wife dynamic duo, have spent the last thirty-plus years bringing an innovative, collaborative voice to issues, causes, and brands. Working with the public & private sectors from boardrooms and classrooms to the world stage, as entrepreneurs, business strategists, executive producers, coaches, authors, speakers, and trainers, their work unites diverse populations across a wide spectrum of business, policy, and social issues in the US and abroad. Their leadership expertise in Business Relationship Marketing, Organizational Change & Cultural Inclusion, Personal Growth, Project Management, Public Affairs, and Philanthropy Strategies has been leveraged by consumer and financial brands, not for profits, Olympic organizers, Super Bowls, Harvard Kennedy School, Archdiocese of LA and NY Papal visits, the White House and celebrities across the arts, entertainment, sports and culinary genres.

With Ken's expertise as an award-winning singer-songwriter, they launched One Song, a songwriting workshop series for novices designed to unleash creativity in individuals and working teams.

Their DRIVE method: Desire, Relationships, Intention, Vision and Empowerment sits at the core of their companies Prosody Creative Services, One Song & Segal Leadership Global to set a path for every client to Build High Performing Businesses & Elevate Personal & Professional Leadership for Maximum Impact & a 360-degree Thriving Life!

Author's Website: *www.ProsodyCreativeServices.com*
www.ThePrinciplesofDavidandGoliath.com

Mary Beth Kellee

JUST A SMALL-TOWN GIRL

Change is inevitable; you can't outgrow the town, but the town can swallow you whole.

Judging a book by its cover—I've always been judged by how I dress and look. As a redhead, I stand out. However, I've always seen it as my personality and my attitude. I came out of the womb wearing lipstick and stilettos! That's just me.

I knew that my small town was fantastic to grow up in, but I had to leave to further myself. The day after I graduated from high school, my mom passed my bedroom door at 6:00 am, and I was dressed and packed; she asked me, "What are you doing?" I said, "I am moving to Buffalo!" I had no job and no path, but it was the best thing I ever did.

No College Education! Fund Raising! Event Planning! Real Estate! How do they co-mingle? Being a licensed realtor since 1998 in San Diego County has had its ups and downs. The real estate market is a fickle industry, and I wake up unemployed every day.

When I first started in real estate, I came from an excellent position as North American Training Director of Laura Ashley. When I was first cold-called by a recruiter while living in Boston, I thought the recruiter was 'KOO KOO Cray Cray Crazy.'

I said, "Laura Ashley, are you kidding me?" I make fun of people who wear Laura Ashley! Well, I went reluctantly to the interview. Unbeknownst to me, it was "casual Friday at Laura Ashley." I walked indirectly from my position as North East Training Director for the oldest cosmetic company globally, Shiseido. So, of course, I was not wearing Timberland boots, a flannel shirt, or, heaven forbid, Levi jeans. I stuck out like a sore thumb.

The head of HR at the time was a cool dude. He was so relaxed that he had his feet up on his desk. I had zero chance of getting this job from the get-go. I was NOT the LA type at all! However, I became the North American Training Director for Laura Ashley, based in Boston, despite the odds. It was one of the best and worst careers of my life. I put on crazy fun and interactive training conferences that included our teams in the USA, Canada, London, and Wales! I wrote the curriculum, created training programs, and had the fantastic opportunity to train from the CEO to our Shop Managers! This education and experience carried over when I moved into a U-Haul truck with a guy I met on another interesting cold-call interview.

Boston to San Diego

The phone rings one day. It is a head hunter who again cold-called me (he was referred to me by someone at Shiseido Cosmetics). I took the call very reluctantly. This position was for the North American Training Director for Jenny Craig in San Diego! Jenny Craig? I am not an overweight person. I wasn't sure it was for me. The head hunter was adamant that I interview for this position and fly out to the point where he booked me a flight. No one, including my own family, knew that I had flown to San Diego for one night.

There had been a substantial corporate takeover, and all of my peers and direct reports were fired on the same day and the first day of my five-day international training conference. I was an unhappy camper when the Jenny Craig call came to me but uprooting myself and moving all alone to San Diego (a city I had never been to). Hmmm, it just seemed way too far-reaching.

I arrived in San Diego, having never seen my recruiter before. I spy a guy who looks like Gordon Gekko of Wall Street. You can see him, french cuffs, striped suit, on his LARGE phone and a bit too cool for school. He spies on me and is relieved at my stature. Suddenly and from behind me, a second guy takes my suitcase. "Geez, am I now kidnapped by two lunatics, and no one in my world even knows I am 3,000 miles from home?" Well, that guy who took my suitcase took my heart. I ended up marrying the guy!

The Jenny Craig interview went so well that they quickly invited me back two weeks later. Still, they insisted I fly out on a Friday and experience San Diego before a lunch interview with the gang on the following Monday. I fell in love with the suitcase swiper, so I said yes to a free weekend in America's Finest City! Right?

That week that I flew out, Jenny Craig's stock plummeted on the NY Stock Exchange, making front-line news. That position and all hiring were frozen - but what about suitcase swiper? We went back to Beantown and quickly packed up a U-Haul. I hastily quit my career at Laura Ashley. After all, I was the company cheerleader, and it was getting pretty hard to cheer when most of my original team were all fired in one fell swoop.

Off we went, passing through my little hometown, affectionately known by some as the "mistake on the lake," Conneaut, Ohio. What would my elderly parents think? I quit my career, met a guy, packed up my home on a cul-de-sac with a beautiful yard and pool, threw a for-sale sign up in the yard, and shuffled off to San Diego. Wait, not yet!

We answered an ad in the Vail newspaper for a couple to host a European 5 STAR Ski Chalet! I don't even know how to ski, but suitcase swiper was a ski bum! I genuinely mean that he lived in a Kibbutz on the Golan Heights and taught snow skiing. Yes, snow in Israel. I was so enthralled with him, and my sole desire was to make him happy. So we stopped en route to San Diego with our U-Haul and met a guy who owned nine ski chalets in Europe. The Vail Chalet was the only one in America. We were interviewing as a CHEF and Ski Host/Accountant. We had zero experience, and we landed the gig.

We were flown to London and then to France to experience what a guest would experience from staying at the 5-star chalet. We were picked up by the ski chalet host and taken back to their romantic ski chalet in Morzine, France. We dined on Foie Gras and Raclette and drank the best wines. We even had a cheese tasting class. We landed a fantastic gig, right? Two days later, the tables turn, and we, the newly hired chalet couple, have to entertain the seasoned and highly regarded staff and friends of the chalet owner.

David, the owner, sought humor in giving suitcase swiper and me the largest multi-level chalet. The kitchen was on the bottom floor, and there was a DUMB waiter on the 3rd floor. The menu was duck three ways, Goat cheese mousseline, Tarte au citron, and one item we could make up. I chose to make celeriac puree. So my partner was not allowed to assist with any food shopping or prep. He was to serve the food. I had to shop in FRANCE! They sell ducks whole. How the heck do you debone a duck? Thank GOD, a drunken and seasoned, oh and real chef, swung by my kitchen late the night before and deboned my ducks in minutes! Another pastry chef stopped by and helped me make the dessert. On the evening of the dinner, I had every item sorted out and done. All the last-minute helpers saved me! Who had the last laugh that night? I would say David, the owner, was smitten by us.

This chalet gig lasted a season. We learned more than ever about how to serve and go above & beyond. This will help as we move into marketing and real estate, trust me!

Alas, we return to our original destination of San Diego only to live with my partner's elderly father. The story, drama, and crazy turn of events didn't stop there. My purpose in sharing this life story is that not once did I ever give up. I followed my heart and beliefs, which led me to today's rewarding and remarkable life. Sometimes, you've got to take what's in front of you, put your stiletto heels in front of the other, and take leaps of faith. That will win you a lifetime of experiences, stories, and unique adventures.

MARY BETH KELLEE

About Mary Beth Kellee: Mary Beth helps clients buy/sell and invest in real estate globally and in San Diego County. There is no too small or too big property for her to tackle, and she gives 110% to her clients! She is uniquely known to the market property by stepping outside the box.

Many refer to Mary Beth as a Master Connector. She has a unique ability to network and introduce like-minded entities to join in a joint mission. Connecting people is a gift that has been the cornerstone of her career both as a fundraiser and in the private sector. Through her connections and coveted Rolodex, Mary Beth's ability to raise awareness and promotion from small start-ups to large foundations has proven fantastic success.

Despite the unchanging judgment of appearance, people refer to MaryBeth as a Master Connector. They say she has a unique ability to network and introduce like-minded entities to join in a common mission. Connecting people is a gift that has been the cornerstone of her life as a fundraiser and in the private sector.

Author's Website: *www.TheKnowInSanDiego.com*
www.ThePrinciplesofDavidandGoliath.com

Maureen Vincenty

DREAM AND BE OBSESSED

My story is different, yet it is the same in many ways as yours. It is, after all, the human experience. My life is a uniquely crafted series of events over the past 38 years leading me exactly here, today. Every single moment played its role regardless of how I interpreted that experience. Good or bad? Exciting or painful? Perpetrator or victim.

When you reflect on your life through a lens of positivity, what do you see? Here is what I see.

I see a woman who has been incredibly blessed, traveling to over 40 countries and counting, living abroad in Rome and Costa Rica. The world was and still is my playground. There wasn't a sport, extracurricular activity, or instrument I didn't know in my youth. As a part of the middle class in the USA, I always was provided with basic needs and then some. I had people around me who loved me, believed in greatness, and supported me.

My educational experience was top-notch (college-prep boarding school, valedictorian, Dean's Honor List at UCLA). After jumping around seven different science majors, I ultimately settled on astrophysics and geology, which landed me a research job for NASA working with moon rocks from Apollo 14, 15, and 17 samples and then as a corporate Geologist for nearly a decade.

In my late 20s, I healed my body from various autoimmune diagnoses after hitting dead ends with western medicine. Thank God for my obsessive passion for research and my relentless thirst for knowledge. This phase of my life sparked my desire to flee the constraints of corporatelaunching my own business helping others on their healing journey while gaining total financial and time freedom. My growing passion for entrepreneurship and service has resulted in additional entrepreneurial endeavors increasing my income, impact, and network of incredible humans around the world.

Wow! What a great life for 38, right? AND it's only just beginning!

Now let me share with you what I've too easily seen when my mindset and belief systems are working against me.

I see a little girl who grew up starving to "get it right" as she learned at an early age that "one can never be too rich or too thin" and that accomplishments, grades, etc. were the most important thing. In fact, I was punished for not being "the best" vs. rewarded for doing well. It started a never- ending need to produce or be better or be the best to be loved.

I see a girl who was independent, strong-willed, stubborn, yet starving for safety and love. I see a girl whose mom was always gone (she was a flight attendant), whose parents divorced at a young age due to her father's severe alcoholism (and probably more things). At fourteen, her mother remarried someone who clearly did not want to be bothered by her young children and came up with the brilliant idea to ship me off to boarding school. That is when a piece of my soul died, and I felt abandoned, rejected, and not a part of one at a core level. I see a young woman in college whose mother was diagnosed with Stage IV Ovarian cancer and watched her struggle for four years before passing. She hated being angry with her mother for abandoning her because she was dying, but the pain of feeling like she missed out on the last eight years of her mother's life was palpable. They "reconnected" emotionally a week before she passed, but it wasn't enough. She still felt like an orphan.

I see a young woman who so desperately wanted to do things "right" and get the best job, best salary, the best husband to "be happy" and make her family proud. Yet, she looked for love in all the wrong places choosing toxic relationship after toxic relationship and unintentionally reliving people-pleasing patterns, trying to fix addict behavior in men, lies, secrecy, infidelity, and more.

The most heartbreaking part of it all: I see a young girl who fought the biggest battle of her life over the next couple of decades. Her biggest GOLIATH was actually herself. Every day was an internal battle of self-beat up, judgment, mentally spinning, and obsessing over everything she perceived she ever did wrong. It manifested into various forms of disordered eating. What started with anorexia turned into the bondage of bulimia which came and went over the years.

How could someone so smart, so driven, so hard-working (who looked like she had it all together on paper) be so messed up behind the scenes? Of course, this led to further guilt, shame, embarrassment, self-beat-up, imposter syndrome, and more. The more she tried to "fix" herself, the more she believed she was broken, and the worse and worse it got.

I am grateful I never gave up on myself. I KNEW deep down there was a life of freedom waiting for me. I just had to figure out the formula.

And then, over time, I realized the secret weapon to winning the war against myself was VISION. So I allowed myself to dream big. I could see the life I always wanted waiting for me, and all I had to do was figure out how to align myself with that vision to get there.

If I could be OBSESSED with binging and purging or focusing on what didn't work in my life, I could be equally OBSESSED with creating a life beyond my wildest dreams of abundance, joy, health, love, connection, and massive impact. My addictive tendencies can be my greatest traits when applied to my faith and vision! Grant Cardone wrote a great book, *Be Obsessed or Be Average,* which I related to.

And yes, it can be scary; facing any Goliath in our life always generates fear. How could it not? But when you get to the point where the fear or discomfort of NOT going after your bigger goal or vision exceeds the discomfort of feeling the unknown, you'll stay stuck.

"Change happens when the pain of staying the same becomes greater than the pain of change." – Tony Robbins

The solution was NOT more therapy and talking about all the things in my life that I perceived to be awful or how much I hated myself. Instead, the solution was to become OBSESSED with all the incredible things that I have already accomplished and be excited beyond belief about everything I get to do.

I now know that 100% is possible 100% of the time. Shifting my perspective to realizing that there are blessings is being an "addict." If I was addicted to self-hate or food, then I could be addicted to my passion and purpose! YES! I can be addicted to healthy habits, building my businesses, generating money to give away to philanthropies, and making a massive impact in this world.

Bad habits can create good habits if you allow them to be a blessing.

EVERYTHING CHANGED when I finally gave myself permission to dream and started going after my vision. NOTHING CAN GET IN MY WAY NOW. It isn't just about stopping a behavior. You must dig into the WHY. It's always the WHY beneath the WHY.

You'll never conquer your Goliath or any huge goals or vision you have for your life unless you're willing to take yourself on in a deeper way than ever before. Give yourself permission to be OBSESSED with your vision and figure out the WHY beneath the WHY. Once you do that, I promise you nothing will get in your way ever again. That brick wall you think you're running towards is, in fact, as thin as a piece of paper that you can rip right through.

After you've given yourself permission, and you've done everything you humanly can remember your ultimate source of power, which can fuel through you to overcome all things. Mine is Jesus Christ who became my personal savior in 2018. It is through His grace and mercy and unconditional love and acceptance that has taught me to unconditionally love and accept myself. I realize that through Him all things are possible. I no longer must be perfect to love myself because He loves me just the way I am. His spirit is with me all the time to remind me of this truth and to encourage me and provide me hope. He is strong when I am weak. He provides me with a peace that surpasses all understanding. He places the massive visions on my heart and promises a life of joy, abundance, and love. After all, He is the one who gave David the ability to defeat Goliath when no one else thought it was possible.

So, in closing, take the next 20 minutes and a blank sheet of paper and write down the following:

- Where in your life have you been your own Goliath?
- If you could conquer that piece of you and no longer had any self-imposed limiting beliefs or destructive habits, what would you really want to go after?
- List five reasons WHY you want to go after this vision/goal.
- Write down how you would feel when you accomplish that.
- Visualize it as if it's already happened.

Now give yourself permission to dream and be OBSESSED with your own greatness. You are magnificent! You are powerful! You are worthy!

MAUREEN VINCENTY

About Maureen Vincenty: Maureen is an experienced coach, entrepreneur, and business owner who guides coaches and entrepreneurs into a greater possibility for their lives and businesses. Incorporating her people skills and love for teaching and empowering has led to her current role as founder of Get Legally Smart. Maureen is an experienced coach, entrepreneur, and business owner who guides coaches and entrepreneurs into a greater possibility for their lives and businesses. Incorporating her people skills and love for teaching and empowering has led to her current role as founder of Get Legally Smart. Maureen has been recognized for her contributions to transformational leadership as student, coach, and her support for various emotional intelligence leadership centers.

Maureen empowers with the education, tools, and community to Protect Their Empire so they can increase their income and impact. From moon dust to legal", Maureen's background may seem all over the place, but she's always been obsessed with chasing everything down the research rabbit hole, and LOVEs helping others. With a science degree from UCLA, she worked in corporate for a decade from NASA to EPA and then left to become an entrepreneur as a peak performance health consultant. Most recently, she founded Legally Smart supporting fellow entrepreneurs with protecting their brands and empires through education, tools, and affordable attorney access, so they can legally scale their businesses to the next level saving lots of time and money in the process.

Maureen is the host of "Health Reboot Series" Summit, and has made media appearances as a featured speaker on Live At The Clubhouse, and an expert in health on the Primal Blueprint Podcast , Female Health: UNLOCKED, Shine Your Awesome Series, and Health Junkie Masterclass.

Author's Website: *www.GetLegallySmart.com*
www.ThePrinciplesofDavidandGoliath.com

Michelle Crites

THE GIFT OF TRUST

Many of us have heard the quote, "Luck is what happens when preparation meets opportunity," attributed to the Roman philosopher Seneca. There is much debate about this statement. Some argue that there is no such thing as luck. Others say we create our own luck. Zig Ziglar made his own quote out of that and said, "Success occurs when preparation meets opportunity." Having spent the last one-and-a-half years focusing on leadership skills, I agree with Ziglar, and I can see how it plays out in the classic story of David and Goliath.

David was the youngest male in his family; he was also the smallest. He was given the job of a shepherd, which wasn't glamorous. Shepherds would spend countless hours out in the fields with the sheep. Their job was to ensure the sheep had fresh food sources, plenty of water, and, because sheep like to wander, find the lost sheep, and bring it back to the group. A large part of the job was to protect the flock from predators. To do this, David's weapon of choice was a slingshot. He had many hours a day to fill as the sheep grazed. David could have sat under a shade tree all day, dozing, and dreaming, but there is a reason God highly favored him. He chose to work at the skills he needed to be the best shepherd possible. David took down bears and lions as they attacked the sheep under his protection; this took practice and confidence. I can imagine him spending many hours practicing his shot on a multitude of possible targets: near, far, stationary, and moving. Over the years, he became incredibly skilled. That was the preparation that met opportunity.

When no one else from King Saul's Army would step up to defeat the giant, David announced that he would. When King Saul had tried to arm David with heavy gear and a sword, David refused it and chose his own weapon of a sling and five stones. Most would have thought him to be nuts, but the "luck" that David had was his trust in his skills, his powerful mindset, and a determination to honor God, whom he loved deeply. I have always loved how this story speaks of perfecting our skills and trusting that inner voice that tells us we are ready. Even when the world around us can't see how this could possibly work, keeping our mind focused on the desired outcome and continuing to move forward will take us to some amazing results.

All my life, even when I was quite young, I remember people really opening up to me, sharing a lot of what was on their minds. I could not begin to say how many times people would say to me, "I really don't know why I'm telling you all this; I've never shared this with anyone before." I have always loved talking with people, really getting to know them. But when I got to my teen years, I remember feeling stressed out when people started sharing their deepest thoughts, especially when it came down to making a decision or coming to some sort of conclusion. I found myself resenting people sharing with me, and I would try to shut down these conversations before they even started.

Then one day, as I was trying to outrun the stress of something a friend had shared with me in confidence, this overwhelming sense of peace suddenly came over me. I stopped in my tracks and got very still. I heard God speaking to my heart. It wasn't an audible sound, but I felt it pressed into my heart. "My child, why do you feel angst and try to outrun my gift?" Gift? I thought. This isn't a gift; it's a curse!

I very clearly heard the question, "Why do you consider this a curse?" "I'm only a teenager," I thought to myself. How can I be responsible for solving their problems? It's too much! How could I possibly resolve their issues? I'm still trying to figure out my own life! I don't have answers for all these people!"

I remember what almost felt like a laugh, and then the response, "I don't expect you to solve their problems. I never asked you to do that. The gift is letting them talk because they trust you. They get to work through their thoughts as they talk to you. You make them feel safe."

The pressure had finally been released! Finally, I could listen; in fact, I was happy to listen to people after eliminating the pressure of resolving their issues. I felt comfortable asking questions or simply saying, "I'm so sorry," and giving them a hug or simply sitting in silence while they talked. My entire mindset shifted, and I was no longer stressed about it.

Fast forward to my adult life: All those years of listening, asking questions, loving on people right where they had led me to a ministry that I am so passionate about today. I had no way of knowing back then that God would take that young girl on such an incredible journey.

I haven't lived the perfect Christian life. I've had my moments in sin, making choices that make me cringe now. I grew up in a wonderful Christian home. I have always been a believer. But I haven't always walked the walk perfectly. At one point, I had someone I loved deeply taken from my life much too early. It broke me, and I let it break my relationship with God. I carried a lot of anger for a very long time. I allowed it to break my relationship with God. But, looking back, He always kept His relationship with me.

Two years later, I moved back to my childhood town. I felt the wall that I had built around myself and knew that my life wasn't working for me. There was a void, and I knew I had to find my way. There was this wonderful ministry that opened its doors once a week, where you could get a prophetic word or word of encouragement. There I met a husband-and-wife team that would start speaking life back into me. They saw gifts in me that I had long since buried and began the journey of bringing them back to the surface. It was a two-and-a-half-year journey because I had come to believe the lies of the enemy that God didn't want to have anything to do with me anymore. Now, I can laugh and admit it was me that turned away; God was always there.

These two people helped me see who I really am and Whose I am. They trained me to use the gifts that I had developed through my life of listening as people opened up and shared their stories with me so freely. Had I not had that internal conversation with God all those years ago, I believe I would not be doing what I do now. Today I'm blessed to be a Pastor, serving in the field of Spiritual Warfare or Deliverance Ministry. All those years of listening helped me hear not only what someone is telling me through their words, but behind their words--what they are not saying that tells so much of the story. Now I support people in getting free from those old childhood wounds that have kept them being whom they were created to be on this earth. Together with the Holy Spirit, we free people from the limiting beliefs, fear, self-doubt, unforgiveness, and more that have taken someone off the path they were meant to walk and free them up to become all that they were created to be!

It's amusing as I look back at that time in my teenage life. Serving in this ministry has shown me how the enemy created resentment that I came into agreement with as He tried to keep me from stepping into my destiny. Thankfully, God stepped in, and I'm so grateful that I listened.

What about David? What if he became resentful when he was made a shepherd? What if, instead of honing his craft with his slingshot, he just sat around in anger? Would he have been able to fight off the predators that came to attack the sheep? Would he have been able to take on Goliath? We'll never really know because that isn't the road David chose, but I would have to guess that the answer to both is no. David's powerful mindset kept him on his God-given path.

How about you? Are you continuing to develop your skills? Are you fully committed to being the absolute best version of yourself? If you aren't, consider taking the time to ask yourself, "What's underneath that? Why am I not committing fully to myself?" The answers will come if you really want to find them. You are worth the effort, and I believe God has a wonderful future planned for you!

MICHELLE CRITES

About Michelle Crites: The founder of Live Your True Calling, Michelle's desire is that every person realize the full potential of their God given destiny. She is an Author, Speaker, Empowerment Coach, founder of several summits, award-winning actress, and her greatest role to date is being a mom!

Michelle has spent the past 12 years serving in Deliverance Ministry, breaking down strongholds and helping people heal and get free from the pain of the past that has kept them from being all that they were intended to be. She is an advocate for health and wellness and teaches classes on natural ways to supplement a healthy lifestyle.

She is currently working on her next book and creating a podcast to inspire everyone to live their best life. To see more from Michelle please find her on Facebook at Live Your True Calling.

Author's Website: *www.linkedin.com/in/michelle-crites-86389563*
www.ThePrinciplesofDavidandGoliath.com

Michael Wolf

4 MINUTES EACH DAY
CAN CHANGE YOUR LIFE

The world we live in today takes demands a lot out of us every single day. First, you do your best to attend to daily responsibilities, your family, your work, and those most important around you. Then, add the mundane tasks of bills and obligations, cleaning, and maintenance. Then add the things you should do, like working out and such. All of this can be overwhelming! Life will ask for more and more of you, and if you don't take time for yourself, each day can lead you depleted, deflated, and in some cases depressed, waking up to another day of the same exact stuff.

That's why 4 minutes a day changed my life completely.

Borrowed from Napoleon Hill's *Think and Grow Rich*, I've created the habit of morning affirmation with the "self-confidence formula."

Each morning, for about 4 minutes, I've been talking to myself for over 15 years now. This simple yet profound habit has provided me with a framework of confidence to create the person I am today (and still becoming).

The process of affirmation at a base level trains your mind to think differently, to think inward. It's a process that grows from you. It's about starting your day as an active participant in your life instead of being on autopilot and reactive to what your daily grind gives you.

Everyone has fears and insecurities, and we deal with them every day. The dominant thoughts and emotions that we have racing through our brains can be the difference between a good day and a bad one. On a long enough timeframe, it's the difference maker between simply existing on this earth and truly living. My 4-minute morning affirmation is a stake that I drive into the heart of doubt and distraction. It's a guardrail against fear and the unknown. It sets the tone for the day. It's intentionally bringing positive, exciting, and motivational emotion into my psyche; it's training my mindset on my terms, and it's being done every morning, every single day.

These 4 minutes are an easy yet powerful exercise of my mind for my benefit, and I am charged with the belief that I can approach the tasks at hand today and experience overall success. By doing so, my day is going to be a great day.

Yes, there will be challenges. Yes, there will be setbacks. Things don't always go as planned in life. But the proper mindset and belief systems that are seasoned and developed each morning through an easy daily routine allow for an intensively positive baseline from which to launch. No matter the challenge that comes, we will take that challenge and turn it into an opportunity. 4 minutes CAN truly change your life.

Why does this method work? Well, you are training your brain to think differently, focusing on the positive and the good that will come rather than worrying about what may go wrong. In doing so, we exercise our brain muscle to function in an alternative way, an INTENTIONAL way, to believe and achieve the primary task(s) or goal(s) at hand.

For me personally, I started a career in real estate, which is a simple business, but easy? It is not. Many people who try this business soon fail within the first couple of years, chalking their failure to a conclusion that "maybe this business just isn't for me." I was determined early in my career not to be one of the many casualties that the real estate industry chews and spits out.

With that being said, I had personal doubts and fears about what I could achieve. I questioned whether I was good enough. I had a fear of sorts for success. Did I deserve it? The unknown pathway to get to a promised land of the goals and dreams that I desired was a personal Goliath that I needed to conquer.

Affirmation is not an overnight cure-all. It requires a consistent and dedicated approach. In the same way that you cannot expect to see significant results by going to the gym for just a week, if you remain committed and dedicated to the goals that stoke a burning desire for success in yourself, the results will come. THE RESULTS WILL COME! You are training your mindset appropriately, and in doing so, you can fend off the worst emotions of fear and doubt and worry – all the nasty tricks that your mind consciously and subconsciously plays on you.

I converted my fear of success. Rather than thinking, "why me?" I turned it into "why not me?" I demanded of myself and my mindset to set the intention to believe I am worthy, that I am good enough, that I deserve success IF I was willing to put in the effort to get to where I wanted to be.

My 4-minute affirmation was like a refinery of thoughts for my mind, by putting my self-talk in the blast furnace and burning off the negative emotions and doubts; by focusing on the positive and setting an intentional personal statement of belief that I CAN, and I WILL be successful in my endeavors.

Call it the secret. Call it the universe acting on your intentions. Call it GOD. Call it what you will, but there is something to this. Successful people worldwide give a ton of credit to *Think and Grow Rich*, and rightfully so. It's one of the most profound books that I've ever read because it's changed my life to a reality that I only dreamed about when I first started my career.

Now 15+ years in, If I could go back in time and tell my former youthful and naïve (yet motivated!) self what the future held, a part of me would not believe it. I am grateful to have been able to train myself and learn by standing on the shoulders of the giants that came before me. It's truly through this meaningful 4-minute exercise in personal growth that I am here today as a manifestation of what I could only dream about from my early years in my business.

Having done this for years, the actual process is like brushing your teeth. If by chance, you forget to brush your teeth, you know that something is just not right. The same applies to habits forged into your personal growth rituals; it will keep you focused and fresh if done consistently.

Suppose I didn't have this 4-minute affirmation habit. In that case, I imagine the first thing I would do each day, rather than focus on positive thoughts and beliefs; I would attend to the tasks and problems that need solving in my business, jump on the phone and start scrolling away, or let the family morning routine distract me and get my mind focusing all the things that take a toll and chip away at my finite level of energy that I have to give to each and every day.

Rather than depleting the tank at the first waking hour of each day, I start on a positive; I pump up my positivity, I give myself a "BOOYAH" to jump out of the shower with the expectation that no matter what happens today, it's going to be great. I'll turn challenges into opportunities and capitalize on what the day brings. How can you deny this level of motivation, concentration, and expectation? What would happen if you did the same thing? It has worked for so many, so why not you, too? The natural destination of this mindset and belief system is the physical realization of goals that you have a burning desire in which to see their fruition.

To do this in the best way possible, allocate proper time and a location where you can be undistracted. Be it during a morning walk, in the shower, or in a quiet space where you can focus. You should be nowhere near your phone during this vital part of a daily routine.

It needs to serve as a conscious and present baseline for your emotional state. You are training your mind to sideline the doubts and fears. You will gain the confidence to get to more "yes" on a given day instead of rejection. You will emerge from this exercise as if taking a gasp of fresh air after holding your breath underwater for as long as possible. You will emerge energized and motivated. Confident and optimistic. This is the energy that gets things done. This is the mindset that is the catalyst of progress. This is the process that forges your mindset to truly see results.

If you have been in a rut. If you are living each day in monotony. If you are not yet realizing the results in your life that you feel you deserve, then what's to lose by taking 4 minutes to yourself to change your life.

I challenge you to be the captain of your life as opposed to merely a passenger along for the ride. This amazing experience of living is so precious that we cannot afford another day wasting away or misallocating our talents, love, and goals.

4 minutes of self-affirmation has made an incredible difference in my life in all circles. This is a whole-systems approach to success in life, and it starts with getting your mind right to believe in yourself and know that success is in the cards. You deserve it. Why NOT you?

Every day represents a new opportunity for growth and change. So, tomorrow morning when you get out of bed, will you dread the day ahead? Or will you make the investment of 4 minutes for yourself that can change the rest of your life?

Want to know more about the self-confidence affirmation? This is borrowed from Napoleon Hill's *Think and Grow Rich:*

I know that I have the ability to achieve the object of my definite purpose in life; therefore, I demand of myself persistent, continuous action toward its attainment, and I here and now promise to render such action.

The dominating thoughts of my mind will eventually reproduce themselves in outward physical action and gradually transform themselves into physical reality. Therefore, I will concentrate my thoughts for 30 minutes daily upon the task of thinking of the person that I intend to become. Thereby creating in my mind a clear mental picture...

I know through the theory of autosuggestion, any desire that I persistently hold in my mind will eventually seek some expression through some practical means of obtaining the object or position I desire.

I have clearly written down a description of my definite chief aim, and I will never stop trying until I develop sufficient self-confidence for its attainment. I realize that no wealth or position can long endure unless built upon truth and justice.

I will engage in no transaction that will not benefit all whom it affects. I will succeed by attracting to myself the forces that I wish to use and the cooperation of other people. I will induce others to serve me because of my willingness to serve them. I will eliminate hatred, envy, jealousy, selfishness, and cynicism by developing love for all humanity, for I know that a negative attitude toward others will never bring me success. I will cause others to believe in me because I will believe in them and in myself.

I will sign my name to this formula, commit to memory and repeat it aloud once a day in full faith that it will gradually influence my thoughts and actions so I will become a self- reliant and successful person.

I profoundly hope you make the choice that puts you in the captain's chair of your life by taking 4 minutes each morning for yourself and your future.

MICHAEL WOLF

About Michael Wolf: Michael Wolf is a professional Realtor, author, entrepreneur, and devoted father of two wonderful kids. He and his wife Jessica founded the Wolf Real Estate Team in 2006 and have served nearly 1000 clients and over a ½ of a billion dollars of real estate sold in the San Diego County area. He's also the Author of "*The First Time Homebuyer Book*" and "*The First Time Investor Book*." Together with his wife and team, they are committed to making a difference in client's lives and helping them make the best decisions as the premier San Diego real estate market experts. In his free time, Michael is an avid traveler, chef & bread maker and sport enthusiast as well as a real estate investor. He's the recipient of the prestigious 30-Under-30 Award by the National Association of Realtors, 40-Under-40 Award by the San Diego Association of Realtors, and Voted as San Diego's BEST Real Estate Agent by the San Diego Union Tribune, among other notable industry accolades. He lives just outside of downtown San Diego with his family of four, and grateful for the opportunity that real estate has brought him and his family. His passion is to share the benefit of real estate to everyone that has a goal of real estate ownership, both locally and nationally.

Author's Website: *www.MikeAndJessica.net*
www.ThePrinciplesofDavidandGoliath.com

Monica Pandele

DOES NATURE LOVE YOU?

When was the first time you recall being in nature and feeling a deep connection?

I was about six, in the deeply forested mountains of Transylvania - the Carpathians. And no, Dracula was not part of this scenario; he was probably busy entertaining foreign tourists searching for extraordinary stories. It was a summer school holiday morning. We were once again, like every summer, at a forester cabin, placed far into the forest, some 15 miles away from the closest human settlement. It was a simple building without electricity, without running water, surrounded by pristine nature. Brown bears visited us every night in search of an easy meal, and hedgehogs the size of my father's hand made a regular appearance in the grass surrounding the cabin. That morning, my father and I searched for spicy white mushrooms called 'iutari,' the main ingredient for an earthy breakfast with sheep cheese and smoked wild pig bacon. My father was highly skilled at spotting the mushroom's whiteheads hiding in the forest debris, and I wanted to impress him. So I turned on my hidden antennas and navigated through the beautifully lit beech trees, jumping across a rapidly flowing stream that filled the entire forest with its loud sound.

Suddenly all turned quiet, and my dad was nowhere, no response to my calling, only the echo of my voice. There were no trails, no signs, only forest. My heart beat faster, and I realized I had to find my way back to the cabin on my own. I had no idea which way to go, no memory of the way we came. I dropped my basket with the few mushrooms I worked so hard to find. As I kept anxiously asking myself which way to go, a sudden calm washed over me as I felt called to follow a voice that I could hear not through my ears but through other parts of my body. It felt like a path opened up between the beech trees. I followed, trusting blindly. After a while, I'm not sure how long, I could see familiar clues, and the cabin's roof became visible between the trees. My mom welcomed me with a heavy spank. It was her way to release the fear I was lost. My dad gave me a sharp look followed by a big hug asking me how I made it back. I didn't know how to explain; it was an inner knowing. We went on and cooked the delicious earthy breakfast. Life never felt the same after that moment. I knew nature loved me.

The forest became my best friend; it still is the place where I feel the safest. My orientation skills never fail; I have my inner GPS tuned-in, a unique navigation system created by my special connection with nature. Seeking my way through wilderness became a way of life. Protecting my best friend became my professional calling. Some 15 years later, I earned my badge as an ecologist, a profession rooted in a deep understanding of biodiversity assessment and conservation, leveraging the magic connection of all living systems.

I spent almost 20 years defending nature from humans I considered careless or spent time cleaning up the mess they caused. I loved what I did, yet I never felt I was doing enough. I was adamant at my job, and I advanced my career rapidly, getting recognized and promoted for my achievements. Yet, I judged myself for not doing enough, given the level and speed of destruction nature suffered around me.

One theme became apparent. No matter how much passion I put into my roles as consultant, activist, teacher, researcher, or civic leader, I kept feeling a lack of joy and lack of fulfillment, despite becoming skilled at protecting nature. Hidden anger, judgment, and resentment built inside me toward those not appreciating mother earth as highly as I did. Interestingly, my confidence in my ability to make a difference also dimmed. Anxiety and frustration became the norm, and all those who disagreed with me, with my views, became my enemies. The more I knew about nature, the less understood I felt by the communities where I worked and lived. I rarely felt I belonged. Looking back, I now see the invisible emotional thrust that lured me to move across four continents, looking for my tribe, for those who would get me, exhausted from trying so hard to fit in, desperately wanting to belong, to contribute to my fullest potential.

Fast forward, two years ago, it was again a summer morning. This time, I was going to Yosemite National Park, my sacred place since I moved to California. I was listening to an audiobook recommended by a friend to boost my creativity. Two questions asked by the narrator intrigued me. First, "Do you love nature?" Daaah! Of course, I replied eagerly, looking at my professional career choices, values, and stand in the world. The second question: "Does nature love you?" made me pause. My instinct replied, "No, nature doesn't care about me specifically; why would it?" I felt a heaviness in my chest, and tears started dropping out of nowhere. It took several deep breaths to reconcile with the emotions passing through. I realized that I lost that enchanted childhood connection I had with nature somewhere along the journey. I separated myself. I denied the unique gifts nature lovingly gave me. I disconnected from myself, from the spirit (and nature) in me, from the nature and people around me.

Who did I become? I am a people pleaser, masterful at assessing a situation and turning into whoever needed me to accept me. I gave up trusting myself, feeling I never know enough to be valuable or competent at my purpose, exhausting myself from making up scenarios that led nowhere. At that moment, it became clear that the price I paid for this choice was no longer bearable. A gate from a different dimension cracked open as I arrived in the magical Yosemite Valley, where I paid reverence to EL Capitan, feeling the sacredness of the moment. Was I brave enough to step through this gate without knowing what was on the other side, willing to deal with the fears I avoided for decades?

"The longest journey you will ever take is the 18 inches from your head to your heart." - Andrew Bennett

The disconnect from my own heart was not an opinion anymore. Some 30 miles of wandering in the majestic beauty of the sacred mountain helped me find the way to my heart. I purged the glut of doubt and anger, finally releasing the ongoing need to know it all. I felt nature's love once again.

To own the gifts nature gave me and to truly live my purpose, I got to drop into my heart, accept who I was, and belong to something bigger than me, the nature that guided me through the adversities of life. Dropping into my heart allowed me to be vulnerable and compassionate. It opened up a window where I could see the people around me with all their gifts, finding common ground in polarizing situations, and being able to build a space beyond the disagreements that otherwise would have put us in opposite teams.

On the way from my head to my heart, I reconnected with self-compassion. In the past, whenever I wouldn't create the results I hoped for, I would judge myself and others, questioning value as if it was a direct reflection of those results. Labeling situations as right/wrong or winning/losing prevented me from being open. I realized that self-compassion was about giving the inner critic a break, seeing the goodness in every situation, thus learning how to serve best those around me and nature.

Leading from my heart and listening to my unique GPS propelled me to contribute to protecting nature in ways I never imagined. I gained access to an inner-knowing that became available only when I deliberately chose to get out of my head. Yes, the head was no longer the only place of my body designed with intelligence. The intelligence of my heart - proven by scientific studies in the last decades, including the Heartmath Institute - became the most valuable gift. It supports me in my pursuit of healing nature, not by doing more but by being more, being in relationship with people and nature, cherishing and leveraging our interconnectedness.

Now I know that when I drop into my heart and accept who I am, I'm in a relationship with myself, nature, and its people. Without questioning if I know enough, I instantly feel I belong because I know I do. Do you want to know how? But that is another juicy story for another time.

I'm a heart-centered warrior fulfilling my life purpose by being in a relationship with nature and its people, accepting instead of denying our common humanity as fuel for my purpose.

MONICA PANDELE

About Monica Pandele: Monica Pandele is a heart-centered leader, global citizen, life-long learner and community builder, a scientist by trade, and a spiritual leader by choice.

Monica is on a mission to scale global awareness of our interdependence with nature so that all human beings create the sustainable and flourishing future they desire from the place of 'being in relationship' with their environment.

In her roles as sustainability expert, leadership coach, motivational speaker, community facilitator, mentor, and guide for transformative experiences, Monica helps unlock the collective wisdom to generate new climate justice possibilities, building unity, dignity, abundance, using diversity and polarity as catalyzers for synergy.

Monica is the founder and CEO of Gefyra Inc, a social enterprise that is literally 'the bridge', partnering with corporate, government, and nonprofits, to create a sense of belonging and wholeness allowing every human-system to operate at its best, creating from its full potential.

Author's website: *www.Gefyra.life*
www.ThePrinciplesofDavidandGoliath.com

Neetu Sing

FROM FROZEN IN FEAR
TO FINALLY FLYING FREE

You may write me down in history With your bitter, twisted lies,
You may trod me in the very dirt But still, like dust, I'll rise.
~Maya Angelou

Have you ever had the thought that you just want to escape it all? Run far away and pretend all the turmoil never existed? Only to find yourself going from the frying pan into the fire? And it seems like there is no way out?

I am a Survivor—a Thriver. I have lived through the horrors of domestic abuse and violence. I share this story with those who need to see the light and feel love and blazing courage. I transformed my beliefs and mindset and created a whole new paradigm and fierce action that finally set me free. I escaped from drama, trauma, and chaos and went from a toxic, violent, and abusive marriage of almost 18 years to living a life of freedom, love, peace, joy, and gratitude.

And you can too!

I still remember his cold bare hands squeezing my neck as he pushed my body against the bedroom door. His choking tightened with an enormous force, the door thrust a hole in the wall, and I felt my breath leaving me. Today, it did not stop after throwing things at me and hitting me. It didn't stop even after dragging me by my hair against the carpet. His rage knew no bounds! His voice shook me as he said, "I'm going to kill you" It got dark, and my future flashed in front of me.

I'm dead. He is in prison. My babies are in foster care. NO. NO. NO! Never!

Then, I saw a dim light and from within me surged this fierce courage I didn't even know I had, and I pushed him away and freed myself from his clutches. Then, still gagging and gasping for breath, my body still trembling, my blue bruised lips still quivering, I picked my two-month-old baby from the bed, ran like the wind, and locked myself with my six year old. For the first time, I did not cry.

My heart burned. My soul churned, and my breath was on fire. My nostrils were flaring, and I was breathing hot and heavy; I could feel every single heartbeat inside of me. I thought, "How on earth did I get here? And when did I get here? And how the hell do I get out? Am I ever going to be free of him?"

From the outside, my life appeared to be perfect. Living in America, successful career, nice home, vacations, I had it all—on the inside was a shattered image of my fake dual life covered in my wounds, scars, blood, and tears, all disguised with my smile.

I was already an expert at concealing bruises with scarves and makeup. My big flashy smile and "I am fabulous" fooled pretty much everyone. I always pretended everything was great, even in front of my own children. It turned out that I was fooling just myself.

My marriage had turned me into a great actress, a very happy soul to the external world. Internally, I switched between being either a trophy wife or a doormat during the day while being robbed of my dignity in my own home at night. I was continually complying and satisfying his every need just so I could be safe and not bear the brunt of his constant yelling and screaming, threats, abrupt anger, and violent rage.

Denial, in the beginning, was the greatest barrier for me to see, realize and accept that the man I trusted my life with was indeed the biggest threat to me. I was in constant survival mode and didn't even know I was simply coping with each waking day. Battered woman's syndrome, fear, depression, anxiety, and PTSD don't even do justice to define what I was dealing with on a daily basis.

I was dancing with the devil and wondering why I was in hell!

"He just gets angry a lot; he's not really a bad person," I said, to cover it.

"You're married for life; divorce is not in our culture. You have a family to take care of. What will happen to the children? Forgive and move on," they said, to hide it.

"You know I love you; I did not really mean to choke you. It just happened by accident. I will never hit you again," he said to defend it.

"Think about the kids. Do you really want to break the family?" Everyone questioned me.

And I believed it all. Once. Twice. Thrice. and soon, I lost count. I had no idea that I was stuck in an ugly cycle of verbal, emotional, mental, physical, and sexual abuse. One that didn't seem to end. It seemed so confusing; I was questioning everything I was doing. I felt helpless and trapped. I tried to escape seven times. He would win me over by saying and doing the right things only for me to see it was just a hoax to keep me hostage. The dynamics of love, hope, and fear kept this never-ending cycle of domestic violence in motion, and I endured an abusive relationship for nearly 18 years!

I found myself in new cities and new circles, but I realized it was short-lived; this gave me fleeting happiness, that's all. I was even proud of myself, baffled at my ability to endure non-stop trauma and still function. The abuse, violence, domestic shelters, hotlines, doctors, hospitals, therapists - I just wanted the monstrosity to end. How did I not exhibit any hostility? What am I made of? Who am I? and why am I being given this experience, to begin with?

I started pouring myself into others, helping everyone else transition from danger into safety while having a voice in my head calling me a hypocrite at the same time. I realized the hard way that all of this was just a distraction, and I needed to find a real solution and fix the root cause of the problem instead of a temporary band-aid.

"The cave you fear to enter holds the treasure you seek."

This quote by Joseph Campbell changed my life. I stuck it on my mirror until I became it.

Nature and books became my confidante. I began seeking solace in small things and was grateful for all the magic amidst the madness. I was ready to find true happiness with no taint of sorrow. And then, I met ME. Not the me the world thought I should be. But, just like Bill Gove said, "If I had to be truly free, I had to be ME."

I had an awakening. I remembered who I was, and I took my power back. I used my imagination for the sake of good, and miracles started happening. In fact, it was happening all along; otherwise, I wouldn't be alive to share this story!

I saw clarity amidst the chaos. I chose faith over fear.

I decided I would never be tortured or controlled by anyone, not even my own Frankenstein frightful monkey mind. After seeing cruelty, abuse and death so closely, yet coming back alive several times, I saw myself as indestructible. Just like the lotus, you too can rise from the mud and bloom out of the darkness. You just have to trust the light inside, and you'll radiate into the world.

God, grant me the SERENITY to accept the things I cannot change, COURAGE to change the things I can and WISDOM to know the difference. I held on to this prayer until I merged with it.

I started reading, writing, journaling and had gratitude with every single step. I started making videos of my future self to my current self. I was willing to do anything to breathe freely again.

Life is such a great teacher that it will repeat itself if you don't learn the lesson.

Once upon a time, I was too ashamed to look for help. I was covered in blame, shame, embarrassment, and guilt. Now, I was willing to fail, willing to die and be reborn again, if that was completely. No more hiding. No more defending. No more proving anything to anyone else! Enough!

Only when I finally broke my internal shackles and got out of my own way did things change. I learned that what other people thought about me was none of my business. I allowed myself the same grace and ease that I would extend another human going through difficulty. I crushed all self-sabotage. I was willing to completely let go of all my limiting beliefs and mindset that held me hostage and kept me in my own prison when I was truly born free.

Detach yourself from the concept that misery is unavoidable, and when you choose to be who you are instead of all the excuses that are holding you back, freedom is all yours.

Today I'm on the path of healing and helping others sculpt their own David and discover who they are so they too can breathe free. We are all born free if only we realize it.

Now, When Will You Wake Up and Live?

NEETU SING

About Neetu Sing: Strong people aren't simply born. They're made by the storms they walk through. As a survivor of violence & domestic abuse, severe trauma & stroke all under the age of 40, Neetu has thrived despite the most horrific circumstances & evolved from it all. In her work as a transformational Master Coach, she has transformed the lives of hundreds of women as she shows them how pain doesn't have to turn the heart into something ugly & surviving can be beautiful.

Neetu is also an award-winning financial advisor who has helped multiple clients & high net worth business owners with their estate planning for 8+ years. She is well known for her work in generational wealth planning & tax-savings strategies.

She is a #1 Best Selling Author, speaker & philanthropist who serves several organizations mainly in the areas of helping women, orphans & older adults.

Authors website: *www.MasterCoachNeetu.com*
www.ThePrinciplesofDavidandGoliath.com

Nicki Hu

TESTING MY RELATIONSHIP WITH SELF-WORTH

I turned down a hundred thousand dollars last year. For a woman who was making almost nothing in her business for three years and was borderline about to give up on all of my dreams, this act was the single most powerful act of surrender, and it would be the final nail in the coffin to the old me.

I know many people would be blessed and grateful to have money drop into their laps just like that. One of my core beliefs was that I did not have to work hard for money. As the universe would have it, I was always provided for financially; not a crazy amount of money, but just enough to give me hope to keep chasing my dreams. Unfortunately, even though I had this belief about money, I also had a broken relationship with it.

It became clear three years ago when I quit my corporate job to follow a calling. I had no idea what that calling was, but I knew I was meant for more.

Even though my intuition guided me, I had a deeply rooted belief that I wasn't good enough. This subconscious belief was ingrained in me at a very young age because this was the belief that my mom projected onto me.

As immigrants, my parents came to the United States with the clothes on their backs and a vision to create a better future for themselves.

The poverty they endured in their childhood was the trauma that would become their purpose in life. They worked tirelessly every day for over twenty years and built a multimillion-dollar empire. But in the process, money and hard work became the benchmarks for success.

Money signified wealth, power, and authority. Marrying rich and having a well-paid and respected job was the epitome of success. As karma would have it, all of my siblings failed to meet my parent's expectations. But I was the black sheep that would break the generational trauma.

The psychology behind a child's actions directly reflects their unmet needs. For example, I catered to all of my mom's needs because following orders and being of value to her met my need for validation. As I grew up, I started looking for that validation externally, but my core wound would always subconsciously be linked to trying to get that unmet need from my mom.

But I was different from my parents. I believed in wealth without the tireless work ethic, and I also promised that I would never treat anyone differently because of their financial status.

For years, I never succeeded in making money from my business startups. I tried a handful of business ideas from personal training, owning my own fitness apparel brand, affiliate marketing, real estate, life, and spiritual coaching. My biggest blockage from all of those careers was the ability to sell myself. I kept switching careers, thinking it was not a right fit. I kept buying programs that taught strategy when in reality, it was my belief system that hampered my success.

I was used to achieving a lot but never recognizing myself for it, self-sabotaging my progress because one failure meant I was a complete failure, and I was so insecure about showing my true self. I couldn't ask people to pay for my services because my value was tied to how much money I made. As a newbie, I didn't have anything to show for it, which meant I wasn't worthy YET.

This is single-handedly the biggest block that keeps people stuck in relationships that don't serve them, jobs that pay too little but demand too much, and self-esteem issues. Not money, but the connection to their self-worth.

My entrepreneurial journey was the beginning of healing my relationship with my self-worth. I never worked out seriously before, but that year I committed six days a week for an entire year because I wanted to become the face of my apparel brand. Fitness made me realize that I had insane strength for a tiny five-foot girl, hip-thrusting about three times my weight. It was also the first time men started giving me attention for my physical looks. That healed the belief that I was not as beautiful as the popular girls because the same attention they got was reflected towards me, which meant I was just as attractive.

My next journey into affiliate marketing was the gateway to finding other individuals who were ambitious but didn't believe in struggling for money. A connection from that program led me closer to home. I met the meditation group that became my soul family and was transformed by belief about pain and struggle. They saw me in my most naked state, baring my trauma and how I felt about myself, they heard my dreams, and this was the first time I felt real community. They helped me heal the part of me that wanted to be accepted for who I was and not what I had.

My darkest moment came when everything I knew about myself came crashing down. I found out I was pregnant in the midst of building my life coaching business. All the trauma I had about self-worth came rushing back. I was terrified of becoming just like my mom and traumatizing my son. I wasn't getting clients, and the last string of self-worth I was desperately holding onto was my body image, and that went as the baby bump grew.

I cried every night, apologizing to my unborn child for being a worthless mother. I didn't even know if I had it in me to live or to love. That darkness led me to faith.

I connected to spirituality through human design, natal charts, and numerology. The charts reflected me like nothing I've ever experienced before. It gave me so much validation because these were traits that I knew I had, but I didn't know how special they were.

I had come to a complete stop during this time because my body was physically tired. I had no inspiration, motivation, or drive. This moment of silence was the universe's way of telling me to stop seeking outside of myself and to look at everything I already had. I experienced a massive boost in my self-worth, but I realized that all my seeking was still trying to prove my worth. I was still motivated by wealth, and it weighed down on me heavily because I was reminded that I was not where I wanted to be.

I hit another wave of depression, and I decided to let the very thing causing my pain go. I didn't want the money or the recognition. I just wanted to be normal, average me, and be okay with it.

The universe tested my relationship with my self-worth once again.

One day, my mom asked me for a favor to drop her off at the airport. I said yes even though my body was screaming no because I had already subconsciously switched my belief that my worth was not tied to what I could do for her. So when I broke my boundary, my body knew, but my brain logic-ed its way into believing that I should because I really wanted to make the relationship work, and she was finally starting to accept me.

That one request led to a windfall of favors. When I finally said no, her trauma triggered a response about how money was hard to make and how I owed her after all she'd done for us. I no longer wanted to be guilted into believing I was not good enough because I prioritized myself and my happiness.

I received a text afterward saying that she would give me a hundred thousand dollars to buy my first house because she gave that to all my siblings, but I can't ask anything of her, and she won't ask anything of me. Plus, I lost my inheritance. We can just spend time as a family as I wanted.

I declined her offer. Showing up unconditionally despite how she treated me was equivalent to staying in an emotionally abusive relationship because I needed external validation, and I was not okay with that. Setting this boundary made me realize that I no longer had an attachment to money and its relationship to my self-worth.

The universe dropped a final test on my path: A potential client who desperately wanted help. I charged premium prices for my services, didn't budge on my offer when they said they couldn't afford me, and declined to work with them after they wanted to pay because they didn't align with my values nor respected my professional boundaries.

I became extremely selective of the things and people I commit to. I am no longer willing to compromise my energy or time for money.

NICKI HU

About Nicki Hu: Nicki Hu is a Florida-based love coach who helps highly successful women attract/ manifest their divine soulmates to create authentic, lifelong, joyful relationships. Though she helps all women, she specializes in helping minorities culturally navigate the world of love and dating to find the one.

Her expertise comes from her own 12 year relationship with her husband and in addition to finding love, many women seek her out to navigate their own personal relationships successfully. Nicki helps by unlocking your magnetism in love through self-mastery, and reconnecting to joy using a variety of tools including human design, astrology, psychology, leadership, and life experience to help women shift from feeling undesirable to radiant in their love life.

In addition to the joy of spending time with her son Luca and her husband she also has a passion for fitness, having new experiences, and creating beauty through her photos and words.

Author's Website: *www.ManifestIncredibleLove.com*
www.ThePrinciplesofDavidandGoliath.com

Dr. Onika Shirley

RESILIENTLY FACING
ONE OF MANY GIANTS

Mindset to me is the set of beliefs that have shaped how I have made sense of this unpredictable, uncertain, and rapidly changing world and how I have made sense of myself as an individual. As a result, my mindset has influenced how I think, feel, and respond in any given situation.

When I had my first child at the age of sixteen, I had to face a really challenging time in my life. I was a sophomore in high school, and one month before she was born, I moved into my own place. When facing the fact that her father and I were no longer talking after being three months pregnant was a lot for a sixteen-year-old to deal with. I had to have the courage to face this adult situation with the eyes of a child. I had to prepare my mindset for raising my baby girl while attending high school and maintaining a stable living. I urged myself to have a positive and open mindset. I knew what I needed to do, and I was committed to doing it. I wasn't going to be another statistic of being a teen mom dropout. I had also determined that I would not be a teen mom where my mother had to raise my daughter.

Can you think of a time you had to face a giant? Can you relate to having to face the challenge being slightly unprepared?

Challenges in life can result in pain, bitterness, anger, frustrations, and even stagnation. The challenges of life have the potential of robbing us of our drive, ambition, and pursuit of the fulfillment of our dreams. It can even defile us of our worth. We may deny it as a way to shield and protect ourselves because there may seemingly be some small comfort in the shadow of negation. Sometimes we privately manage the pain by avoidance, but our healing comes from acknowledging and confronting. Everyone has a story, but not everyone is willing to tell it or even admit it. My personal story is very eventful and has many thrilling twists and turns. Each of our stories is a part of a journey, and in the end, it leads to self-discovery, personal healing, and inner strength. Can you recall someone being a single teen mom? Have you ever thought to yourself what that must have felt like?

The Struggle

It is so easy to become trapped within the thoughts that consume our minds. At some point, we have to accept our reality, move from disbelief and denial, and accept the facts. There is liberation in acceptance. The road ahead may be long, but it will lead to a place of peace that surpasses all understanding, and it will lead you to a place of genuine contentment. Deciding to acknowledge our truth immediately puts us on a different path and launches us towards our new journey. Being a single mother revealed the presence of my inner strength. I had to start figuring things out at a young age, and some things cost me more than I should have been willing to pay. I accepted my failures, asked for forgiveness for all the wrong I did and started to follow the steps ordered by the Lord. We cannot overcome things that happen to us in life alone, but we can do anything with God. Charles Swindoll said, "Life is 10% what happens to you and 90% how you react to it." Do you feel like you responded to the ten percent of life happening in your life effectively?

There are three elements of resilience that I will expound upon: challenge, commitment, and control. Resilience for me as a single mother is my God-given ability to adapt and bounce back when things in my life don't go as planned. I learned not to wallow and dwell on the failures in my life but to acknowledge the situation, learn from what life dealt me, and then move forward.

Challenges

As resilient people, we tend to view difficulties as a challenge, not a paralyzing encounter with life. It is a moment. It is a thing. It is only a chapter in our story; it isn't the entire book. In our weaknesses, He is strong. We should look at all our failures, bad decisions, and mistakes as a lesson to learn and an opportunity to grow. Don't view them as negative reflections on our abilities or self-worth but as an opportunity for God to show us His power and for Him to demonstrate His love.

Commitment

As a resilient person, I am committed to the life that God gave me and to the goals that He has allowed me to establish. I am compelled to get out of bed every day and face anything laid out before me in His strength. I must say that I could do nothing without God. I am committed to God and His righteousness. I am committed to the task that's necessary to achieve my goals. I don't do things for me to be seen, but I am committed because there is a need for what I do. The commitment isn't limited. The commitment must be to everything. The commitment is to be the best parents we could be, relationships, friendships, movements, and causes we care about, and most of all, to God. I had to be committed to being a great mother.

Personal Control

As a resilient person, my time and energy are focused on situations and events that I can control. When I place all my efforts in areas that I can control, I find that I can have the most impact. I feel empowered and confident. I am encouraged to act because I am optimistic and feel powerful. I am not wasting time worrying about uncontrollable events. My life's journey is now to share how I overcame the hurdles and obstacles in my way to achieving unexpected success as a single mother.

And what I learned from that is that my mindset and belief system really catapulted my success as a parent. The first secret to facing your giant is having belief in yourself. Nothing will change in your life until you believe you can conquer any obstacle. And if you have a low belief in yourself, nobody else is likely to be able to raise it for you. It's an inside job. I had to have a mindset shift about the whole situation at a very young age, and now I have a five-step system I would like to share with you that's much like David and Goliath when David had to conquer his giant Goliath.

The Process

Good thing, bad thing, who knows?

When things happened to me, I learned not to label them as bad things, and I found that I didn't suffer, but I was able to pick up the broken pieces and start to put things back together.

I asked God to reveal to me my life's purpose.

I found that finding a sense of purpose played a vital role in my purpose discovery in the face of difficulties. Life as a single teen mother was difficult, but I decided to focus my energy on helping other single mothers realize their lives and dreams mattered.

I built positive beliefs in my abilities.

It was important for me to have confidence in my abilities. I reminded myself of my strengths, of all the things I was good at doing, and my accomplishments. I did not permit myself to dwell on negative things that I couldn't control. A positive mindset in every situation has helped me build resilience for future challenges, and it helped me raise my children with peace of mind.

I learned to invest in the process, not the outcome.

I started to focus on the process of making my vision a reality and not the vision itself. The vision set the direction, but I had to concentrate on the actions necessary to accomplish the vision. I focused on the joy of pursuing my dream, the process, the journey, and not the destination.

I learned to envision completed processes.

I started to envision the actions I needed to take to ensure the process was completed and that I had done all that I could do to reach my life's goals. So I didn't focus on the failures, but I focused on finishing.

Resilience is that indescribable quality that allowed me to be knocked down by some of life's toughest situations. However, it has helped me to build inner strength and, in some cases, to come back at least as strong as I was before. Resilience is not magical; it takes real mental work to transcend hardship. Inner strength is about having the courage to face the pain and disappointment without allowing them to crush our spirit.

DR. ONIKA L. SHIRLEY

About Dr. Onika L. Shirley: Dr. Onika L. Shirley is the Founder and CEO of Action Speaks Volume, Inc. She is a Procrastination Strategist and Behavior Change Expert and known for building unshakable confidence; stopping procrastination, and getting your dreams out of your head into your life. She is a Master Storyteller, International Speaker, Serves in Global Ministry, International bestselling author, International Award Recipient, Serial Entrepreneur, and Global Philanthropist impacting lives in the USA, Africa, India, and Pakistan. Dr. O is a Motivational Speaker and Christian Counselor. Dr. Onika is the Founder and Director of Action Speaks Volume Orphanage Home and Sewing School in Telangana State, India, Founder and Director of Action Speaks Volume sewing school in Khanewal and Shankot, Pakistan. She founded, operated, and visited an Orphanage home in Tuni, India for four years and she supported widows in Tuni, India. She is the founder of Empowering Eight Inner Circle, ASV C.A.R.E.S, ASV Next Level Living Program, and P6 Solutions and Consulting. She has served for 13 years as a therapeutic foster parent for the State of. Of all the things Dr. O does she is most proud of her profound faith in Christ and her opportunity to serve the body of Christ globally.

Author's Website: *www.ActionSpeaksVolum.com*
www.ThePrinciplesofDavidandGoliath.com

Peter Mendiola

A WINNER'S MINDSET

People ask me how I got here, owning seven plus businesses. "I started with nothing and faked it until I made it," is my usual response. I'm an example of someone who doesn't know everything but has my hands involved in everything. I started a company where I knew nothing about that industry and then surrounded myself with people who knew the industry. Then I faked it until we became successful—the concept of "faking it until you make it" has guided me in many cases.

Now, don't be fooled by this mindset. My businesses are legitimate and perform exceptionally well. However, my attitude has always been that I can do it if it's been done before. To this day, it still feels like I'm faking things, even though I've built this entire empire and sit in board rooms full of the top qualified and talented professionals throughout my industries. I have no ego in any of this. I'm a problem solver who takes on challenges when Goliath stares me right in the face.

I didn't grow up with money or in the best neighborhood. However, I was fortunate enough to go to college because I played football. That background has nothing to do with my business success, but I've utilized my sheer willpower and strength in many situations to overcome challenges. But I started with nothing when we built our first company. I knew nothing and had nothing, yet that was all I needed to succeed.

I could envision what I wanted to do, and I've "tricked" many people into working with me. At least that's how I feel. It's incredible because I've somehow convinced the most outstanding professionals in the industry to work with me and work well together.

My David and Goliath story is that I started with nothing and built this empire with literally, I mean, zero money. People ask me, "How did you begin the company? How do you create a mortgage bank? Did you have one million dollars?" I tell them all no. I'm just resourceful and work with other great people.

I've been fortunate to be surrounded by great people, starting with my parents and marrying the right girl. I've also been fortunate to have all the best mentors around me. I've attracted some of the business's best people, and I don't know what they see in me. The most incredible compliment I've received from all these mentors is that I remind them of themselves. And I've heard that from many successful people that I remind them of them. That's probably one of the biggest compliments I ever received when someone's super successful says to remind them of when they were younger.

I tell my daughters that you must do what no one else is willing to do in your work ethic. Sports have played an enormous role in my success as a leader and professional. I played football and pretty much any sport you could think of in my younger years. I wasn't the biggest guy, the fastest, or even the most talented guy—but I worked harder than anyone else.

I worked on getting stronger because I knew somebody out there could be outworking me and trying to take my position on the team. It's that champion mindset that I still have today.

Sure, I have all these people working for me. Sure, I'm selling a bunch of houses and creating a bunch of loans, but there's someone out there that's just as hungry as we are, probably more brilliant, and they are coming to take my spot.

The 4 Secrets to maintaining a winning mindset:

1. Surround yourself with the right people.

2. Have perseverance and a knack for working with great people.

3. Don't be shaken by the small challenges.

4. Find out what your highest and best uses are.

I think you must find a way that works for you. So many companies are figuring out your top uses and skillsets. Find more intelligent people to help you do the other things you're you lack. Even when you think you're the best at something, there's someone better and be open to learning it. I hate ego. It's the worst thing in life and business. Instead, be genuine.

An excellent example of this is when my managers came to me and said, "I have a suggestion for you. You know, you should try and be more of a leader. You have everyone's attention and respect." I think he meant I should be a more eloquent-speaking leader when speaking to people on zoom or in front of a room.

That's why I feel like I still fake it today. I'm never going to act like someone that I am not. I speak the same way to you as I do in a business executive boardroom. I'm still faking it, but I'll tell you what I'm going to do is win, and no one will stop me. I think that's why people want to work with me. They trust me and know what they see is what they get.

I'm not brilliant or anything, and I wear shorts, sandals, and T-shirts to functions. I remember stuff that people say. I say things to people like "I'm hungry" or "I'm a shark, and I got to eat if there's blood." The people I work with eat that stuff up because of the positive mental environment for winning.

You've got to have a drive that is different from most. I'm so scared of failure. I'm afraid of letting anybody down. I thrived on making my parents proud, so I succeeded. Now, I thrive off making everyone in my organization proud.

I'm making it up as I go, but I'm making it work because I work with people and people pour into me.

When I started this business, I knew nothing, had nothing, but started anyways with nothing. I'm not stupid. I knew that the markets were crashing in 2008, but I never thought it was bad enough to quit. I thought to myself, this is an opportunity for me to grow if other companies are shutting down. When most people go one way, I want to see what the other way looks like before forming definite opinions. The real estate markets are crazy, and companies will lay people off and consolidate while I'm over here thinking, "What will happen if I go and try to grow."

All the mortgage banks were shutting down, the real estate offices were consolidating, and I did the opposite. I got on a phone call from the owner of another company, and he said, "How's everything going? I'm so good, and everything's excellent right now (knowing that the markets are crashing). How are you doing?" His reply to me was, "Let's be honest with ourselves. No one's doing great right now." I thought I didn't have time for this and said to him, "I must go. I don't have time to talk." Years later, his company went out of business, and ours is one of the biggest ones in the country. A winner's mindset doesn't focus on winning.

Everything you're confronted with is an opportunity, good or bad. It is how you handle it. Decide how successful you're going to be. I share with my entire company a principle I hope they live with every day—Everything we do right today and in the coming months will dictate our lives for the following years.

So, I told everybody in the company that I chose that route, let's go, let's make this an opportunity to be more successful than before. With that mindset, we're stronger.

PETER MENDIOLA

About Peter Mendiola: Peter Mendiola is the President & CEO of CEO at Point Mortgage. Peter has been President and owner of Coldwell Banker West, Inc., and served as President of the Pacific Southwest Association of Realtors. Peter has been interviewed by the media on issues facing the local housing market and was the host and moderator for the San Diego Real Estate Economic Summit.

From an early age, Mendiola was an entrepreneur when he co-founded a web design company that managed sites for Hewlett-Packard Corporation and Hollywood movies like "Gone in 60 Seconds". While attending college, he received his Salesperson License in 2000 and worked for Prudential CA Realty in La Jolla. In 2003, Peter received his California Real Estate Broker License. In 2006, he purchased the Realty World franchise. When he launched Realty World West, with ten agents and 12 listings, production was doubled each year they were in business.

Peter attended the University of San Diego School of Business, where he emphasized in Real Estate, Finance, and Marketing. While at USD, he also played on the football team, was a member of Delta Tau Delta Fraternity, and was the University's Student Director of Marketing.

Peter is married and a proud father of two daughters.

Author's Website: *www.linkedin.com/in/peter-mendiola-99294696*
www.ThePrinciplesofDavidandGoliath.com

Phillip McClure

THE WOLF GOLIATH

Wolf Goliath definition:

One who disguises themselves and/or their motives in order to take from you for their own gain. Often one who is respected or in a place of influence or power.

The preface of meeting this Wolf Goliath:

As David and Goliath prepared for battle, there was one thing that David knew that Goliath failed to recognize. The important maxim that David recognized was that you must know your enemy. In the book, The Art of War, Sun Tzu states, "If you know the enemy and you know yourself, you need not fear the results of a hundred battles." I once experienced a situation where understanding my enemy and myself allowed me to make a choice that set me free and put me on the path to success.

I was in the middle of a briefing with about 30 other soldiers when my supervisor came in and had me excused. We walked down the hall together, and he said that I was pulled out of the briefing as I had been summoned for an interview. It felt just like the first time I had to walk down the hall with a teacher or counselor to go to the principal's office. You might have had a similar experience, where your mind is racing, wondering what you did, what was going on, were you in trouble?

You may have had so many racing thoughts accompanied by an increased heart rate and were unable even to try small talk as your mind was all over the place. Now, what happens when the person or people across the table from you are indeed your enemy but are a Wolf dressed up as a friend, a business associate, or even worse, a mentor or center of influence. I met this Wolf Goliath alongside two other individuals. The stage was set, and all I had to do was walk in, get wrapped up in their cause and aspirations, and not think about my desires. They had designed the situation to have me sacrifice my goals, my time, and my dreams in exchange for a false sense of success that once realized would be devastating to my desires and my true future.

I was about to be presented the opportunity to either advance in rank and retire as a Sergeant Major or take the job I had been advocating would be best for the organization and myself. As I walked into the small room, I saw my supervisor and their supervisor waiting for me on the other side of a large wooden table in a room. The door was then closed, and they asked me to have a seat across the table from the three of them. Yes, I was nervous; "where was this going?" I thought. Once I sat down, they began asking me about my career aspirations as they had heard I was looking to move into a different organization. This was when I started to understand what was going on. I was then told I would receive my promotion within the next couple of months and get sent to Sergeant Majors Academy soon after. They explained the career path set up for me and all the great things I had been doing and that they knew I would continue to do, as well as the mentorship and the influence of soldiers that I would have. This all sounded awesome as I had been busting my ass for years for them. That's when it all came out, though; here was my Wolf Goliath. The conversation went to, do this, or your career is over.

I knew then that my working hard would always be for someone else's agenda, and I would not be able to create my own path. I was then told I would still be allowed to take the job I had advocated to get for years. Then listened to the discussion on why it was not good enough for me and why it would not be in my best interests.

I was still holding onto the belief that the other position I had advocated for would suit me better. I could impact others in the best possible way and have people better positioned right out of the gate starting their careers. This job was as a Recruiter. I believed that I could make a difference in the atmosphere if I could put the best people in the best jobs, the career paths that fit them. I know that someone will work harder and longer for a cause they like or believe in, so it would benefit everyone to start them outright. It seemed backward to look to fix people after the fact. Get it done right the first time, in the beginning, and the machine will work better with more fluidity and passion.

Unfortunately, this is not the job they wanted me to do. Taking the career digression to enhance the organization the way I believed and desired would mean committing career suicide. After much discussion, it was determined that I would be granted my transfer if that was my final decision. Who would give up the promotion into a position that they out-qualified hundreds of others to do in their right mind? I was then told I would have to sign papers that stated I would not be promotable for the next three years if I chose the job I wanted. My retirement was four years from that date. Thus, I would forever be unable to accept any promotion and would be ineligible for career advancement, even though I had the highest marks in multiple categories. The kicker of all of it was that if someone turned down a promotion, they were taken off the list for that year only. Not in my case, though.

I was then dismissed from the meeting and needed to report back with my answer.

I am thankful that with the help from a friend, I was able to see it. I was almost convinced through their flattery and what I believe now to be false pride until my friend Chris said just a few words to me. "I don't know what was said in there, but I have a good idea." He said, "Does a few hundred dollars more a month in retirement pay outweigh your dreams"? That was the jolt I needed. I immediately stood up, went into the room, and found them still there. I chose "career suicide." I took the position as a recruiter, which would allow me to fix problems from the beginning before they even started. This was at the cost of saying no and forfeiting so much that I had worked for. Everyone thought I was crazy! Who would ever turn that high of a promotion down? Well, I did, and my life has been amazing ever since. After I turned it down, the best part was the number of people that simply gave congratulations for having the fortitude to stand up for myself, my career, and my desires. This is not something you see happen in the military.

I followed my desire; I knew myself, and I understood my enemy; I slung my stone. I David slayed the Goliath that stood between me and my burning desire to reach my dreams. Those dreams have now positively impacted so many lives within that organization and those I have dealt with in my company NorthStar Coins. Where I build the tools to help people all over the world achieve their goals and dreams.

For all of us who have faced a similar opponent and succeeded, congratulations, it was not an easy beast to slay. To everyone who still has that chapter left to write in your lives, learn to recognize those who would take your talents and dreams for their own gain. Listen to your heart and arm yourself. So, if that time comes, you can smile deep inside and know your enemy and not fear the results of the battle. You are the champion; you will be victorious as David was. You are the only YOU and the only one who knows your true desires and aspirations, so fight for what is yours to receive and never let it be taken from you.

Desires and Intuition

Most people believe in their intuition. People just have issues with changing their current homeostasis, whether they consciously know it or not. They stay with the flow and not in flow. Even though they know that something is wrong, they let themselves be directed by a source that will continue to keep them from following their desires, let alone give them the time to even think and dream about them. There is a current that bombards us for our attention, never to see or to capture the time to take care of our futures and ourselves. The known situation is comfortable as it is known, even if it is not rewarding or pleasurable.

Working hard to improve yourself in confidence and purpose will allow you to break free. The reason this is true is we constantly hear so many people after the fact state things such as, "I knew I should not have been involved in that relationship, investment, or decision. It simply just did not feel right. They just made it sound so good."

PHILLIP D. MCCLURE

About Phillip D. McClure: Phillip is married to the love of his life, Maaike McClure, and is a very proud father of two exciting kids. He was raised in the Great state of Montana before moving to Utah. Phil lives life to the fullest. His accomplishments consist completing a full Ironman, deploying four times with the Army, earning multiple decorations along the way. Including two Utah crosses! Which makes him the only Soldier in history to receive that medal twice. Currently Phil is the Owner of NorthStar Coins, Events by NorthStar, the co-owner of P.B. Fast cars and recruits' pilots for the Army Aviation program. It was during his last deployment that he accidentally created his first Master Mind and it has forever changed his life as well as the others involved. He mentors and coaches in self-improvement and physical fitness.

Phil is an exotic car enthusiast that spends as much time behind the wheel as possible, weather it is carving through canyons, ripping around the racetrack, or coaching others to see their potential. Competitive driving is the best therapy in the world.

Live life to the fullest and have fun while doing it. You don't get a rewind in life so take mistakes as the lessons they are and improve, don't make the same mistakes twice.

Authors website: *www.NorthStarCoins.com*
www.ThePrinciplesofDavidandGoliath.com

Rachel E. Diamond

LOST AT SEA: A LIGHTHOUSE OF LOVE

Until recently, my life had been a series of challenging events I was quite certain had manifested to shake me and ultimately break me. To be honest, I'd wondered more times than I can count, "How am I going to make it through this? What's coming next? How could it get any worse? Why is this happening to me… again? When will life be easy? Who am I here to be?".

Childhood Trauma. Family challenges. Toxic relationships. Infidelity. Working multiple jobs to pay my way through college. Marriage. Divorce. Single Parenting. Co-Parenting. Braving the dating scene as a single parent. Toxic work environments. High-stress profession. Demanding work weeks. Exhaustion. Corporate mergers. Economic downturns. Layoffs. Career changes. Vehicular accidents. Financial strain and uncertainty. Side hustles. Leaping into entrepreneurship. Loss of loved ones. Miscarriage. Loss of pets. Loss of friends. Crippling grief. Anxiety. Depression. Self-isolation. Health challenges. Carrying the world on my shoulders. Falling apart. Rebuilding. Starting over. Risking. Failing. Risking again. Losing myself. Soul-searching. Starting over. Discovering and recovering pieces of my identity. Weaving together a new version of myself.

I felt lost in the sea of life, tossed around in my little lifeboat, taking on water, bailing it out, and pausing to catch my breath before the next big wave came crashing in. I was choosing this existence and had convinced myself it was the only way.

Thinking back to early childhood, I can see where I attached my worthiness to personal performance. I told myself concepts like, "If I could be perfect, maybe then I would be noticed and celebrated. If I was perfect, maybe then I could escape feeling judged or inadequate, maybe I would fit in, maybe I would be enough." I poured myself into everything I attempted and sacrificed whatever was necessary to achieve my personal best. Trusting others to support me, from my view, wasn't an option because I feared if I let go of control and someone else got it "wrong," I would be seen as incompetent, inadequate, unintelligent, unworthy of love and appreciation. No one would ever want to choose me. I wasn't willing to be vulnerable and take that risk. The strange thing about it was that I thought I was being a "good girl," responsible, humble, and doing the right things by being this way. I couldn't see that I was living and acting unauthentically while being governed from a place of fear. I'm not even sure these underlying thoughts and emotions about the rewards of my behavior were conscious at the time. These subconscious patterns became a protective encasement as time went on, and the limiting beliefs continued stacking into my lifeboat like weights. I accepted and took on the challenge, never courageous enough to say no, as if a trophy would be given for carrying the most cargo without sinking. I bought into a story that suffering showed strength and requesting support showed weakness, that nothing came easy.

I had to work hard, be successful, achieve more, juggle everything with ease, be a superwoman. I had to prove I could handle whatever came my way, do and be everything on my own; no one was here to save me, nor did I want anyone to—especially a man. The source of that conviction also formed early in life as a pre-adolescent. My goals out on the horizon were independence, self-sufficiency, acknowledgment, wealth, security, safety, and stability. I told myself that only then could I have and enjoy the magical life of freedom and adventure I had envisioned for myself as a young girl. And, of course, I was going to do this on my own. I was the captain of the ship I had built with my blood, sweat, tears, soul, and sacrifices. I was stubbornly fixed on doing it my way, from my safe zone, lost at sea with a broken compass, and unwilling to admit defeat by firing off an S.O.S.

Until I was.

One morning I found myself waking up to a new reality. I felt as if I were now stranded on the sandy shore of an unfamiliar land alone and deserted, no longer tossed at sea where I had safely spent many years by choice. The greatest storm of my life had come out of nowhere to rock me like never before, just as the future I thought I wanted and had worked so hard for was within view yet just beyond my reach. My course was forever altered, and the map I had been following was floating out atop the waves with the fragments of life I had collected.

For the first time, something cracked my protective shell wide open, unsalvageable, and I was finally able to see all that I had been hiding from myself. And for a moment, I was terrified. The scarcity mindset and limiting beliefs that I held onto so tightly had been the anchor that kept me wandering lost at sea, safe from others, a prisoner to myself, and leaving a vicious path of destruction in my wake. I had never braved looking back to take inventory of my journey until now when I had no other choice. This was my giant to be defeated. A silent monster made up of fear, self-righteousness, superiority, judgment, control, self-doubt, distrust, conditionality, rules, stubbornness, perfectionism, unworthiness, sadness, despair, grief, abandonment, manipulation, lies, and self-sabotage. For the first time in my life, I recognized that these deep and dark places within me were the real captain of my life. Not me. It was the great deception.

Here's the irony. I had been creating that storm my whole life. I WAS the storm.

What I had always wanted to have in my life, what I truly wanted deep down inside at a soul level, was precisely what all of my fears and doubts were fighting so hard to protect me from. Because I wasn't ready for its greatness, the responsibility and what it would require I let go of to receive it. And, since I was so intently focused on protecting myself from a place of fear and scarcity, my greatest fears are exactly what I manifested as the perfect storm. The Big One that threw me off course just as I was about to crash into a great precipice camouflaged as the shoreline of my dream destination.

And I'm grateful for it. So incredibly grateful.

It created an opportunity for me to begin anew truly. When everything had been stripped away, the waves no longer crashing into my raft to distract and busy me, and my white-knuckled fingers pried away from the helm, I was able to look each fear, each story, each limiting belief directly in the eyes one by one, sit with it patiently, feel it, listen, understand where it came from, and lovingly relieve it from duty with an appreciation for caring enough to protect me all of these years. The pain I had been causing myself and the people I care about, while unintentional, was very real. I received this new reality as a gift, an opportunity to see a new possibility and create deep long-overdue healing. My self-created destruction had rescued me.

Before the storm, I had been unknowingly sailing off course because I was looking outside of myself for directions and validation rather than connecting to my highest source, God and intuition (a.k.a. my "inner compass"), for guidance. I hadn't trusted that everything I needed was already inside me and the cargo in my boat did not contain my worthiness. I was born worthy, whole, enough, perfectly and wonderfully made. We all are.

Tapping into my intuition created trust, which began with unconditional self-love, integrity, consistency, recognition of values, and alignment with my life vision. I was then able to trust others because I first trusted myself to recognize alignment or misalignment and choose accordingly from a place of integrity. Knowing I am solely responsible for that choice was empowerment.

From trust came the ability to surrender. Surrender was a powerful release of control and a deep leaning into what was possible. It created freedom from judgment, expectation, conditionality. It was an invitation to step out of what's comfortable and into acceptance that I am supported and provided for according to what will best serve me on my journey. It was an opening to give and receive all that is and all that will be in perfect timing.

Support through surrender and trust had been the missing coordinates for me. When I finally released myself from the grip of my fears and all of what wasn't serving the highest version of myself, it became clear that I had been craving connection and belonging my entire life. Fear and control kept me bobbing along the surface, unwilling to receive because I was afraid to truly let someone in. To let them see what was hiding within the depths of my ocean, to know me as vulnerable, messy, struggling, imperfect. Human. The intimacy created by allowing others to witness us in our rawness is what connects us to the realness of life, humans-being, and the many dimensions of this shared experience. We truly are One. And we need each other. Until now, I wasn't able to admit that I needed anyone. But I do.

When I am trusting, surrendered, and open to being supported, I am made stronger in unity with others. I am powerful in my authentic being. I can love others and myself unconditionally. My unique gifts are amplified, and I can serve my family, friends, clients, humanity, and all living beings from within my purpose and life vision in a much bigger way.

I am no longer a lifeboat tossed at sea. Instead, I am the lighthouse guiding others out from the darkness, safely onto the shore and into their greatness. Standing firmly in gratitude for every obstacle, every storm, for I now hold the answers to the questions that used to paralyze and separate me from my greatness—three words: Trust, Surrender, Support.

From an Island of One to a Lighthouse of Love. What a fantastical journey of transformation and becoming it has been!

RACHEL E. DIAMOND

About Rachel E. Diamond: For more than 30 years, Rachel has been touching lives and sharing her gifts in the Architecture and Construction industry. Her award-winning Interior Designs can be experienced in public/private facilities and residences across North America and Europe. She has written and contributed to industry-specific articles published in Architecture and Construction magazines. Utilizing this collective experience, she continues to leave her creative fingerprint on the world as the Visionary and Owner of Radiant Artistry and Design, providing planning, design, photography and artistic services. Additionally, Ms. Diamond is in the process of creating Radiant Life: Wellness and Coaching.

When asked about her life vision, Rachel will passionately express her deep desire to discover, capture, and express the heart, soul, and dreams of each person whose life and energy intersects her own; share the beauty of our human experience; and empower humans on their journey of self-discovery and creation of their best life. She is an advocate and contributor to various non-profit organizations who also share her vision for leaving the world a better place than they've found it.

Contact Rachel via email: *RadiantArtistryandDesign@gmail.com*

Author's Website: *www.RadiantArtistry.Design*
www.ThePrinciplesofDavidandGoliath.com

Rachel Ivanovich

MIND THE GAP

Have you ever heard of the Unhappy Triad? The name is fitting. If you have ever experienced this condition, you know. But the lessons I learned from my experience from this are more than happy.

It was a beautiful spring day in Munich. Sunny days in Munich were rare. I was in a particularly joyful mood, and not just because the sun was shining. My best friend from high school, Susy, was visiting from the States! My heart was full. I had just given birth to a healthy baby boy, my sweet Sascha. I was happily married and a blessed mother of two. My daughter Julia was two and ahalf years old, and although she was a handful, I couldn't imagine a better life for myself.

For Sascha's baby shower, I received a super cool new pram. I have to elaborate here as these are not so prominent in the States. You have to envision one of those old-fashioned English baby strollers. We didn't have a car. This was pretty typical for Munich in the '90s. The subway system was amazing. You really didn't need a car if you lived in the city. But an awesome pram? That was akin to having the best minivan ever.

The pram I received had all of the attachments. Everything a mom without a car could ever dream of, especially if you had another young child, which I did. Julia was only two when Sascha was born. So, my friends got me the pram which included a "kiddie-board." Best. Thing. Ever. You could push the stroller with the young child in it (imagine a bassinet on wheels), and your older child could ride along, standing on a small attachment attached to the rod of the back two wheels. I felt on top of the world as we set out that morning.

We had a great day out on the town. I had been in Munich for almost ten years at this point, and I was so excited that Susy had finally come to hang out and check out my new scene! I took her all over town until the kids started to get tired. "Let's go home and chill," I said, so we got onto the subway and headed home. We had no idea why the subway line which was supposed to take us home ended early. We will never know. But we will never forget how the stop changed things.

We were packed in like sardines. The subway doors opened, and everyone flooded out. I found myself being rapidly pushed towards the doors. I tried to maintain my balance, but I couldn't control the situation. I did my best to hold on to my stroller so it wouldn't get pushed over. As I was shoved out of the subway, my foot didn't hit the platform. I missed it. My right leg pummeled into the gap; my body twisted backward. I went down screaming. Everything happened faster than I could have imagined but looking back, it felt like things were in slow motion. As I went down, the pram went up, turning into a catapult. WHAT? My BABY! I screamed as the pram launched my newborn into the vacating subway. "HILFE! HELP!" I yelled. I desperately tried pulling my leg from the gap so I could get to Sascha. But I was stuck. Panic set in. I couldn't even find my friend Susy! Where was she? Someone, help me! I can't find my baby! Then Julia began to wail, and I was brought back to the present moment. I tried to focus. What can I do? What should I do? Where's Sascha? Where's Sascha? I was near hysterics.

The next thing I knew, the conductor was in my face. "Fraulein, I need to move the train along." Susy finally appeared amidst the swarms and thankfully helped me yank my leg from the gap.

Madness! I had imagined the train leaving the station dragging me along behind. I was so frantic and fearful.

After Susy freed my leg from the gap, I finally was able to crawl into the empty train car to search for my missing child! My heart was breaking; where was he? I tried to stand up, and my knee and ankle buckled from my weight. I couldn't bear weight at all. I held back the tears. I didn't have time for emotion right then. My friend Susy was fruitlessly screaming at the conductor to call the paramedics. We needed help immediately!

Suddenly I had one of those mom moments. "Check the pram," I thought. And Sascha was there. Indescribable relief swept over me. He had slept through the whole episode. He had slid down under the blankets and was so small that no one had realized he was there. "He's here; he's okay!" That was the only thought that mattered to me at the moment. After that, I didn't care what had happened to me. My baby boy was okay.

The next thing I knew, I was being loaded up on a stretcher – someone had called the paramedics. First, they loaded me, then Julia, then 13 week old Sascha, and up we went on the escalator. The cops took Susy in a police car - talk about adventure. I tried calling my husband at work. He didn't pick up. I felt so alone.

The paramedics took me to the emergency room, kids and all. And then we waited. As the shock of potentially losing my newborn wore off, I started feeling the pain. I was shaking. Finally, they took me into an exam room for an X-Ray. They found nothing that night. No broken bones, they said. They gave me crutches, called us a cab, and sent us home.

By the following morning, my knee had tripled in size. It looked like an oversized watermelon and was the color of a plum. The next three weeks were a blur of doctor's appointments and a struggle to figure out what was actually wrong with me. Remember, I was in Munich without a car, with a 13 week old and two-and-a-half-year-old. Have you ever navigated cobblestone streets? On crutches? In the rain? With two kids? Just getting to each of my appointments was a significant challenge. I can't even tell you how many times I cried. But then it got worse.

They finally told me I had a severe injury called an unhappy triad. Not only had I severed my ACL, but I'd damaged the medial meniscus and severed the tibial collateral ligament, among other things. In other words, I'd blown out my knee BIG TIME.

The doctors told me I would need major surgery. How on earth could this be happening? Who was going to take care of my babies? I was still breastfeeding Sascha - the poor boy was only 13 weeks old!

I was devastated. The doctors told me that I would have to learn to walk again after the surgery. One particular doctor said that I would walk with a limp for the rest of my life, even after surgery. And even if I did all of the prescribed PT and the surgery was successful, I would NEVER run again. I was a runner. I had been running almost every day for over ten years. I cried for days.

But then a resolve took over. I had done hard things before. I could do them again. This was not the toughest thing I would ever have to overcome in my life, nor was it the easiest. I had to stay positive and open to what was to come. With all of my heart and soul, I had to believe that I would persevere and come out stronger on the other side.

Remarkably, the German government paid for me to have my good friend Nicki come stay with us during this trying time. I spent two weeks in the hospital after the surgery. After that, I spent two years in PT. It was HARD. These were some of the most challenging times in my life.

If you are anything like me, you struggle to ask for help. One of the biggest lessons I learned during this time was to let go and let others help me. I had no choice. Nicki, my dearest friend, played mom. She woke up every other hour while I was in the hospital to feed my newborn son, Sascha. By day, she brought him to me to nurse. In between, I pumped, and she fed him. She brought my sweet daughter Julia to see me while in the hospital. We were better together. We need community. This was my community. Together we were stronger. Nicki and I decided this was a minor setback: a bump in the road. Nothing would stop me from being the best mom I could be.

Nine months after being on crutches, I had to learn to walk again. I will never forget the feeling when the physical therapist took my crutches away. I felt so helpless. But at the same time, so determined. I would walk again—without a limp.

No. Better. I'd run again. I'd run marathons. To prove I could do anything I put my mind to.

As of today's writing, I have completed one full marathon. 26.2 miles. I have run over seven half marathons. I have six screws and two pins in my right knee. I am always in pain. But it is a reminder of what we can all do.

Four years after my surgery, I mailed my first half marathon medal to the doctor in Germany, who had told me I'd walk with a limp for the rest of my life. He had told me I would never run again. I included a thank you note. I simply said, thank you for inspiring me to be a better version of myself.

What, dear reader, is holding you back? Where have you been told you won't succeed, or you can't do something? As the saying goes, what doesn't kill us makes us stronger. I believe this. We must take the adversity handed to us in our lives and use it. This tenacity fuels us and makes us stronger. Right now, I am training for the Niagara Falls International Marathon. I challenge you to take some adversity from your life and convert it into something beautiful.

RACHEL TERESA IVANOVICH

About Rachel Teresa Ivanovich: Rachel Teresa Ivanovich, MBA, EA, is the founder and Chief Leadership Officer of Easy Life Management, Inc. She is a business coach, an Enrolled Agent and earned an MBA from San Diego State University with an emphasis in Finance and Taxation in 2010.

Born and raised in the Pacific Northwest, Rachel and her family moved over 40 times by the time she was 30 years old. Selected to represent the USA in Germany in 1988 by the Congress- Bundestag Youth for Understanding program, Rachel developed a love for other cultures and a deep empathy for peoples of different backgrounds. After spending a decade of her life living in Germany, Rachel and her two children landed in Carlsbad, California. Longing to put down roots, live more simply and find a place to call home, Rachel started a tax practice and named the fledgling business Easy Life Management (ELM). After having grown the original tax practice and business management firm to over 700 clients and a team of six, Rachel transitioned more than half of her tax practice in 2019 to another tax advisory firm to follow her lifelong dream of helping fellow entrepreneurs to develop their vision, grow their businesses and live to their full potential.

Rachel is married to a California native and is the mother of five amazing young adults. Community service is one of Rachel's biggest passions. She serves as Chair for the Agua Hedionda Lagoon Foundation and is a board member for the Carlsbad Chamber of Commerce. She is also an active member of the Carlsbad Hi-Noon Rotary Club.

Author's Website: *www.ELMtax.com*
www.ThePrinciplesofDavidandGoliath.com

Roxanne Felton

THE TRUTH WILL SET YOU FREE

Like David, my Goliath story is one where I go up against the most significant internal battle, and winning this battle will ultimately set me free. In this journey, I have found my inner champion.

I'm a small-town Catholic girl from Biloxi, Mississippi. As a life-long learner, I understand how your mindset is critical to growth and happiness. Having a mindset focused on growth helped me conquer my biggest fear. I've been carrying this fear around for 40+ plus years. But I've learned that if your mindset is positively greater than your trauma, your subconscious will elicit unexplained feelings and behaviors until you address your greatest fears.

At 60 years old, I allowed this negative influence to run the controls of my everyday life. The lingering signs of my trauma leaked into my adult life. I severely lacked confidence. I couldn't say no to people. I experienced internal anxiety to please everyone. I would allow that negativity to kill my daily productivity. I had daily battles with my inner-critic (inner-voice).

Growing up, my mom had six biological kids. Then I had a stepfather. My stepfather wasn't a perfect man. He pushed my mom into drinking. I would escape the toxic home environment by volunteering at the church rectory. When at the rectory, I was the only female nearby. I didn't pay any attention to it because I'd been a tomboy and always hung out with the boys. But I felt something different about going to the rectory. For me, the rectory was my solitude and escape from home. I had keys to the rectory and nobody knew I could go and come as I pleased.

I was a little girl. I didn't know a lot, but you know something isn't right after seeing the priest alone and all the boys have left. Since my stepfather never went to church, he was never with us. The priest had me start doing some of the readings, and everybody knew that only altar boys do that. I was getting special treatment. I still didn't know any better. This is a priest who I looked up to as a leader and role model. My father figure at home was my brother, and the priest treated me as a proper father would treat a daughter.

It started with smooches on my forehead, then a couple of months went by, and then he would start kissing me on my cheeks, and then he started kissing me on my mouth. Suddenly, it no longer was like a role model or a fatherly kiss.

I internalized and buried my discomfort. After a couple of months, my mom said I had been acting differently. She asked me, "What's going on? Do you want to talk to me about something?" My answer was always, "No."

The priest made me promise not to say anything to anyone, and I was good at keeping my word, too good. It felt different having such attention from an adult since I never received that treatment at home. I wanted to go to the rectory and see what, and we shall call him, Father Kenny, was doing. He made me feel special and gave me things to do. When I was bored, or things at home weren't that great, my mom advised me to go to the church, and I always said, "Absolutely, I would love to go."

Father Kenny's patriarchal treatment initially felt like mentorship and fatherly love, but that quickly evolved beyond what any child should ever have to experience. My commitment to our secret challenged my inner champion as I let my inner critic win, and I buried my trauma every day. He'd make me promise that I wouldn't tell anybody. As the leader at the church, he asked my mom if I could sleep over. That's when I knew my secret enabled him to take things too far, and it got worse. But, do you muster up the courage to stand up against your Goliath, or do you keep a promise you made? I was raised to keep my word, and I did all these years.

Every day since then, I wanted to release this secret. I wanted to defeat this Goliath that I've been dragging around my neck my entire life. My brother, who was the only person I ever told recently, asked, "Why didn't you come forward when they had all of those lawsuits against all the priests?" I said, "I was ashamed." While at the height of my career, I didn't want people to speculate and treat me differently. I did not want to go through the pain again. I've been trying to figure out the right words to speak my truth for so long, but any time I felt courageous, my inner critic would dissuade me from breaking my promise.

Mom Was My Saving Grace

If my mom knew what was going on, she would have confronted him, and I would not let that happen. My mom would use profanity very loosely. So, to this day, I don't swear. I don't drink either because of what I witnessed growing up. Despite those bad examples, my mom is paramount to my story. Her mindset and beliefs were built on education, fortuitous for me and my siblings' futures. My mom was strong, and her vision for us made a huge difference with my story and secret. I had a big secret that I promised my mentor that I wouldn't tell anybody.

My mom's main goal was to ensure that we all received an education. I relied on my belief system and trust in her words. My mom's mindset was that all of us were going to college. I knew that my mom, even though with only a high school education, had a belief system, and I know that she would have been very disappointed if I had told her what was going on. However, as she dreamed, all of her children, including me, went to college and obtained good jobs.

When I was in college, I had a boyfriend who wanted to serve in the Navy, and he called me. He said, "Roxanne, I want to go join the Navy and want you to go with me, so I said, "Well, I have to ask mom." I didn't know any better, but I thought I could go to school later. She said, "Hell, no!" She said, "You are to finish college!" I am the kind of person who finishes what I start. My boyfriend moved on to the Navy and married somebody else, but I stayed in school, made the honor roll, and graduated as my mom demanded.

I wasn't used to talking to my mom about problems or issues because she was always working, trying to provide for her children. She was more intelligent than her education in all cases.

Despite the positive growth in my life, I still allowed the memory and secrets of Father Kenny, for the longest time, to torment my soul. I kept our secret. But now, like David, I took a slingshot of faith and power by writing this chapter and my story. I take my slingshot of power and toss the weight of pain, abuse, and secrecy from my life with my revealing words. I'm going to be honest with myself because I've been in denial. I want to conquer that giant with the truth.

Mindset is essential. There were many times that I wanted to say something, but my inner voice, my inner critic, kept that from happening.

I know I'm a child of the highest God who asks me to open the doors of truth and freedom. I know now that I can pray to God almighty. I slew the giant in my life through faith and forgiveness.

A Message To The Youth and Adults

My inner critic fought so hard to keep me from publishing this so many times. It told me to keep the secret. The pivot is when you align your inner critic with your inner champion. When they are out of line, the critic wins every time, causing doubt and fear, keeping you from taking any action.

When you feel like something's not right, you must know that you can always break a promise and ask somebody to help you. Use your God-given intuition of discernment, and you'll find that your heart will guide you to safety, freedom, and deliverance. You may feel helpless as I did for so many years, but the truth can and will set you free.

Father Kenny probably would have had some charges brought against him had I told someone when it was all happening. He was a pillar in the Catholic community. I knew that if he treated me the way he did, there were probably others at the church. He was the priest everybody loved in the community. Abuse is abuse, period.

He was my Goliath, and now I have conquered the giant. My story is out there, and I have said his name. I am free.

ROXANNE FELTON

About Roxanne Felton: As an Agile Advocate and Productivity Coach, Roxanne has shared her knowledge with diverse local and international project teams. She has held numerous projects roles ranging from Senior International Project Manager to Project Executive. Her unique style of training is a result of bringing thirty-five plus years of experience as a Program and Project Manager in Information Technology. Roxanne's current skills have afforded her opportunities to travel globally to deliver coaching and training in places such as Ghana, Nigeria, and Kazakhstan. Roxanne holds many certifications including Project Management, Release Train Engineer, Scrum Master, and Enterprise Agile Coaching.

In her spare time, she is an avid reader, competitive tennis player, global traveler and enjoys playing with her west highland terrier, Moritz.

Author's Website: *www.linkedin.com/in/roxannefeltonchristopher*
www.ThePrinciplesofDavidandGoliath.com

Samantha Roberts

YOUR CHALLENGES, YOUR GREAT CONTRIBUTIONS

'You are enough.'

'There is absolutely nothing you need to do to prove yourself.'

These are two phrases that I have read about countless times throughout my youth and my early adulthood, but I, for myself, never embraced them.

I had been raised outside of a traditional home; my grandfather gifted us a second chance after our mother put my siblings and me into the foster care system a few years after divorcing my father and stripping him of his parental rights. Furthermore, a few years later, she married a man unfit for fatherhood or even child proximity.

My grandfather was a traditionalist. He didn't understand the new age of women who would go to college, where they wouldn't start a family in their early 20s, and they wouldn't settle down.

Before any of these societal pressures were relevant to me, we used to have the most incredible conversations about strength, tenacity, ownership of our own destiny, and how anything was possible with focus, dedication, and hard work.

In those years, he raised me to be tough and independent. He raised me to think for myself. He raised me to trust that I can make anything happen if I put in the 'good work.'

As we both got older, his demons came into the conversations. My fundamental limitation as the daughter of his life's biggest failure and the fragility of his own health wore down his 'knight in shining armor' exterior, and his words became double-edged swords.

In my youth, he had fostered so much strength and self-belief within me. And in my early adulthood, our conversations filled me with a debilitating belief system. As I felt so indebted to him for the position in life he had saved my siblings and me from, I continued to seek his approval and praise. Today, I refuse to demonize him, but I cannot pacify the impact I have witnessed his words have on our family.

Yes, he is indeed a person who has endured extreme challenges, loss, and heartache. But no level of darkness defends the negative impact we make on others. So, I choose to honor and hold true our good memories and cast aside the effect of the tough times.

There were moments in my youth that were so powerfully beautiful that I would wish to gift them to anybody. And then there were subtle, dark, awful, disgusting moments that I wouldn't wish on an enemy.

I started asking myself in my early 30s, "Whom would I have been if not for the experiences between four and ten years old?" because there were moments so dark and devastating that I lost my innocence.

Not only my physical innocence – at the transgressions of my stepfather. My inquisitive nature, lost in the years of uncertainty and general challenge, and my dreamers' innocence, continuously present in my storytelling and songs.

Early on in my life, I started feeling this sense of 'the little guy against the world.' I had this awareness that something in me was different—fundamentally different.

Having been raised through the different challenges that I had experienced at such a young age, I sensed that I had a different awareness to the rest of the world of 'what else is possible.'

I may have been a small-town girl, and I may have overcome childhood molestation. I may have overcome time in the foster care system and overcome depression and debilitating chronic pain. I may have overcome growing up without a mother, but I was gifted a first for my family. I was given the opportunity to be raised by my father.

Other than the years that were stripped from him, he raised me. They were not easy years. We scarcely had enough money for food and heat, but fundamentally, he taught me about honor, working diligently with the resources at hand, and how to create opportunity with abundance.

I don't remember us talking much in my youth, but I remember working in the shop, on cars, on the house, and in his business. We watched science shows while we worked. I earned the things I wanted. At his insistence, I rewrote my homework if it was sloppy. I mowed the 7 acres if I wanted to play at a friend's house. I learned that money is not the only currency, and the barter system is alive.

Looking back, I believe he taught me how to seek abundance and to believe that living with a sense of lack was a choice you could ignore or simply filter out of your awareness. I also learned how to read others without the incessant need for words.

This played out powerfully in my twenties after I chose to stop speaking following two car accidents and flipping a quad down a rock quarry. These accidents left me with post-concussion syndrome and completely changed my personality and short-term memory. Unfortunately, it also severely altered my beloved love of language.

The crushing, crippling, and debilitating pain that I endured throughout my twenties opened my eyes that all this hardship must have been for a reason. So I started unpacking my choices andthe lens required to select them.

I uncovered that the lens through which you view the world would dictate the patterns that continue to show up. If you have unresolved issues with poverty, poverty will continue to show up in your life. If you have unresolved issues around the scarcity of food, you frequently find yourself making choices that satisfy that story of lack.

After ignoring my patterns and naively keeping my head buried in the sand, I discovered, uncovered, and realized that I needed to reframe my mindset; it's not 'me against the world', it's me 'impacted by the world.'

This realization helped me to slow down and to bear witness to myself to choose to look at things that I had endured and experienced as challenges were, in fact, gifted into me because I can give their knowingness to somebody else, so they don't have to get lost in it as I did.

Before this sense of ownership entered my life, I lived in a progressive pity party. I had left my hometown and moved to NYC to pursue my career and engross myself in a community of people who had all overcome extreme hardship and pain.

This provided a new sense of normalcy about how much people can endure. The problem was that it also showed me how highly productive and motivated people could mask or bury their trauma and leverage its darkness as a strength. I spoke earlier about the power of a double-edged sword; this new life was the very embodiment of that.

If you choose to bury parts of yourself, your truth, your past, or your life – fair warning, it will resurface at the worst possible timing. Or it will simply serve as a reminder that you are human, and if you ignore facets of your life, health, or well-being, a natural reset will set you right again.

The challenge with choice is that it has consequences. When you choose to diminish your worth or your contribution, it comes with consequences.

My mission now is to share my life experiences with others in raw transparency and irreverent truth. I now trust that challenge is a gift; it isn't shameful to have weaknesses. It can save a life if we each share our lessons in real-time.

There are so many stories in my life that I now can leverage as a source of strength. I diligently work through new memories long since buried and forgotten. I am pursuing their gifts. I wish to share with others that it is never a competition and that trauma dumping is not the only way to get things off our adult chests. We can purposefully integrate ourselves into communities where we open, share, or hold space for others to unpack or work through our truths and challenges.

On my darkest days, I reach into my community and pour love into them, one voice memo at a time. I share the insights I have witnessed in them or the contributions I have seen them make. Nearly without fail, I receive a note back, thanking me because the individual I was called to reach out to was having a tough day. They may have been in a spiral, or they may have felt overwhelmed or underappreciated.

I offer this encouragement: stop now if you are reading these words and have made it this far. Then, please take 10 seconds, send someone a voice note, and let them know they are on your mind.

Every human faces challenges, every person on this planet has overcome something they wouldn't wish on an enemy. We have the opportunity to alleviate their darkness by 10 seconds of our time. We can share stories of hope and possibility.

In closing, 'I love you – just because,' please remember: 'You are Enough!'

'There is absolutely nothing you need to do to prove yourself.'

SAMANTHA ROBERTS

About Samantha Roberts: After 12 years, mute and non verbal, following back-to-back car accidents and narrowly escaping death upon flipping a quad down a rock quarry, Samantha reached her own personal rock bottom.

Through the power of Community and Mentorship, she found her voice again and her conviction to live a life of contribution and service.

During the quarantine of 2020, she became a Grant Cardone Licensee and launched her podcast, Storytelling by the Numbers, and the Proximity is Power Summit Series.

She is committed to lifting 1,000 voices in Courageous Conversations in our newly invigorated virtual economy.

Author's Website: *www.StoryTellingByTheNumbers.com*
www.ThePrinciplesofDavidandGoliath.com

Shane Laufman

A SIXTH-GRADER CAN DO IT

Imagine yourself in a dream. Your mom whispers to you, "wake up." In typical fashion, you hate it when she does that because you are reminded that it is time to go to school in the freezing cold. It is bright out—blue sky. You wait until the very last minute to pop out of bed in fear of getting punished.

Fast forward: you are on the bus. The kids on all sides of you are smiling and laughing, and you just sit in deep silence.

Thank God the ride is over.

It is painful to look at the clock. The clock is just the sick reminder of how long it will be until the school day is over. Each class has another name. Each class is another prodding as you feel like cattle being herded to a slaughter that just never seems to end.

Over and over, this happens, but today is different. It doesn't faze you. In fact, the verbal,mental, and physical abuse lost its edge over the past couple of weeks. Every time another punch, scratch, name, accusation, blatant lie, and hours tacked on to the 'children jail,' affectionately known as 'detention,' is just another opportunity for you to question one thing: "Do I have any worth?"

Fast-forward to after your 2 hours of undeserved detention. Home is not better. Your mother can't connect with you. She is sick. She doesn't seem to know anything but physical "correction" that could possibly rival a warden's approach to the saying, "spare the rod spoil the child." The kids in your poor neighborhood hate America. You are American. You are the enemy. All the kids with their homes in ruins, take out their pain and anguish on you as they lost their loved ones to a war-torn country. More running, and you treat it like a game in hopes they don't catch you as all 30 kids are chasing you down. Sometimes you win, which is you being faster and smarter just long enough to be alone, but most of the time, the loneliness is even worse, and to ease that pain, you give in. They pile on you and give you another beating for the books.

There is no escape and not a single friend. No relief for years because what led to this was the lie that your father was trying to kill you. And how could you not believe that lie when you are on the run, homeless multiple times, and move across the country to cover your tracks? Whenever he tries to call, it is another outburst of anger, fear, and on the right day, convulsions. "This man must be that evil to make your mother have such strong reactions, but why would he keep on calling?"

You have been in this hell for three years straight without a break. You have nothing to hold onto, and for the two weeks leading up to this day, you cannot come up with a single reason why you are valuable. Today is going to be different, though. You've known that mom won't be home today. You know that no one will check up on you.

You move to the kitchen, pull out the bleach and soap, and start pouring all other chemicals you can find into your cocktail that will help alleviate your pain. You have been careful to consider your worth and the impact if you go. Your conclusion: Your mom will have no ties to the evil, murderous father. Your sister won't miss you as she is in a different world. The cost savings of one less mouth to feed will actually help those around you, and you hope the hate that is harbored by the middle school kids that you just want to be friends with will dissipate so they might be happy. Chemical cocktail it is; you learned this while searching on the internet.

You move to the living room and sit down with the drink in your hand, double-checking that there wasn't anything that you could find of value about yourself. You ponder for an hour in the dark and tranquil, hoping for a single moment of inspiration. Nothing.

You have made your choice, but a thought does come into your head, "I want to do something for myself just this once. I'm going to disobey mom, knowing I won't get the 'correction'", and that alone makes you smile. So you turn on the radio to a station that is not the usual monotonous Christian station. You want to have a single moment of inspiration—a good feeling before you go.

Rebelliously (because mom never let us change the channel in fear that the evil would come out), full of guilt, however, calmly soul searching for light, patiently flipping through the stations, seeking that feeling, that dopamine hit of good and light, to finally have something for me. You want your last moments to fulfill a need to feel alive.

This move was calculated. Knowing my mom wasn't home. I was disappointed that I couldn't even find one station to feel for myself. The discovery was transformational in the form of a discovery that I had zero value. I couldn't even find one station to make me feel good. Nothing comes on any of the other stations that satisfy your last wish. Finally, you decide to be courteous, your last silent gift to mom and turn it back to the Christian station, and THERE IT IS!

A song using your favorite instrument in a way that you had never heard before. It captivates you and draws you in so fast like it was made for you and this moment. You know you have never heard this song before! The first phrase hits you so hard in this song that you fall to your knees and get as close to the speaker as you can, like it was a warm fire on a winter night. "Why do you run? Why do you hide? Don't you know I just want to be with you?" Tears swell in your eyes.

The song goes on and speaks of God, who is sitting there watching you as you run through life. All he wants to do is be with you, and you keep turning away from Him. You keep ignoring, slandering, hurting him, but regardless He thinks of you and continues to be patient while only wanting to be loved by you as much as He loves you.

This is the exact moment that my entire world was shaken to its core, and my belief in everything was changed so much that I was a completely different person as of that moment. A sixth grader had an epiphany where he could empathize with God in this song. All of the years being forced to read and memorize and attending only adult services that preached this message were consistent, but this was the first time you actually felt it.

In an instant, I believed that I had value that transcended my peers' approval. At that moment, I realized how selfish I was. At that moment, I thought about the pain that God was going through from the moment that his trust was broken by all of humanity, and my pitiful little existence on this earth, seeking approval from children, was child's play. I didn't deserve to be loved. The children around me didn't deserve to be friends with me, but if God could do it and He loved me as much as described in this song, I could change the hearts and be a healer of those around me.

My belief went from nothing to the potential of what I could become. The belief that I was selfish led me to seek the reasons WHY the kids were hurting around me so much so that they felt the need to gang up on me. My belief in God, that He was real and felt the same as I did, but on an even grander scale, led me to have no fear of anything yet to come. That day my fear was replaced with hope, my pain turned to empathy, and the next day when the first kid in my morning math class attacked me, I asked them about their family and consoled them when I found out their pain. It was the pivotal point that led to me going from the most hated person in the county to making my enemies my friend, my equals, and one of the most popular kids by the time I was a graduate of high school.

From my childhood to David's story, there are many parallels. I want to mention something that I learned while facing these many goliaths in my life. It is not cool to be David. It is brutal to absorb the responsibility of those around you that don't deserve it. It is miserable to see those who should be leading you cower in fear. It is disheartening knowing that you must take on challenges that you are seemingly not prepared for. I can confidently tell you this: Your belief in God, yourself, the goodness of others, better outcomes, impossible dreams just being a step away, and, to quote the bible, "faith like a mustard seed can move mountains" is absolutely true! It is just a matter of time before it happens.

The crazy part is that this very personal event is one of the key moments that have led me to take on many seemingly impossible challenges. I became a genuinely kind-hearted individual. I have had the pleasure of becoming a licensed investment advisor training hundreds of newly licensed individuals a month, owning multiple companies, brushing shoulders with elites, helping officials get elected, and having a beautiful family with the "white picket fence" even though I never wanted it. And all of this before the age of 30.

For any decision, two elements must exist: belief and value. Belief is overcoming logical barriers such as "humans can't fly," and value is the emotional drive to act on your belief. I am excited to explore more about strategies and actions you can take to improve your belief and develop your values in the following books in our series. You must have a simple RESOLVED choice, a covenant you can create! You can, at this moment, choose radical, conclusive, constitutional change, yet, a single and straightforward decision can make transformation simple. If you ever need encouragement, just remember that if a sixth-grader can do it, "so can you," no matter what phase of life you may be in currently.

See you in the next book!

SHANE LAUFMAN

About Shane Laufman: Shane is a serial entrepreneur, business owner, executive marketing director, national top trainer and educator, sales coach and trainer, investment advisor, broker and expert teacher. Shane has accomplished all of the following without ever obtaining a college degree.

Shane's first true entrepreneurial experience began in high school when he borrowed a friend's guitar and busked tables in the lunch cafeteria while playing songs for couples and friends, earning a living and 3 meals a day from his peers.

At 18 years old, Shane was given the opportunity to become a financial advisor. Shane has built a successful career in training brokerage services for fortune 500 companies and brokerages worldwide. Shane also focuses his expertise in financial training and marketing by helping and advising high-profile professional athletes.

Shane has helped over 12,000 students and clients worldwide with their financial needs and investments. Shane has been a partner and founder in educational courses. Shane is a co-partner in a remote entrepreneurial incubator program which is currently expanding.

Shane is experienced in crypto currencies and NFT's and loves exploring and sharing investment tools and services through creative investment products and strategies. Shane is a master networker and has been featured on podcasts and is actively broadcasted as a professional speaker on the social media app Clubhouse.

Author's Website: *www.LaufmanShane.com*
www.ThePrinciplesofDavidandGoliath.com

Steven Wener

TRANSFORMATIONS

We're born into this world without a rule book, and most of us have parents who really haven't lived their lives according to self-discipline or goal setting. Nor do they know much about developing success habits, taming the overbearing negative voices in their heads, or dealing with the stress of the unknown.

So as a child born into the environment I just described, I felt lost in life. Don't get me wrong; I had an incredibly fun childhood. I was athletic, adventurous, and part of a huge family, as my mother was the oldest of 10 kids, but my father would commute to another city for work and be gone for years during the week and back on weekends.

Not having my father around while growing up was challenging for me, and it took me decades to understand he was simply trying to take care of his family, as his father was a poor shoemaker and his mother passed when he was a young man. When he was home, he was a very dominant personality that didn't nurture; he was harsh with his wisdom.

I made monumental mistakes growing up. My scarcity mindset had me gripping onto cash without understanding that I was developing a reputation with my family and friends as a cheap person. Between being selfish, cheap, lazy, and late for almost everything, I lived in this delusional pattern that only suited me. My guard was up, and I was fully protected; the world couldn't hurt me, so I thought. I was afraid to change and be vulnerable. I lacked the conviction to set goals because that would mean I would need to be held accountable, and I wasn't into responsibility. I preferred to be the big fish in a small pond, not the other way around. How far does that get you?

So let's take stock of the old me or my inner team: selfish, lazy, late, frugal, and insecure. There was also fear, envy, insecurity, and self-loathing on the bench. Now let's put this team on a court, and what kind of a team did I have? I had the one with a huge losing record that repeatedly got fined for foul play or kicked out of the game.

With everything that I'm sharing about my old self, could it be possible that I could turn my life around and create a winning team? Absolutely! Did I have any idea how to do that? Nope. I had to learn my lessons by being forged in fire. It took pain and loss for me on a monumental level to finally realize that there was a better way to live, a better way to treat myself and others, and I also began to think about legacy. How would I be remembered? There wouldn't be much memory at that current pace other than things I wouldn't want to hear because they weren't flattering by any means.

The first memory that stuck with me about being able to achieve was when I went on a trek to Mount Everest. I was 31 years old and on a trip with a friend, and one of his dreams was to see Everest. So we booked a six-month trip to Southeast Asia, and part of that trip took us to Nepal. In life, I often called myself the 70% guy, as my 70% could achieve what it would take others 100% of their effort to accomplish in certain areas, so for that reason, I typically took the lazy way out. Little did I know that 70% wouldn't cut it in that mountain range. I hardly trained, didn't break in my boots properly, and suffered during the 13-day trek.

I was finally on my own, surrounded by people, but alone in my struggle with altitude, where nobody could help me other than my own determination. It was the first time I can recall where I had to dig so deep for an extended period of time that I told myself I would sooner die on that mountain than turn back.

On our final ascent day, we needed to decide to go down to the basecamp of Everest or summit Kala Patthar? We decided to summit the 18519-foot peak. I cried my heart out on that mountain as I finally found enduring strength that got me to the top. Now think, how often do you push yourself beyond your own limits? And were those your limits in the first place? That moment became my benchmark.

The next event that truly transformed me was marriage. I was so stuck in my ways, single for so long, a spoiled bachelor, as I had successful real estate practice, toys, and very few bills. As I was never in what I would call a serious relationship, I had experienced enough dating that I knew I wanted something more meaningful and permanent. Still, I had no idea how scary that would be once I went down that path. Again, remember, responsibility was something that didn't suit me very well, as I never prepared myself to be responsible. Avoidance or excuses were my defaults, and there was very little recourse.

Nothing serious enough that could affect me enough to change, not at that time. So, I married someone beautiful and who was tough with me when I was acting like a fool. That didn't mean that I made it easy for her or myself. I also fell into a massive depression, as I had just uprooted and left everything I knew back in Canada and had to start over and rebuild in San Diego, as this is where my wife's roots were.

Once I began to get my bearings in San Diego, I worked to get relicensed and back into Real Estate; as I started in Canada back in 1993 (a recession in my province), it was now 2008, and the United States was in an economic freefall with real estate and the stock market taking unprecedented hits. I had monumental hurdles in front of me, but I was finally ready to begin growing up and tackling the things that held me back for most of my life.

I started to excel in my profession and quickly grew my real estate practice to become a top agent in San Diego. I began to take my future seriously, as I was no longer responsible for just myself, and the explosion that took me over the top was finding out I was going to be a father to our beautiful son. As I began to take on even more responsibility, I began to rewrite my story and define what I wanted out of life and how I wanted my future to play out.

Fast forward to 2022, and I've established myself as one of the premier real estate agents in San Diego, have spoken nationally around the country to lead masterminds, have fantastic friends, and have three incredible children. My wife keeps challenging me in ways that keep me improving on who I am. I am building out a coaching business designed around priming the mind with daily morning calls. This gives my students and me the extra juice needed to take on the day with a smile and purpose.

I've created a daily task list to remind myself of what needs to be done on any day to feel accomplished and understand that capacity can always be stretched further. I don't live life like I'm lost any longer. My foundation is made out of reinforced concrete, and my absolute passion is looking for the truth in vulnerability.

We meet others in their finest or worst moments, and we can embrace and share that life isn't so bad or scary, regardless of our scars. Those scars are simply reminders that there cannot be good without bad or bad without good. It's up to us to choose the path once we understand there is a path to choose.

STEVEN WENER

About Steven Wener: Steven Wener has been a licensed residential real estate professional since 1993. His aim is to question, consult, and execute a plan in order to achieve your desired result. He has taken the lessons learned over the years and published *The Communication Code,* a book describing how to create relationships around the selling experience. This has allowed Steven to find his way onto podcasts and stages locally and across the United States, where he describes these methods to help others elevate the way they think around effective communication and its importance. Steven is a Broker-Associate at Elite Real Estate Team at eXp Realty of California, Inc., Full-service Realtors® that represent all of San Diego County & South Orange County. His father led him down the path of becoming a Real Estate Agent and an independent business owner at the age of 23.

After two decades of smart work, Steven is so thankful to have helped over 1000+ buyers and sellers while practicing my father's philosophy. Check out how Steven's community at breakthroughmornings.com where vulnerability is our common connection, so we can remind ourselves that we're not alone in our struggles.

Author's Website: *www.SDSoldbySteve.com*
www.ThePrinciplesofDavidandGoliath.com

Susan Carpio

BELIEVE IN YOURSELF – AND BE OPEN

A dream vacation became the setting for an event that changed my life and put me on the course for the biggest battle I have ever faced. What I learned in that fight — how to believe in myself and find trust and strength in the resources put in my path — are the lessons that guide me today.

My teenage son and I had landed in California for a family gathering in Disneyland. Imagine my horror when I discovered a lump, the size of an egg, in my left breast. I decided at that moment that I did not want to spoil anyone else's good time, so I ignored it, and that mindset of literal denial would be where I lived throughout that trip.

But while my mind was away, my body was not. As we were driving home, I heard the word "cancer" in a song, and I experienced a frightening feeling of ice in my veins. I assure you, that feeling was pure bodily wisdom telling me that I couldn't ignore it!

I set up discussions with friends in the alternative health world. These were people who I had been running with for years, people I trusted in and believed in their approach to health. Long before I discovered the lump, I was convinced that Western medicine's approach was unsurvivable. Which would be worse, I thought: cancer or the treatment? In addition, I just couldn't believe that I could have cancer. I mean, I didn't even eat eggs that weren't organic! I didn't try to truly find out just what that lump was with that mindset. I didn't visit a doctor, I didn't schedule a test, and I certainly didn't share what was going on with my loved ones.

However, I did change my diet. I stopped eating sugar after I read that it feeds cancer. Looking back, I marvel at the irony. I did not believe I had cancer, yet I changed habits and chose to eat foods that were known to be cancer-fighters. Was I really in denial?

It is well documented in psychology that fear dictates the actions we take. The actions can fall into four types: fight, flight, freeze, and fright. If you decide to fight, you face the fear directly. If you choose to flee, you work around the fear to avoid it. If you freeze, you hope the fearful stimuli will pass. If you go into fright mode, you become paralyzed and do nothing.

I wasn't in denial. I was in a state of fear. I had the kind of fear that was so overwhelming that it paralyzed me. I was in such a frightful state that I didn't even know I was in a fear mode, and that was my enemy. The Goliath became larger and larger as I kept trying to push it out of my mind.

One day, a woman called me and told me, "I am a doctor, and I know your parents. I know your friend, and she has told me what is going on with you." This woman, whom I did not know, was quite frank with me. She flat-out said, "Susan, what you have going on can kill you if you do not address it. So go get it checked!"

And something clicked; this woman was David's smooth stone who popped me hard enough to knock me out of the fright state I had unknowingly been in.

You may be thinking, "Oh, good – she finally went to the doctor after five long months!" Nope.

I went to an alternative doctor in Texas who did thermal temperature screenings. He pretty much told me that it looked like cancer. As I went back to my hotel room in a town hundreds of miles from home, I sat in my room alone and crying, not knowing what to do. I was so scared – of the cancer, of the treatment, if I would live or die. Finally, I started looking at places I could go to get treatment other than traditional medicine. I was prepared to leave the country.

I was fortunate to have a woman in my life as a spiritual teacher, and I confided in her what was going on. She told me with much love, "Susan, you will be OK. Go see the doctor." When she told me I would be OK, it was another stone in David's sling. I grabbed onto her words and scheduled the appointment.

The diagnosis was breast cancer: a 5-centimeter tumor, two other spots of concern, and an enlarged lymph node. I wept; I felt weak; I felt paralyzed; I was lost and scared. I never dreamed this could be my story. I cried for my parents. I cried for my son. I cried for myself.

I called my spiritual teacher to accuse her of lying to me. This was my very first lesson on how beautiful she is. She said, "I never told you that you would not have cancer; I told you that you would be OK." It took me a minute to internalize what she said, and her message resonated for several days afterward. Sanarie Boyet started me off on the right path.

With my eyes swollen and red, I went to a health food store to find more anti-cancer supplements. A sweet woman at the register told me of a brilliant functional medicine doctor nearby whom she believed saved her mother's life and helped her heal from cancer. I found Dr. Roger Billica, and he explained how his treatments would fortify my body to withstand chemotherapy. For the first time in this ordeal, I had hope when I left his office.

I faced my Goliath again and again in doctor's offices as I listened to their treatment suggestions while my sister, my angel on Earth, went to every appointment with me. I kept hearing: "You need surgery. You need chemotherapy. You need radiation." As the doctor was talking, I would look at my sister and subtly shake my head left to right, giving her that sister-to-sister sign language of "I can't do this." She would respond with a stern lip, nodding her head up and down, suggesting, "Oh yes, you can!"

I then called a dear friend, and he said immediately, "You need to meet my friend, Erin Ley." Again, I wasted no time calling her because of my trust in him. Erin, a cancer survivor, became the next smooth stone in my sling – she helped me realize that I needed to look at chemotherapy as my ally. It was there to help my body fight something we couldn't fight alone. Erin also shared visualization techniques. I snatched up her lessons and instantly set my mind to them.

This new mindset helped me get into a treatment plan. I was in for six years of treatment consisting of eight chemotherapy treatments, then surgery, then six weeks of radiation, and five years of hormone therapy.

Eight months after I found the lump, my treatment began. It was time to put my faith in my Lord and Savior, Jesus Christ. I transformed my thoughts and truly believed that He not only created chemotherapy and radiation because He knew I would need it, but He would also supervise every tiny drop of it in my beautiful body. All that was needed would be utilized, and the rest would harmlessly pass through.

When my treatment was all over, I started thinking more about how I got here. It was that moment of introspection when I realized I had lived the life of a people pleaser – I was a good mom, a good friend, a good daughter, and a good employee, and I gave myself up in many instances. Unfortunately, I forgot to be good to me! After this realization, I decided that I would always speak when uncomfortable and represent myself in truth.

Do you know that child's toy where a round-shaped object goes into a round hole and a square-shaped object into a square hole? Have you ever watched little kids as they learn that no matter how hard they try pushing that round object into the square hole, the toy doesn't flex? I recognized that I had been flexing; I allowed others to force me into things I didn't really want to do. I had lived that way for 48 years, and my illness might have been the result.

My Goliath was born from my state of fright and not believing that I had the strength to fight back. But I opened my mind to people who locked arms with me in my battle and helped me change my mindset. I encourage you to believe in yourself and in whom you represent – you are a unique and splendid individual and precisely whom you are meant to be. Smile from the inside out; let it start deep from within and bring it out into the light. Know that it is perfection to be shared with the world!

SUSAN CARPIO

About Susan Carpio: Susan has worked in the high tech industry for more than 30 years starting her career with an electrical engineering degree. Her experience encompasses deep technical roles in electronics labs, front line project management, and senior level leadership roles in both the commercial and aerospace and defense sectors. Currently Susan is a technical business development manager for integrated test systems supporting aerospace and defense applications at Keysight Technologies based in Loveland, Colorado.

While working for technology companies, she also has an entrepreneurial spirit and heart. Her son, Jase, his wife, Shilo, and their three children are the light of her life, and watching that young family start on their own has created her dedication to helping young mothers find a sustainable income so they can stay home with their children.

Susan is a cancer survivor and thriver for 10+ years and she attributes this to the mercy of Jesus Christ, the loved ones who surround her and her heartfelt thankfulness for life!

Author's Website: *www.SusanCarpio.com*
www.ThePrinciplesofDavidandGoliath.com

Thomas Malagisi

DEVELOPMENT OF A MINDSET AND BELIEF SYSTEM

Well, we all know the story. It may be found in the Old Testament book; Samuel 17. The small guy beats the big guy.

The unruly beast of a human. Six cubits are how his height was described. Truly a huge person during that time. He was wearing a helmet of brass, also around his shoulders and legs; he was laden with armor. Copper and zinc make brass. Copper yields formability, and zinc provides strength. Brass being a soft metal being able to flex somewhat but was strong. Indeed a protected huge person with that armament. Intimidating.

David was a small guy that lived most of his life alone with his flock. His slingshot was the tool of this trade to ward off intruding animals. He most likely prayed, sang songs, and built his belief in himself during his alone time.

Whether the story is fact or fiction, there must be some reason why it holds true through time. Looking at today's time, we know of movies that emulate the story to some degree. Open Range 2003, Braveheart 1995, and Gladiator 2000. All were movies that moved the audience.

But is the slaying of Goliath the only part of the story?

I may interpret the persona of Goliath as poor outcomes, the negative in our lives. Notice that the people of Israel are said to be free if Goliath can be fought, then loses, and is killed. But not just fought and killed—His head must be taken.

My personality type has been classed as a Myers Briggs, INTJ. With that, I, too, have found that I spend much time alone. Not the socialite. Liking people well, but not always the first choice for gatherings.

This part of the David and Goliath story is not one that I had to deal with externally, but I believe it is one that most people deal with and never really speak of. It's an internal thing. It's what Greg Reid talks about in the book *The 13 Steps to Riches V3 Autosuggestion*. Here he talks about APES and ANTs. He describes a method he uses to cut off the head of things that lead to negative results.

As a young child, I remember the story that I gravitated towards. It was the story of the *"Little Engine that Could."* What a powerful story that original story must have had on many.

Growing up, my mother taught me that I could do anything. She stressed hard work and diligence through things. To learn and apply what was learned. Always having a chore to do or a job to kept me busy towards some end, which was good. At this early age, it taught me the power of having a purpose. We never got an allowance in our family. The thing we got from doing the chore or the job was the gratification that we did it to the best of our ability.

My father was a hard man but loving. He was a WWII US vet from the Philippines zone. He used to use an expression. While I'm not sure if it was the jingle of that day or one he learned from experience, it went something like this: "Believe nothing of what you read and half of what you see. Think for yourself." I liked that. Think for yourself. Be independent. David thought for himself while all others trembled. He had confidence and faith in his ability.

Posters and clocks. Growing up in the '70s, posters were a big thing. I remember playing with friends at their homes and seeing that they had pinned up posters of their heroes on the walls in their bedrooms. Famous basketball players, baseball players, even Farah Fawcett, and Charlie's Angels. Were they good at those sports? Yes, all were above average. But, they practiced, practiced, and practiced. They knew what shots they could do with complete confidence and those they questioned. Did they marry supermodels? I'm not sure.

When my sister was ready to give birth to her children, I saw something strange. Of course, she beautified the upcoming child's room, but she had scenes hand-painted on the walls. At the time, I honestly thought, "What a waste." I didn't understand, but they were works of art. Those kids, now grown, turned out well. I now know that what you surround yourself with penetrates your mind. First your conscious mind, then your subconscious.

I never did that stuff of trophies or posters. Instead, I had a friend whose grandfather collected clocks. He was very generous to loan me some. I took them to our basement, where I proceeded to clean and oil them. I was intrigued by what made them work, how the pendulum provided energy to the mainspring, what each gear did, etc. I was impressed that this procession could be done by handcraft. This was probably originated from my gravitating to the movie "Willie Wonka and that Chocolate Factory." Here I was training my mind to bottom-line things swiftly. Learn cause and effect. David meeting Goliath in the valley between the two mountain ranges, David had to bottom-line the situation. Surely, he knew that going into hand-to-hand combat would not work.

Recalling that I wanted a Raleigh 10 speed bike when I was young and asked for one, the response was, "What are you going to do to get it?" So, I started shoveling driveways in the winter and cutting grass in the summer. I remember when I finally got the bike, I solicited my grass cutting services to a surrounding affluent area, and I got some work there! Wow. I could do that on my own. I was affirming my belief in myself. Next was the problem of how to get my newly owned lawnmower to that affluent area. Well, I devised to way to ride my bike those miles, hold on the lawnmower and pull it along on the street. Truly a great experience. I had a purpose. I had those who liked my work, and I got paid for it.

So, I guess my mother and father set my mindset that I can accomplish anything with a bit of work and direction. Nothing is given but earned. So, make up your mind, stick to it, and make it happen.

See, during that time, it was also stressed that "a person is only as good as his word." You didn't need a contract or a signed document. If you said you'd do something, then that is what you'd do—Commitment.

Until my school closing in the 11th grade, I went to a parochial school. They taught us the curriculum and, more importantly, discipline in structure. As a young boy, I needed that structure.

Later in life, going to university and working for large corporations, I became "normalized." I recall that this was the beginning to get self-doubt. This was when I started to really question myself. I'll tell you about that in the next writing.

THOMAS MALAGISI

About Thomas Malagisi: Thomas Malagisi, BSME, MBA, has over 30+ years of Manufacturing and Business experience. Thomas enjoys working with teams in many capacities. He thrives on accomplishing that which previously was thought of as something that couldn't be done. He celebrates the achievements of those types of goals. Thomas loves building upon group and individual strength through leaders and teamwork. Thomas utilizes Development-of-Management skills when leading groups and teams. He is also focused on employee retention for companies as well as the growth of individuals. Thomas holds his standards to world class business skills.

www.ThePrinciplesofDavidandGoliath.com

.

Valeria Mironov

FIND YOUR "ENOUGH" POINT

Everyone is predestined to experience different situations in a lifetime, which usually makes us feel happy or sad. Typically, we feel low and overwhelmed when faced with life struggles and obstacles that prevent us from moving forward. In this chapter, I will take you on a life journey of self-discovery, healing, and self-growth.

Have you ever felt like being an obstacle in your own way?

The human brain feels uncomfortable and unfamiliar when we experience something new. As a result, it provides various signs for you to give up on what you've just started and go back to how it used to be. There is faith that you can do it on one side, and yet the doubts, insecurities, and fears destroy that faith. The lack of confidence and negative self-talk has ruined more opportunities than the actual failure. If you don't try, you will never know how it could go.

Looking back at my life, I can confidently say that fear or doubt has been involuntarily wired in our brains through past experiences, family, and friends. At some point in my life, I felt like an impediment to myself because of my limiting beliefs and negative self-talk. Especially when things were going quite well and not so well, the skeptical voice was lighter and at times stronger and much deeper.

Even though I felt like I was on track (doing the right things, meditating, journaling, having a vision board, attending events and webinars), something subconsciously kept me from pursuing my dream life and taking the right actions. Having the right mindset and attitude to succeed is essential, but unless the limiting beliefs, the brain hand breaks, are released, things will still be and happen the same way they used to. For something to change in your life, YOU must change first.

The ENOUGH and TURNING point in my life was the unsuccessful purchase of our first house. How would a simple sale of a house be so impactful on someone? The strong, brave, and resilient girl gave up after the third day of finding out about the news. It was the beginning of a great transformational journey. I was ready for change, and I found the courage to share my story over zoom to a wonderful coach.

Soon I realized that the root of my reaction to financial obstacles was deeply embedded in my childhood and linked to the relationship with my dad. When I was a kid, my dad spoiled me and bought or did anything I asked. I grew up knowing that all I want is given to me, and things always work out my way. I love my dad so much, and it is completely okay to have massive desires and work on them, but "my way" is not always the best; there could be something even better waiting for me. The resistance I used to put on things/events wasn't really benefiting me. Still, the small child within me was hurt, demotivated, and low when things didn't play out the way I desired.

I've learned that everything happens for a reason in life, it is good, and it is an invaluable learning experience for me and others. Looking back at the events, I can see that the house sale falling through was the right thing to happen because I ended up working with a coach, finding a much better property, and became aware of limitations that prevented me from unleashing the power within me. At that time, the struggle, worries, and fears were unnecessary and only energy-consuming.

So, how to discover the healing and self-growth pathway?

The starting point would be to find someone who can assist you in noticing your blocks and limitations. These are sometimes deeply hidden in your mind and are difficult to spot. The next step is to release and heal these limitations or stories so that you can overwrite them and apply the new stories in your life.

The repeated thoughts that constantly come to your mind become your manifestations and reality. Imagine having only positive, empowering, and incredible thoughts about your life, business, job, relationship. Would you feel happier and live a much better life? The quality of your self-talk, beliefs, and ideas define the quality of your life.

To have a better life, first, start working on your belief system. Then, become aware of what is not serving you and release these obstacles from your way.

Secondly, surround yourself with like-minded people who share the same values and vision and inspire and support you. Find a trustworthy person to whom you can communicate anything, particularly when you feel low and face obstacles. It is so essential to deal with negative emotions and not just cut from them. When having a low moment, discuss your feelings and thoughts with a reliable person and do not get stuck on them. It can be your coach, friend, accountability buddy, or whomever you trust the most. By releasing and healing these feelings, you clear your mind and pathway to get anything you want.

Thirdly, the right attitude and mindset are crucial. The first time I came across the "right mindset" concept was in Robert Kiyosaki's book *Rich Dad Poor Dad*, which was a great learning and self-discovery moment. I've noticed that various people perceive similar sentences or events differently because of their different mindsets and belief systems. To succeed in any area of life, having the right mindset is the starting point. There are so many miracles hidden in our brain; find your ways to unlock them. Embrace each life obstacle with a strong, empowering, and positive mindset, and everything will work out in its best way.

Along with your healing and self-growth journey towards becoming your best version, often remind yourself about people, events, or things you are grateful for. Focusing on what you have now and being thankful for it will attract more and put you in an excellent state of mind. Try to attach some emotion while thinking, visualizing, or journal what you feel grateful for. This exercise will take your mind away from fears, lack and scarcity and put you in a loving, thankful, and kind mood.

Whenever you catch yourself blaming or thinking negatively, stop your thoughts and remind yourself that everything happens for a reason, and that is good for you! Connecting the dots between the events that happened, I see how things were meant to occur at a specific time and stage in my life. I was meant to start coaching and face my obstacles and limiting beliefs. I took power in my hands to overcome the fears living with me for decades and began the journey that changed my life forever. As a result, I found my purpose and my WHY in life. I discovered my passion for helping people transform their lives the way I did. It feels so incredible and fulfilling to see how people can change considerably in such a short period. I signed up for two public speaking clubs, which I have been thinking of for years, but procrastinated. I got involved in a project of writing this book, which was one of my dreams, and without getting on that zoom call with my coach after I found out about the house, I would have still lived with my limitations and fears that used to surface every time things were difficult.

Isn't it astonishing to see how releasing limiting beliefs empowered me to unleash the power in me and pursue my dream life?

What's stopping YOU now from living your dream life?

Be brave, face your obstacles and fears, and overcome your limitations, becoming invincible. Find your "enough" point, where there is no more tolerance for old self-beliefs and finally get control of your life. Any situation/event is happening for a reason; take something positive from it. Surround yourself with great like-minded people, and don't stick to negative thoughts and low moments. Release and heal them. Give more to others when you feel down; that way, you will shift your focus from problems and negativity to helping others and feel much better. Concentrate on what you have now and what makes you feel appreciative, re-live these moments of gratitude and be in a thankful state of mind.

I am celebrating you, my dear reader, and I am deeply grateful for you having the curiosity to familiarize yourself with my story of self-discovery, healing, and self-growth. Sending my love and great appreciation!

VALERIA MIRONOV

About Valeria Mironov: Valeria is an aspiring mindset coach and she is keen to leave a legacy of change and transformation through her positive impact and coaching. Valeria is looking to become a successful public speaker, she recently became a member of Toastmaster International and Public Speaking Association.

Valeria found her passion for helping women transform their lives. She founded VM Super Coaching and is looking to have a positive impact on many lives.

Valeria is a member of Tony Robins Inner Circle community and is Reiki Certificate I qualified Valeria graduated Law with Accounting BA and MSc in Corporate Governance and Leadership in United Kingdom. She sets herself massive goals and always achieves them. She continuously self-develops herself and takes any opportunity that comes her way.

Valeria speaks three languages, strives to read one book a week and embraces any life obstacle and challenges with a positive mindset.

Author's Website: *www.facebook.com/valeria.mironov*
www.ThePrinciplesofDavidandGoliath.com

Vera Thomas

THE MIND OF DAVID

David was the apple of God's eye (Ps 17:8)
In spite of his multitude of sins,
he was not denied Being called a man after God's own heart
His trust and reliance on God At an early age was the start
Of unwavering trust even in the midst of his wrongs
He knew God was with him all along
He felt remorse as we all do
He knew his God would help him through
God's forgiveness was unconditional
As David's walk was untraditional
Like when he danced with all his might
David was criticized and scorned for such a sight
To dance as David danced
To live by faith, not circumstance
To have the faith and unfailing assurance
On the God who was his fortress and rock
A God who is not to be mocked
That unwavering trust Is necessary for all of us
- Vera Thomas, 1/24/2022

The Book of Psalms, written by David, is my favorite book in the Bible. Knowing that despite David's flaws, weakness, and even wickedness, God was with him. He felt God's wrath, love, and forgiveness. Like David, no matter the circumstances,

I can rely on Psalms to strengthen, encourage, confirm, chastise, to allow honor and praise to the Most High. The 23rd Psalms is my daily meditation as it addresses every need or concern.

David's son Solomon wrote, "In all thy ways acknowledge Him, and He will direct your path" (Proverbs 3:6). Clearly, the fruit does not fall far from the tree. This scripture is unconditional! As you read this, you might ask, "Was David acknowledging God when he committed adultery or murder, among other sins?" David, like all of us, had human frailties, weaknesses, and in his case, lust. While he did not acknowledge God during his sin, he recognized and felt great remorse after the fact. In Ps. 51, David confessed his sins and poured his heart out to the Lord. It begins, "Create in me a clean heart Oh God and renew the right spirit within me." That is a part of my daily prayer.

I believe God saw David as the apple of his eye regardless of his sins because God knew David's heart. There is another scripture, "And you will seek Me and find Me when you search for Me with all your heart." (Jeremiah 29:13). Seeking God is a daily walk. It is not just for Sunday morning! How do we seek him with our whole heart? When we pray, it can be as simple as, "God help me!" "Lord forgive me and help me to forgive others as well as myself." Prayer does not need to be long and drawn out unless led by the Holy Spirit. I talk to God as my Father, my friend, my confidant. He already knows everything about you and me. However, he gave us free will to follow the steps he orders us to take, or we can choose to go our own way. It is clear David did both. However, his heart never swayed from his faith, trust, and awe of God. That is why he was the apple of God's eye and called a man after God's own heart. (1 Samuel 13:14, Acts 13:22 KJV).

David's belief system seems to be centered around believing and trusting God, period! Not without flaws, not without pain and guilt. He had his moments, as we all do. But, David knew the source of his being and could talk to God to regain whatever he needed at the moment.

David trusted God to protect him from his enemies and all demonic forces that tried to take him out! He relied on God to handle everything. David believed, "No weapon that is formed against thee shall prosper, and every tongue that shall rise against thee in judgment thou shalt condemn. This is the heritage of the servants of the LORD, and their righteousness is of me, saith the LORD." (Isaiah 54:17). Weapons against us may be formed, like David, I believe to no avail. David reveals this belief in over 123 verses in Ps. Including Ps. 20, 37, 91,140, just to mention a few. His trust that God would handle his enemies and adversaries without him needing to do anything; even in times of battle, he trusted God and had the victory! Goliath is a prime example.

I grew up in a minister's home; however, it was not until I was out on my own, going through more trials and tribulations caused mainly by not having that faith to seek God in all things, for all things, and through all things and going my own way. I began to realize from whence cometh my help! To have the mindset to trust God no matter what reminds me of those times in my life when all I could do was trust God to lead and direct.

I remember times in my life when I experienced God's protection. Most recently, I believe this COVID pandemic is a force with which to be reckoned. Since its beginning, I have read Ps. 91 and trust God to protect me. Now don't get it twisted; I have had my vaccinations, load up on vitamins and wear a mask. As I am pursuing my dreams, I also rideshare. I always pray and ask God to put in my car who He wants in my car, and they must wear a mask. I am doing His work as I drive, and I am protected.

There was a time when I literally slept with the Bible opened to Ps. 37 under my pillow. It was during a time when I felt demonic forces attacking me. There was a spirit of heaviness all around me. I met a person who tried to encourage me to follow their spiritual way, which seemed contrary to my belief. As a result of my rejection of the faith, all kinds of strange things started happening that seemed demonic. I was renting an apartment from this person, and I felt spirits in the place. That is why I slept with the Bible under my pillow.

During that same time, one early morning, I was driving down a dark country road headed to a rural school district as part of my position. There was absolutely nothing wrong with my car, yet it seemed to keep trying to veer towards the edge of the road that was a ditch. I know this may seem strange. "For our struggle is not against flesh and blood, but against the rulers, against the authorities, against the powers of this dark world, and against the spiritual forces of evil in the heavenly realms." (Ephesians 6:12). I was experiencing the spiritual forces of evil. It was confirmed when *that person* pulled up beside me at a red light and said, "God is really with you, girl!" and I said, "I know because you tried to destroy me."

Like David, God takes care of my enemies. I was one of two African Americans on a board of directors. Because of my training background, I was asked to assess a training by an independent contractor. The participants were socio-economically disadvantaged. The instructor was condescending, berating the class, and using profanity during his instruction. I was appalled and embarrassed that the agency would contract with such a person. I reported my findings at the next board meeting. The Executive Director went back to the independent contractor and told him about my report. Somehow, he got hold of my home phone number and called me. I was not home. He left a threatening and ominous, full of profanity message on my recorder. I took the recording tape to the board for them to hear it. Nothing was done about him or the Executive Director, who was totally out of line to divulge board meetings info, particularly to an independent contractor. I resigned from the board. A few months later, the independent contractor died of a heart attack.

You cannot treat people any kind of way and expect good to follow you. "For we know him who said, "Vengeance is mine; I will repay." And again, "The Lord will judge his people." (Hebrews 10:30). I believe David understood and trusted God's Word, and so do I. In my opinion, there is no need to hold grudges or be revengeful when you trust the Word of God.

There have been other instances where God took care of the matter, but time does not permit elaboration. I want to encourage you to consider David, his faith, trust, and unwavering reverence of his God. Even amid his mess, David knew God would never leave or forsake him. Believing and trusting God will always prevail even when we cannot see what he is doing or wants to do in our lives.

I pray spiritual eyes will be open and that each of us seek the love, joy, and peace of God that David writes about in the book of Psalms.

VERA THOMAS

About Vera Thomas: Vera Thomas lives in the state of Georgia. She is to date a 4x best-selling author, podcast host, certified transformation coach and family mediator, Classroom Management Advocate/ Trainer/Speaker/poet. She works with parents, children, schools, organizations and churches.

Vera's life story directed her towards work with organizations that provided hope and empowerment to people like her to better themselves. It is her goal to help others overcome a circumstance that diminishes and help them to surge ahead with their dreams. Vera graduated "Cum Laude" with a Bachelor in psychology from Walsh University in Canton, OH.

Vera's work as a facilitator, for more than three decades and includes developing training programs for youth and adults. Hear her story and think about your own. Vera is available for companies who want to transform their teams or individuals who want to transform their lives.

Author's Website: *www.VeraThomasCoaching.com*
www.ThePrinciplesofDavidandGoliath.com

Habitude Warrior Questionare

It's time to reflect on these stories and journeys of triumphs from these 33+ authors. Consider the lessons you have just learned from these chapters and how you can enhance or change your mindset and belief systems. Please take a moment and list them below.

- _____
- _____
- _____
- _____
- _____
- _____
- _____
- _____
- _____
- _____

Time to create new habits! Snap a photo and post it on social media and tag us #PrinciplesDavidGoliath and also at #HabitudeWarrior. It is also super important to share these habits with people who you trust will support you in your awesome journey. We are here to help! Visit the website below and mention this book to receive a free pass to join one of our Habitude Warrior Mastermind sessions:

www.RideAlongGuestPass.com